BOVINGTON
TANKS

GEORGE AND ANNE FORTY

WINCANTON PRESS
NATIONAL SCHOOL, NORTH STREET
WINCANTON, SOMERSET BA9 9AT

dpc
DORSET PUBLISHING COMPANY
KNOCK-NA-CRE, MILBORNE PORT
SHERBORNE, DORSET DT9 5HJ

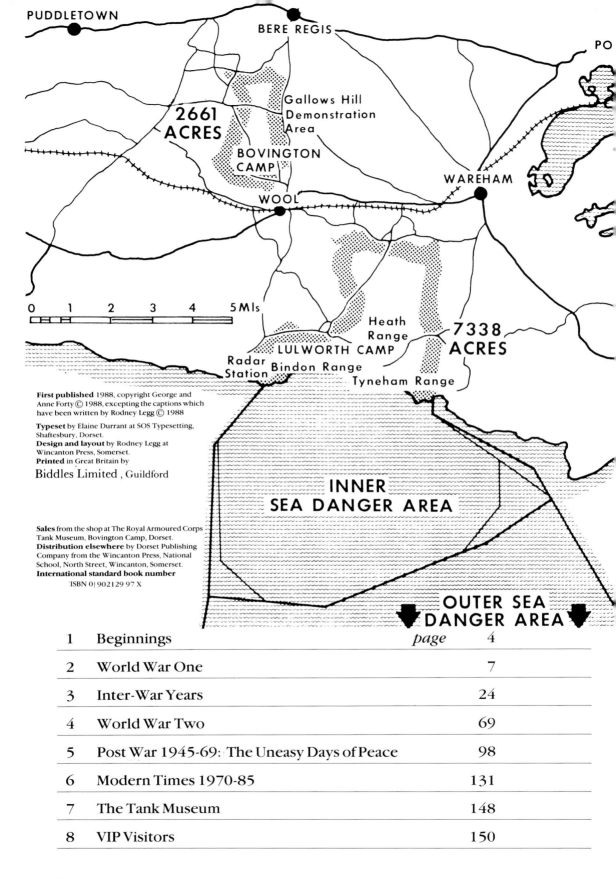

PUDDLETOWN

BERE REGIS

PO

2661 ACRES

Gallows Hill
Demonstration
Area

BOVINGTON
CAMP

WOOL

WAREHAM

0 1 2 3 4 5 Mls

Heath
Range

7338
ACRES

LULWORTH CAMP

Radar
Station Bindon Range

Tyneham Range

INNER
SEA DANGER AREA

OUTER SEA
DANGER AREA

First published 1988, copyright George and
Anne Forty © 1988, excepting the captions which
have been written by Rodney Legg © 1988

Typeset by Elaine Durrant at SOS Typesetting,
Shaftesbury, Dorset.
Design and layout by Rodney Legg at
Wincanton Press, Somerset.
Printed in Great Britain by

Biddles Limited , Guildford

Sales from the shop at The Royal Armoured Corps
Tank Museum, Bovington Camp, Dorset.
Distribution elsewhere by Dorset Publishing
Company from the Wincanton Press, National
School, North Street, Wincanton, Somerset.
International standard book number
ISBN 0 902129 97 X

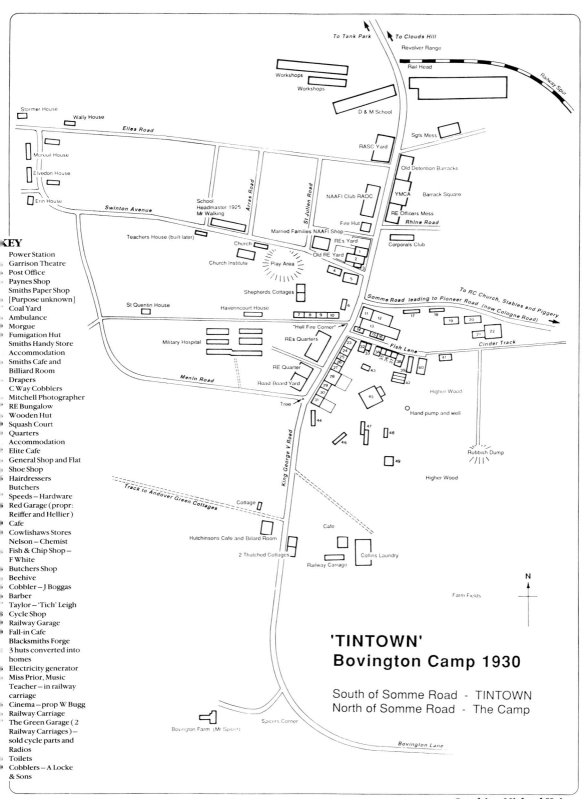

'TINTOWN'
Bovington Camp 1930

South of Somme Road - TINTOWN
North of Somme Road - The Camp

KEY

Power Station
Garrison Theatre
Post Office
Paynes Shop
Smiths Paper Shop
[Purpose unknown]
Coal Yard
Ambulance
Morgue
Fumigation Hut
Smiths Handy Store
Accommodation
Smiths Cafe and
Billiard Room
Drapers
C Way Cobblers
Mitchell Photographer
RE Bungalow
Wooden Hut
Squash Court
Quarters
Accommodation
Elite Cafe
General Shop and Flat
Shoe Shop
Hairdressers
Butchers
Speeds – Hardware
Red Garage (propr:
Reiffer and Hellier)
Cafe
Cowlishaws Stores
Nelson – Chemist
Fish & Chip Shop –
F White
Butchers Shop
Beehive
Cobbler – J Boggas
Barber
Taylor – 'Tich' Leigh
Cycle Shop
Railway Garage
Fall-in Cafe
Blacksmiths Forge
3 huts converted into
homes
Electricity generator
Miss Prior, Music
Teacher – in railway
carriage
Cinema – prop W Bugg
Railway Carriage
The Green Garage (2
Railway Carriages) –
sold cycle parts and
Radios
Toilets
Cobblers – A Locke
& Sons

Graphics: Michael Haine

3

1   BEGINNINGS

THE FIRST written evidence of Bovington's existence is in 1086, in the Dorset section of the Domesday Book, where it is said to have been a farm held by Alvric the huntsman. However the name itself is Saxon and means "the farm of Bofa's descendants." Many years later it became part of the Bindon Abbey estates and eventually, in 1776, Bovington was sold to James Frampton of Moreton House whose estates were already extensive.

In 1896 the War Office, looking for land to be used as a rifle and revolver range, approached the Frampton family and protracted negotiations began, for the sale of an area of heathland which included Bovington. The discussions dragged on and it was two years later, on 16 February 1899, that the War Office agreed to pay Mrs Louisa Mary Fetherstonhaugh Frampton £4,300 for just over 1000 acres of heathland in the parishes of Bovington, Turners Puddle, Affpuddle, Wool and elsewhere in the county of Dorset "to be used as a Rifle Range or for any other Military use or purpose ..."

Work soon began on the building of the ranges and involved a considerable amount of hard labour. Over a hundred men, working under the direction of an officer from the Royal Engineers Department of Weymouth, worked steadily over a period of months to produce a range 1000 yards long and 150 to 200 yards wide, containing twenty butts of the most modern design. A caretaker was then appointed; a Mr Woodrow of the Bryantspuddle brickyards, three miles from Bovington, formerly of the Dorsetshire Regiment.

The accommodation supplied for the camp at this time was a collection of tents about a mile south of the range. On 4 June 1900 some thousand men of the 1st Battalion of the Royal Southern Reserves became the first unit to move into the tented accommodation, when they arrived for their six weeks musketry firing. The men of B Company 1st Volunteer Battalion, Dorsetshire Regiment also arrived at that time and they were the first unit to actually fire on the range.

Originally, apart from Bovington Farm the only permanent building at the southern end of the track was an estate keeper's cottage. Shortly after the range came into use, a bungalow was built for the range warden.

Bovington Farm: before the army arrived.

4

Top **Wool Station: arrival point for the Dorset heaths.**

Centre **Bovington tented encampment: YMCA tent wrecked by a gale, 16 April 1914.**

Bottom **Drum-head service: on the site of the present Tank Museum, Bovington Camp.**

Top **Improvised bread-oven: learning to live in a field.**

Below **Bovington Camp: a postcard from the Great War.**

As more troops arrived to use the range the keeper's cottage was let, as a shop, to the Purchase Brothers. They sold general groceries, fizzy drinks, tobacco and all the small items required by troops in the field, who were unable to get to any other shop.

Firewood for heating and cooking was bought from the Framptons. According to their estate diary for 1900, 236 tons of firewood was bought by the military at £1 7s 6d per ton. Water was at first brought in by Charles Cobb of Bere Regis, on his horse-drawn tanker. Gradually the camp was used more frequently and a well was sunk and water pumped up by an oil-driven engine into large iron tanks with a capacity of around 3000 gallons; the water was then piped to hydrants and standpipes around the camp.

It soon became necessary for two extra rooms to be added to the Keeper's Cottage, which became the post office and canteen. Whilst the officers were waiting for a mess to be built they too used the Keeper's Cottage and when the mess was eventually in use, the Purchase Brothers became "Officers Mess Caterers, general providers and tent kit suppliers."

When firing was in progress, guards were placed at all entrances to the camp, but there was little real need for them as the few civilians in the area, other than those employed by or providing services for the military, had little social contact with the army.

Many battalions used the ranges in the decade before the First World War. Some camped for the whole of the summer, whilst others just spent short periods there. The Territorials also used the range for their annual meeting of the Dorset Territorial Rifle Association.

As more regiments made use of the camp and range the War Office had to enlarge the camp and in 1907 they bought a further 290 acres of Chamberlains Heath. In 1910 another 15¾ acres were addded. This was to increase even further when the Great War commenced.

2   WORLD WAR ONE

WHEN WAR began in August 1914, Britain had the largest Empire in the World. To protect this great empire of self governing dominions, territories and colonies, she not only had a powerful Navy but also a small, but well seasoned, Regular Army. Some of its soldiers had seen action fourteen years before in the battles of the Boer War.

Britain had no conscription but her small highly trained Expeditionary Force of 150,000 men – six divisions – could be speedily mobilised in an emergency. Kitchener knew he would require more volunteers and hoped to recruit about 100,000 in the first six months and perhaps 500,000 altogether. He had not reckoned on the wave of patriotic fervour which was to sweep the country – 500,000 men volunteered in the first month alone. In Dorset, in the first month, 2,258 volunteers reported to the barracks at Dorchester and were sent to Worgret Camp near Wareham. The flood of volunteers caused chaos in the army. There were no uniforms or arms and insufficient accommodation. Every available camp was brought into service. Bovington became the initial training camp of the newly formed 17th Infantry Division.

"The 17th Division belonged to the north. In a happy moment the War Office turned an eye on Dorset and sent 12,000 men to invade the windy sunlit spaces round Bovington and Wareham. It might be a distant journey but here was ideal ground for training; wide hills, great heaths and tracks of pinewoods. So the twelve battalions drawn from between Trent and Tweed were exiled from their crowded cities, or their fields and farms, to learn the business of War where there was little temptation or opportunity to do anything else."[1] Of course the soldiers rapidly proved the latter statement to be completely wrong and soon discovered the 'flesh pots' of Poole, Bournemouth and Weymouth.

The 17th Division was made up of the 50th, 51st and 52nd Brigades. The 6th Dorsetshire Regiment, the 7th East Yorkshire Regiment, the 10th West Yorkshire Regiment, and the 7th Yorkshire Regiment made up 50th Brigade and were sent to Worgret Camp. The 7th Lincolnshire Regiment, 7th Border Regiment, 8th South Staffordshire Regiment, and the 10th Sherwood Foresters formed the 51st Brigade. These together with 12th Manchester Regiment, 9th West Riding Regiment, 9th Northumberland Fusiliers, and 10th Lancashire Fusiliers which comprised 52nd Brigade, were all posted to Bovington.

They certainly did not appreciate their arrival in Dorset and a 10th Lancashire Fusilier found that at Bovington "the first night was spent on the verge of the road, no tents or rations having arrived." The Northumberland Fusiliers also spent their first night 'al fresco,' and were not too happy about it. In fact it became quite a scandal when the local headlines read "Kitchener's Army stranded with no food or covering."

It wasn't until around 9 September that the first tents arrived but these were inadequate as they could only accommodate half of the troops and the rest were left to cope as best they could, out of doors. The weather was wet and became wetter. Many men were sent to hospital with pneumonia and pleurisy. A young soldier from the Manchester Regiment died of pneumonia and was buried at Wool parish church.

The first uniforms were issued towards the end of September but they were not new. These had been re-issued and were thin and patched. The first consignment of arms – outdated Lee Enfields and Lee Metfords – were met with derision and were actually used only for drill practice. The existing manufacturers of both arms and clothing just could not cope with the tremendous surge of manpower. It was not until the following March that a supply of modern rifles arrived and the soldiers were not to see their full complement of uniform, arms and equipment until they were on the point of leaving for France in the autumn of 1915.

On 13 September four trains, containing 4,000 recruits from Manchester and Stockport, arrived at Wool Station and marched the two miles to Bovington. The numbers in camp swelled to 11,000. Gradually the camp became more organised and the weather showed some improvement. Squads of soldiers could be seen doing drill, physical training and, in whatever spare time they had, playing football. The YMCA did yeoman service trying to keep pace with the vast numbers of men. They served refreshments, provided a writing room, sold stamps and kept a supply of games for the few leisure hours.

Concerts were the main form of recreation and one was held most nights, the entertainers being mainly local and the camp's brass band played regularly. This band, the first formed in the Volunteer Army, was the creation of Reverend P A Butler, vicar of East Stoke and Chaplain to the camp. He was a larger-than-life figure, very much a countryman, with fishing his great hobby. When he discovered that several of his new congregation were musicians without anything to play he went off and bought several musical instruments at a cost of £40, and then put an

Bovington's band marching to Wool: its first instruments were provided by a clergyman.

Bovington Camp: off on a route march.

advertisement in the local paper for subscriptions to pay for them! The band played at the evening services in East Stoke church, on route marches, at weekly church parades, and at the YMCA concerts.

At this time a visitor to the camp found it "pitched in a large field situated on the slope of a hill [Bunker's Hill]. The tents were placed high up and the remainder of the field – a large plateau sort of patch – was reserved for drill, while at the bottom of the field were the camp fires and cooking offices." The weather turned wet again as winter approached and torrential rain flooded tents and brought mud. The authorities now moved to alleviate the situation, rashly promising to house the tented troops in wooden huts.

As the 51st Brigade were now at Lulworth there was only the 52nd Brigade left in Bovington, but despite employing every carpenter, and even semi-skilled woodworkers, in the entire area, and even with help from troops, it became obvious that the promise was not going to be fulfilled. It was then decided to put the troops into civilian billets until the hutted camps were ready. This move was not looked on with any pleasure by the civilian population, though when appealed to, on a patriotic level, most of them came to terms with the situation and in some cases made firm friends with their lodgers. On the last day of November 1914 the 10th Lancashire and 9th West Riding Regiments marched to Wimborne. A few days later the Northumberland Fusiliers went to Canford and Broadstone and the 12th Manchesters to Ferndown and Kinson. They only expected to be billeted for about eight weeks but it would be four months before the camp at Bovington was ready for them in March 1915.

The hutted camp was laid out in 'lines' and were denoted by letters – running from A, B and C to the west of the main Wool-Clouds Hill road, to D, E, F, G and H on the eastern side. Each set of huts was given to a battalion of 1,100 men. Each hut accommodated 30 men. There were also guardrooms, canteens, battalion offices, churches. A large hospital block, also hutted, was built to the south of A, B and C lines.

When the huts were ready the battalions returned to Bovington and began training. A trench system was dug out on the heath at Gallows Hill and the troops were soon involved in trench exercises both day and night "... twenty four hours were spent in trenches, units relieving in the

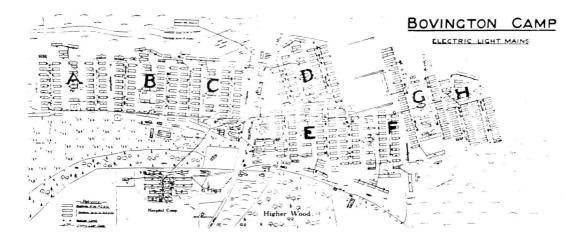

Bovington Camp: plan of the original hutted layout, 1915.

dark. They were odd trenches with no parapets and so narrow that two men, even if thin, could not pass one another." Machine-gun training was also included.

The 17th Division finished its training and departed. Their place was taken by the 7th Reserve Battalion of the Dorsetshire Regiment. The role of this battalion was to train local volunteers as reserves for the battalions fighting in France. The 7th continued in this rôle until it was disbanded in 1916.

The Australian Army now began to use Bovington as a Command Depot for toughening up their wounded, who had been discharged from hospital, ready for their return to the front. After the horrors of the Battle of the Somme, Bovington was soon overflowing again and so Worgret Camp was also used by the Australians, but as soon as possible, when pronounced fit, they were sent back to the front.

As the fighting on the Western Front reached stalemate, both sides were looking for a way through, or over, the barbed wire and trench systems. Among many schemes suggested to the British authorities, was one of an armoured vehicle on Caterpillar tracks. Yet it was not until Mr Winston Churchill, first Lord of the Admiralty, diverted naval funds on his own responsibility, to create the first experimental Landships, that positive action was taken.

Colonel Ernest Swinton, a Royal Engineer, was given the task of forming the new force which was going to be required for manning the revolutionary machines. It was a difficult task as he could not tell would-be recruits just what they were volunteering for, as the whole landship project was highly secret. They were merely told that they were being recruited for "a Company for carrying on an undertaking of Great Advantage but no one to know what it is." Their only requirement was to have a knowledge of mechanics or engineering.

On 3 December 1915, the pilot model of a vehicle called **Little Willie**, produced by William Foster Ltd of Lincoln, underwent trials at Lincoln. **Little Willie** was not a fighting tank, being eventually used for training tank drivers, it can now be seen at Bovington Tank Museum. In 1916, the first fighting machine, known variously as **Mother** or **Centipede** had a successful trial at Hatfield. Like all the first tanks, she was rhomboid in shape and later was to become the symbol on the cap badge of the Tank Corps. To those VIPs watching the trials – including HM King George V and Lord Kitchener – it was an impressive sight as **Mother** was put through her paces, lumbering along at three miles an hour, over battlefield obstacles laid out across Lord Salisbury's golf course. The success of the trial is shown in a letter from a member of the Landship Committee to Winston Churchill:

Dear Colonel Churchill,

It is with great pleasure that I am now able to report to you the success of the first landship (Tanks we call them). ...The official tests of trenches etc were nothing to it, and finally we showed them how it would cross a 9ft gap after climbing a 4ft 6ins

Above **Workshop and D & M School, with the road to Clouds Hill.**

Below **Main Street, Bovington Camp.**

high perpendicular parapet. Wire entanglements it goes through like a rhinoceros through a field of corn. It can be conveyed by rail (sponsons and guns take off, making it lighter) and can be ready for action very quickly. The King came and saw it and was greatly struck by its performance, as was everyone else ..."

Production of this new secret weapon was ordered and the tremendous task of training tank crews, with instructors who knew little more than their pupils, began. Siberia Camp, Bisley was the birth place of the new arm, but soon proved too popular for secrecy, so training was switched to Lord Iveagh's estate at Elveden, near Thetford in Norfolk.

Tanks to Bovington

IT SOON became quite obvious that the Elveden training area was too small for training tank drivers, so Colonel Swinton "with two officers from the War Office, ... made a tour of inspection to find a more suitable training ground than Elveden for the projected enlarged Heavy Section. This visit resulted in the establishment of the unit of Bovington, Dorset, which has ever since remained its centre."[2]

Bovington at this time was still a simple hutted camp and the accommodation was totally inadequate for a tank battalion, having been built to house six infantry battalions. The lines were therefore altered. Young officers came off worst in the reorganisation, and as there was no room in the mess, they were allotted ordinary huts with camp beds down each side, and a row of canvas wash stands down the centre. Another hut was used as an anteroom. The CO had to have a room squeezed in at the end of one of the bath houses and another officer had a shack in the woods where Cambrai House now stands. E Battalion; Centre HQ and F Battalion were in the huts to the west of the main road through camp and G, H and I Battalions were on the eastern side. The few tanks there were, were parked between the trees below E Battalion lines.

When the first tanks arrived, picquets were posted and from the station at Wool to the camp at Bovington the road was closed. All civilians – pedestrians or cyclists – were turned back. The inhabitants of any house en route were ordered to close their blinds and sit in their back rooms. James Spicer of Bovington Farm, told that he had to turn his back to the road, thought it was rather ridiculous as one of the tanks, which had broken down, had been towed by himself and his four-horse team, into his farmyard and remained there for 48 hours! A shepherd is reputed to have refused to leave his sheep, so the soldiers screened him from the road with hurdles until the tank had passed. I am told by a local resident that this is perfectly true. The tanks remained in the tank park overnight surrounded by armed guards – sentries with bayonets and orders to shoot.

**Brigadier General
F Gore-Anley:
first Commander
Tank Training Centre,
Bovington Camp.**

Above **Trench-crossing: demonstration at Bovington.**

Below, both pictures **Sinking feelings: there are bogs between the sandy knolls.**

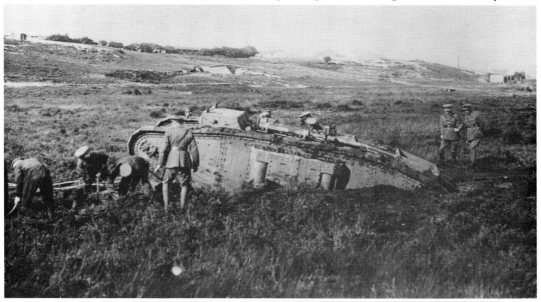

'An easy ride': life in the Machine Gun Corps.

Tank Training Centre

IN MID-OCTOBER 1916 the first Commander of the Tank Training Centre, Bovington Camp, was appointed. Brigadier General F Gore-Anley was chosen for this command. A week later, in great secrecy, the whole establishment of the Heavy Section moved from Elveden to Bovington.

There were still a few Australians in the camp that autumn, "khaki slouch hats, turned up on one side were everywhere. A few days later they departed." The new men who moved in, looked a motley crew with hardly two uniforms alike – kilts, breeches and trousers, leggings, puttees and field boots; buttons of brass, silver gilt, leather and bone were to be seen. They trained for hours on end carrying their kit, in single file, at the double until they dropped from exhaustion. Actually those who did were sent to other units and those who had the stamina to continue became members of the Machine-Gun Corps, Heavy Section. Their day consisted of:-

6 am	Reveille
6.15	First parade. Shave, clean buttons and boots for Roll call and inspection.
6.45	Parade in singlets and shorts or slacks for exercise until 7.45.
8 am	Breakfast
8.35	Parade – Bayonet fighting
9.45	Parade – Musketry
10.45	PT
11.45	Platoon or Company drill
12.45 pm	Lunch
1.30 - 5.15	Vickers, Lewis or 6pdr gun instruction, more Company drill.
5.30	Tea
6 - 7	Lectures followed by cleaning kit.

The rest of the day was their own!

This was the sort of life the Tank Corps personnel would recall:

"It was a bitterly cold day in November, 1916, when, with about 40 others, I arrived at Bovington Camp. We were all ASC men and had been transferred into the new branch of the Army then styled the Tank Corps. We had left comfortable billets at Osterley Park in London for the wilds of Dorset, and I must say we were by no means impressed. Bovington in those far-off days was a dreary spot indeed, and the wintry weather (snow was falling when we reached Wool) did not help to cheer us. On arriving at Wool, we dumped our kit bags at the station and marched the half-mile or so to the camp. Here we were divided up and sent to various battalions then in the course of formation. About a dozen of us had to report to H Battalion where, of course, we had to go through the usual procedure of having our particulars taken. This over we drew some blankets and eventually were directed to a hut in F Lines, which was particularly

BOVINGTON 1917 CAMP

T'WAS AN ISOLATED, DESOLATED SPOT— IT MAKES ME FEAR TO MENTION

WHERE ALL YOU HEARD WAS "STAND AT EASE"— "SLOPE ARMS— "QUICK MARCH" ATTENTION

T'WAS MILES AWAY FROM ANYWHERE BY GAD IT WAS A RUM 'UN A CHAP LIVED THERE FOR FIFTY YEARS AND NEVER SAW A WOMAN

THERE WAS LOTS OF LITTLE HUTS ALL DOTTED HERE AND THERE FOR THOSE WHO HAD TO LIVE INSIDE I'VE OFFERED MANY A PRAYER

INSIDE THE HUTS WERE RATS AS BIG AS ANY NANNY GOAT, ONE NIGHT A SOLDIER SAW ONE TRYING ON HIS OVERCOAT

T'WAS SLUDGE UP TO YOUR EYE BROWS YOU GOT IT IN YOUR EARS BUT INTO IT YOU'D GOT TO GO WITHOUT A SIGN OF FEAR

AND WHEN YOU'D HAD A BATH OF SLUDGE YOU JUST SET TO AND GROOMED AND GET CLEANED UP FOR NEXT PARADE OR ELSE YOU'SE "ORDERLY ROOMED"

WEEK IN WEEK OUT FROM MORN TILL NIGHT WITH FULL PACK AND A RIFLE LIKE JACK AND JILL WE'D CLIMB THE HILLS OF COURSE T'WAS JUST A TRIFLE

"SLOPE ARMS"—"FIX BAYONETS"—THEN— "PRESENT—THEY— FAIRLY PUT YOU THROUGH IT AND AS YOU STAGGERED TO YOUR HUT THE SERGEANT ROARED JUMP TO IT!

WITH TUNICS, BOOTS AND PUTTEES OFF WE QUICKLY GOT THE HABIT —W'ED GALLOP UP AND DOWN THE HILLS JUST LIKE A BLOOMIN' RABBIT

"HEADS BACKWARD BEND"—"ARMS OUT WARD STRETCH"— HEELS RAKE"—THEN RANKS CHANGE PLACES!

AND LATER ON THEY MADE YOU PUT YOUR KNEE CAP WHERE YOUR FACE IS!

COLIN CAMPBELL 35.

uninviting as there was no fire and only one small electric light bulb. I think we all felt pretty miserable, but were cheered up somewhat a few minutes later when a Corporal appeared and told us to go to the cook-house where we could get some hot soup. I don't think I ever enjoyed Army soup more than I did then. It certainly warmed us up and helped to dispel some of the gloom that was hanging over us.

"Next day we sorted ourselves out, and after breakfast had a wander round the camp. There were no brick buildings and Tank Park only possessed about three hangars with about the same number of tanks. We were naturally greatly intrigued by the antics of one of these, which we

15

were fortunate enough to see working, as it lumbered and rolled along spitting and spluttering and stopping every minute or so. It was the first tank we had seen, and I'm afraid we were inclined to greet it more with merriment, judging from the facetious remarks passed, than as a serious fighting proposition. We little realised then what a force tanks would eventually become.

"We discovered the YMCA and C of E huts, and spent most of our time in these for the first week or two. Men were arriving every day and H Battalion began to take shape; 22, 23 and 24 companies were formed as well as the various sections to each.

"There followed an intensive course of instruction on tanks, the six-pounder gun, Lewis and Hotchkiss guns, map reading, morse, judging distance, lectures on explosives, Mills bombs and German bombs, as well as having to do guard duties, PT, squad drill, route marches and night operations. As there was no wireless in those days each tank had to carry pigeons, which were used as a means of communication, so everyone had to learn how to handle those birds.

Bovington's pigeon loft: the birds were the only means of communication in the first tanks, a basket with two being carried in each vehicle. They were soon abandoned in favour of semaphore 'arms'.

"As time went on more and more tanks began to arrive, and the crews which had been formed were soon at work on these, learning their various duties. These early buses had one great drawback. It necessitated having a gearsman inside the tank on the left and right to work the gears, as otherwise the driver could not turn the tank while driving. To swing the tank either left or right one or other of the tracks had to be stopped, and this was where the gearsman came into action.

"Various experiments were tried out at Bovington with regard to the unditching of tanks, and we spent many an interesting time watching tanks being got out of almost impossible situations by means of the unditching beam. Major Strickland was the leading light in these operations, and I believe he could guarantee getting a tank out of any plight so long as the engine was running. "Spuds" fitted to the tracks were another means of ensuring a grip, and most tanks carried a supply. They were easily fitted and could be removed when not required.

"Tank crews consisted of the commander, driver, four gunners and two gearsmen, but later these were cut down when the driver became independent of the gearsmen. The foregoing refers to the male tank which carried two six-pounder guns. I think the female tanks, which carried only machine guns, had a smaller crew.

"One incident which occurred when I was at Bovington made a very great impression on me. It was seeing a Sergeant stripped of his stripes before the whole Battalion. I don't remember what crime he had committed, but I remember everybody had to appear on parade, even the cook-house staff and others not usually required to 'fall in.' With the whole Battalion formed up on the parade ground the culprit was marched out between two Sergeants and the charge and court martial sentence read out. Immediately afterwards his escort tore off his stripes and he was marched back again.

"In spite of the arduous work put in during our training our social life was not altogether overlooked, for we had several sports events, which included football matches, cross-country runs, sports meetings, concerts, etc. Rambles to Lulworth Cove, Bere Regis, Gallows Hill, Black Hill, Moreton and Wool are among my pleasant memories of our sojourn in Dorset, and on rare occasions a late pass enabled us to visit Poole, Bournemouth or Dorchester, which were all within easy access."[3]

Wool represented the chance of escape: and Poole (left) the dream of the flesh-pots.

Training now started in earnest with Instructors courses being run by Centre HQ while the rest of the Battalion were kept hard at it with drill, PT and route marches. Many of the men had just been called up from civilian life and were considered 'unfit.' There were many special courses to instruct in tank driving and maintenance (when the tanks finally arrived); map making; bombing and demolition; rifle and revolver shooting; bayonet fighting; compass and navigation; topography; PT; and pigeons (the care and feeding of). It took twice as long to train for the new unit as it did for any infantryman. One young officer recalled his training:

"My first course was Driving and Maintenance, and I found it was really good fun. The Tanks, although very slow had a magnificent cross country performance and as four of the eight members of the crew were required solely to manoeuvre the vehicle, good team work was required to get the best performance. There was no tactical driving and the main object was to get the tank over the most impossible places and when stuck to get going again with the aid of pick, shovel, crowbar and brute strength. This training was essential as each tank had to be self-supporting and recovery was in its infancy. Maintenance was very heavy, especially greasing up as there were nearly 60 points on the outside of each tank alone which required the grease gun at the end of a day's run.

"The Gunnery courses were also carried out at Bovington. These courses included indoor instruction in the huts below G Bn lines and firing the Lewis guns into the butts on the training ground north of the camp either from the ground or from gun sponsons removed from the D & M tanks.

"... I was next sent on a Revolver Course and the Pigeon Course. The latter was necessary as each tank carried a basket of two pigeons into action. I cannot recall any incident when they proved of much use, as either the tank had to be evacuated in a hurry, the pigeons were stupified by the fumes, or as has been reported they were used up as an emergency ration.

"F Bn began mobilising on April 14th [1917] and final intensive training commences. This included some tactical training on a trench system which the Battalion had helped to dig on Sunday rest days in the Gallow Hill area.

"... On May 12 F Bn paraded at Bovington for the last time and marched to Wool Station from where we embarked in two trains, for Southampton.[4]

As one Battalion marched off to war, so another took its turn at the Bovington Schools, for three months of intensive training. Another young man, from G Battalion, wrote:

"After three months training with G Battalion of the Machine Gun Corps, Heavy Branch, in a somewhat pretty but quiet little village [Bovington] in the sunny south of England, we were informed that the Battalion was fully trained and would proceed overseas immediately. Of course, final leave was the first thing to be considered, and we proceeded to our respective homes or relations in large batches by every available train which left the sleepy little hamlet, the nearest railroad station being 2¼ miles from our camp ... then we returned to prepare for our departure to France. Quite a long time was spent in issuing equipment such as pay-books, anti-gas equipment, revolvers, ammunition, field dressings etc which the soldiers on home service knows nothing about and is lucky in this respect that he does not have to carry it about and keep it always under his eye."

After collecting all their equipment the next item on their agenda was the goodbye parade, in full kit:

"... we loaded ourselves up like a Christmas tree and stood about on the parade ground waiting for the GOC's inspection, which is always the way the staff have of saying goodbye to a battalion on the eve of its departure for active service. When we were feeling properly fed-up and our backs nearly broken with the weight we were carrying, the GOC arrived and made a farewell speech. He was quite a jolly fellow and said he had every confidence in sending G Battalion overseas ... The Depot Band commenced a march and we strode off the parade ground, the General taking the salute from each of the nine companies as they passed him. We then fell out for half an hour, and I can assure you that it was only a matter of seconds before every man had unbuckled his harness ... Then came the final march out of Bovington Camp. We started away about 11 am, headed by the Depot band, and the road to the station for nearly a mile was lined by members of other battalions who were not yet ready to take the plunge we were taking that day. Here and there were scattered little groups of 'WAACS' [Women's Army Auxiliary Corps]. Those invaluable girls acted as cooks and waitresses etc in the different messes of the camp. Loud and many were the cheers that rang through the quaintly pretty country road as G Battalion marched away, in full review order, to entrain for France ... About 12.15 we arrived at the station and very soon our special train backed into the 'up' platform."[5]

From E (5th) Battalion there comes another view of the days before embarkation:

"The formation of "E" Battalion took place at Bovington on November 7th 1916 and consisted of a nucleus of 30 officers and 40 other ranks. It was shortly made up to strength by transfers from other arms of the service and also by a proportion of recruits, who were thought to, and did, give a strain of fresh blood so necessary in a fresh venture.

"The training of the Battalion was marked by exceptional keeness of all ranks in work and play. The wooded country around Bovington is particularly adapted to the training of a Tank Battalion, the rolling downs, the woods, and the small streets being very similar to and as equally deserted as the battlefields of France.

"The last four days before the Battalion entrained for France, were perhaps the most stirring ever experienced by that Battalion. In addition to the breaking up of the Officers Mess, the arrival of the long expected 'transport' brought joy to some company commanders and envy and hatred to the hearts of others. The 'transport' was new and needed considerable running in before it could be considered fit to stand the strain of active service. The main Bournemouth road is considered an admirable testing ground!

"On June 25th 1917, the Battalion paraded for inspection before marching to Wool Station. The inspection was good but possibly marred by a certain unsteadiness in all ranks. This was afterwards discovered to be due to the heavy wind prevailing at the time!"[6]

OPPOSITE. An extensive network of practice trenches was built across Bere Heath, Higher Hyde Heath and Stoke Heath: most represented the German lines that were to be attacked. They were faced on the Bovington side by the British defences – Robert Trench and Gordon Trench; approached from Piccadilly, Regent Street and Bond Street from Lovers Valley, Blighty Valley and Happy Valley respectively. Foreward of the enemy's main kaiser Line were Boar's Head, Mad Point and Wunder Work with the Hohenzollern Redoubt on the right flank. The next strong points were Big Willie, Little Willie and Fritz Redoubt with Three Sisters Redoubt blocking the western approach to Gallows Hill and Stuff Redoubt, Kluck Redoubt and Schwaben Redoubt. Hulke Trench, Willoughby Trench, Hankey Trench, Woods Trench and Colson Trench weaved up the slope to the Hansa Line and Serb Line defences on each side of the sandy lane from the Ladies' Lookout on South Heath to Fort Anley on the south-west side of Gallows Hill. That was the ultimate strong point, the Gallows Redoubt. Its rearguard were the Potsdam and Berlin Lines on Warren Heath and forward of the Black Castle pinewoods.

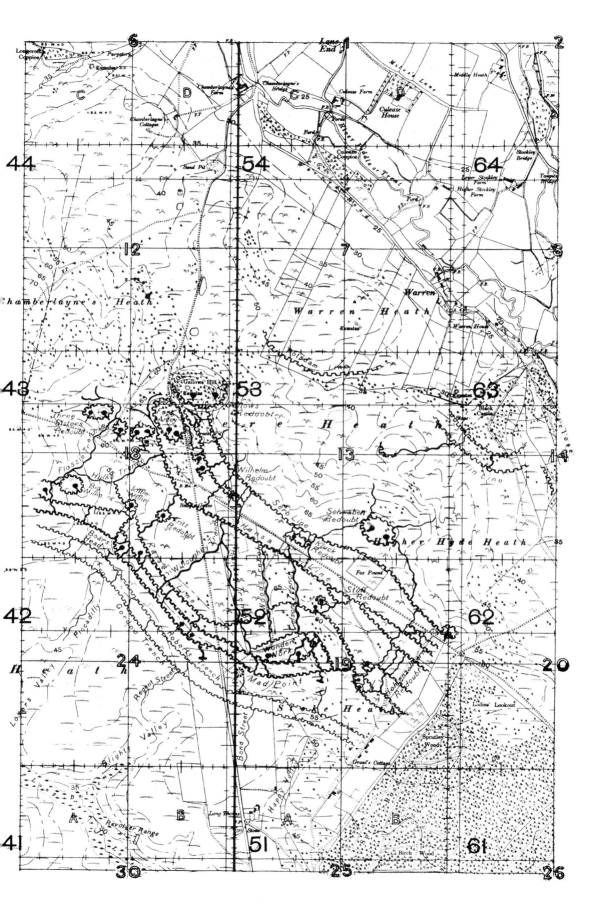

Bovington Workshop, with a tank and line of engines:
note its mineral gauge light railway set in the middle of the floor.

Workshops, mechanics, and cleanliness

WHEN THE Heavy Section, Machine Gun Corps, received their first tanks at Elveden in June 1916, No 711 Company, Army Service Corps was attached to the Section. Its brief was to do all the driving and maintenance (even in action) of the tanks, and this arrangement held throughout the Somme battles of 1916. Most of the personnel of 711 Company went to France in September, with the tank crews, however, a small nucleus was left in England. The tank companies moved to Bovington Camp in November 1916 and the remnant of the 711 Company was transferred to the Heavy Branch Machine Gun Corps. Five battalions were formed at Bovington with a Workshops Company for each. A Depot Workshops was also formed to repair all the tanks used at the Training Schools in Bovington.

At first the mobile workshop, which was brought from Elveden, was adequate for the repair of the first few tanks but as the numbers grew so workshops had to expand. Two canvas hangars – each capable of holding two tanks, were erected on the south side of the Tank Park, under the lee of a bank – unfortunately the area flooded in winter. One engineer recalled it vividly:

"I arrived at Bovington Camp on December 2nd 1916, having driven up from Wool Station in a one horse wagonette with a lid on it ... At this time there was nothing at Bovington but the Rifle Range and a tent-bottom store. It was a summer Training Camp... I reported to Lt Col Strickland (OC Schools and Workshops). The latter consisted of a canvas aeroplane hanger and few tents, with only the most primative tools and other necessary adjuncts. After a short examination as to my capabilities in instructing ... I was placed in charge of such teaching in a canvas hut, carefully sited in the bed of a stream.

"Inevitably this accommodation became even more inadequate and early in 1917 three more hangars were put up, on the eastern side of the tank park, and four more on the south side. However, without lifting equipment it was difficult to cope with the removal of engines, and with the hard treatment the tanks were getting from the soldiers learning to drive, this was becoming vital. So a permanent, galvanised iron, steel framed building, fifty feet by thirty five feet, with concrete floor and an overhead crane, was built. Half was used as a tank repair bay and half as an engine bay. Some old stables near by were converted into a machine workshop and two field smith's hearths were fitted up in an old tin lean-to."[7]

Those recruits with any sign of a skill or interest in mechanics were automatically placed in workshops but as the Heavy Section was the newest unit it had the least 'clout' with the selection board so "about half joined with the knowledge and experience of the average motorist."

Except at weekends recruits were usually kept fully occupied. Every moment was spent in cleaning something – themselves, their kit, their equipment and their hut. First thing in the morning, and again at night, it was a tedious routine of scrubbing, polishing, sweeping and shining. They cleaned windows; dry scrubbed the floors which then had to be swept; blackleaded stoves, the iron legs of forms and tables – even the insides and outsides of coal bins and tubs. Forms, broom handles and other such items had to be scrubbed daily, but despite all this cleaning once a week everything had to be scoured with soda and hot soapy water. This intensive cleaning continued through the year regardless of the weather. At the weekends the huts had a more untidy, lived-in look; shelves were cluttered with personal items normally neatly hidden in a cupboard. All the miscellaneous objects so dear to a soldier were mixed together and left lying around on tables or chairs.

The wall behind each soldier's bed was usually plastered with photographs of wives and sweethearts, fathers and mothers, children and other relations, all looking rather serious, and pinned up with them were cut out pictures and cartoons from newspapers and magazines.

Cleaning, apart from individual care of personal kit and equipment, was done in rotation, but it seemed to most recruits that their turn came round very quickly.

Towards the end of 1917 the Heavy Section became the Tank Corps and was expanded from nine to eighteen battalions. This meant that there were now over 300 tanks in Bovington and further expansion of workshops was required.

"Ten repair bays were erected with a travelling crane running the length of the bays. The tank park was laid to proper falls, drained and given a hard formation and a rolled surface. Standard lights were fitted in the park to enable night work to be carried out when necessary. Additionally, a smithy, a foundry, a coppersmith's shop and an acetylene welder's shop were erected to the west of the new machine shop."[8]

These extensions produced a demand for electricity which was far beyond the capacity of the existing camp generating system. It was necessary therefore, to install first one and eventually a second, additional generating station. The whole plant was run by the regular Royal Engineers Camp Servicement.

"A further improvement was made by laying a narrow, eighteen gauge, light rail track across the repair park with branches leading into the repair shed, engine bay and equipment store to enable stores and materials to be transported more easily. This was found to be especially convenient when the tank park was inches thick in mud after a long spell of wet weather and the passage of many tanks. These various improvements proved adequate for the growing number of repairs which were required as the number of tanks and upkeep grew to 529."[9]

Lulworth Camp: tents below Bindon Hill.

Lulworth – the Gunnery School

LULWORTH HAS been the home of the Gunnery School since 1916 when it became necessary to find a suitable area to practice tank gunnery, away from prying eyes, and it has been there ever since. There had been tented camps at Lulworth prior to this – the earliest photograph we have seen is dated 1866 – when the camp was used for infantry training for Volunteers, but the site of those tented camps is totally different from the one chosen for the tanks. They were much nearer to the Cove.

At first the only guns used were the 6 pounders. Firing was carried out on the new ranges, and also at Whale Island, Portsmouth, but this was found to be impracticable and by the Spring of 1917 practically all firing was done at Lulworth. It was not until 1919 that the small-arms ranges at Bovington and Moreton were finally closed and moved to the Gunnery School.

Initially this camp was entirely under canvas, which proved chaotic in the south-westerly gales sweeping up Bindon valley. These strong winds were inclined to blow the tents, with their belongings, hundreds of yards away. They would probably have disappeared altogether but for a strategically placed barrier of trees at the north-eastern edge of the camp. Then, about the same time as at Bovington, a hutted camp gradually took the place of tents; but Lulworth was always behind with improvements and it was indeed a very gradual process.

Bovington WAACS: the girls were cooks and waitresses in the messes.

Mechanised man: the concept of the armoured fighting vehicle.

With apologies to Heath Robinson

3 INTER WAR YEARS

IN AUTUMN 1918 the War Office decided to double the size of the Tank Corps. This meant raising seventeen new battalions at Bovington and spending a great deal of money – around half a million pounds – on new technical buildings. Work began immediately, and by the end of November nearly half the programme was complete, but the Armistice had been signed and the War Office cancelled all tank production of the new **Medium C & D** tanks.

There followed a very unsettling and contrary period, when decisions as to whether the Tank Corps should remain or be disbanded, were sought. If it remained what would its rôle be? Should it become part of the Royal Engineers or part of the Infantry? Finally it was decided that the Tank Corps should remain a separate unit of the regular army, with an establishment of four battalions.

Bovington was still a large camp, faced with tank repairs and a training programme whilst also coping with demobilisation. One soldier, coming into camp from the Clouds Hill end, wrote: "Bovington was a much larger camp than I imagined it to be. Seen under a formal constellation of electric lamps it appeared as a veritable city of wooden huts set down in a waste of barren moorland. At intervals along our road clumps of secretive pines loomed dark and menacing in the December dusk, and as we drew nearer I saw that these were the outposts of an extensive wood which curved away to the south-west, mantling a shoulder of the ridge on which the camp was built. A long straight road took us past hangars and corrugated iron sheds, which the driver said were workshops. Beyond them I saw the dark, toad shapes of tanks. We passed a power station, a cinema, shops, a post office, and presently stopped in front of a large barrack store."[10]

The Tank Corps, although greatly reduced in numbers after the war, was still operational. Five Battalions were part of the Army of Occupation of the Rhine. Armoured Car Companies were aiding the Civil Powers in several Middle Eastern Countries. One Company was sent to help the police during the troubles in Ireland. In Britain special units were formed to help the police during the strikes of 1920-21.

Throughout those years the training of newly joined recruits for the newly formed tank battalions and armoured car companies continued. They were being prepared for service in all the trouble spots around the Empire and the world.

The Central Schools

IN 1919 the Central Schools consisted of:

Headquarters

Machine Gun School

Tank School

Signalling School

Intelligence School

Compass School

Revolver School

Anti-gas School

Bombing School

Pigeon School

Economies caused these Schools to be cut down and merged. In 1922 the Central Schools consisted of:

Headquarters

The Gunnery School

The Tank Driving and Maintenance and Armoured Car School

Tank Driving and Maintenance School

FROM JANUARY 1919 to January 1923 the D & M School emerged from the chaos caused by the change to peace time conditions. Rapid demobilisation of skilled men greatly reduced the number of instructors. Obsolete tanks had to be disposed of – mostly through the Slough Trading Company – and newer ones sought for instruction purposes.

The Tank Driving School had two branches, at Bovington and Wareham. In 1919 neither of these was used to full capacity. At irregular intervals small classes of officers and men came to be trained on **Mark IV** and **V** tanks. A special course was also put on for Royal Army Ordnance Corps personnel as they knew little of driving tanks. The Maintenance School was fitted up with instructional benches of various parts of the Ricardo engine and transmission and a skeleton tank was used for demonstrating working parts.

'Siberia': Bovington Camp in the snow.

Both branches of the Driving and Maintenance School were commanded by a Chief Instructor but the CI at Bovington was responsible for both branches. The Bovington branch was also sub-divided: The *Mechanical School*, with an establishment of 5 officers and 9 NCO's; The *Maintenance School* with also 5 officers and 9 NCO's; and the *Driving Parks*, in four sections A, B, C, D, with an establishment of 3 officers and 12 NCO's to each park. Each one of these six divisions was commanded by a captain.

In order to help men to find employment on leaving the army in the early part of 1919, efforts were made to teach them to drive cars. A Hupmobile chassis, found in the camp, was used as an instructional model and an Army Service Corps lorry was used for driving instruction. About 100 men passed before the scheme was dropped.

In April 1919 the Wareham branch was closed down, and all instruction in D & M was now done in Bovington. Tanks were still arriving from the manufacturers – completing their war contracts – and many more were shipped from France. Many excellent sectional models were made for instructional purposes, which was a great improvement for the school.

From late 1919 instruction was on the **Mark V, Mark V*, Mark V**** and the **Medium C** and the **Rolls Royce Armoured Car** were also used. The D & M School mechanical side had the RR Eagle engines, the Liberty Engine, the Siddlely Puma, Daimler Lorry-engine and an Austin as well as using running engines in jacked-up tanks.

Bovington Tank Park: its mechanics repairing something lighter.

Bovington Heath, 1919-20: tanks from France await breaking up, or dispersal as war memorials – of a hundred used for that purpose only the one at Ashford, Kent, survives.

By 1923 the standard of instruction had risen considerably. The instructors were periodically moved from one department to another so that they were efficient in all of the Mechanical, Maintenance, and Driving classes of the School.

Ten Commandments for Tank Drivers

1 *Thou shalt not time thy magneto by the battalion guardroom clock*
2 *Honour thy sergeant and thy corporal, for such is the command of the RSM*
3 *Thou shalt not 'pinch' thy neighbours tools lest thou be found out*
4 *Thou shalt not blaspheme, even when thy big end knocketh*
5 *Thou shalt not bear false witness concerning thy pay, for the wrath of the QMS is very terrible*
6 *Thou shalt not scrounge whilst in thy seat, for thy actions will end on CB*
7 *Thou shalt not race thy neighbours engine*
8 *Thou shalt not envy the corporals girl, for pride goeth before a fall*
9 *Thou shalt not divulge thy knowledge in Bournemouth, for the ears of the Military Police are very keen*
10 *Thou shalt not contaminate thy petrol with water lest it be likened unto the waters of Jordan.*

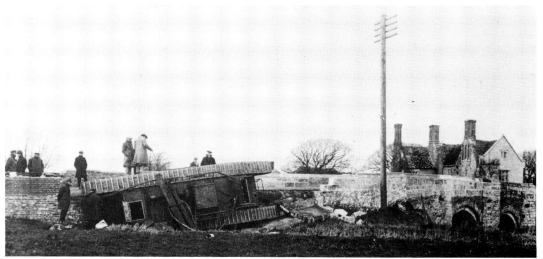

'Dee' (named after the river) on another river-bank, at Woolbridge: the road had subsided.

Lulworth Camp: armoured cars just visible between the ranks and the wooden huts.

Lulworth's changes

1919, BEING the first year after the war, brought changes to Lulworth School as well. Demobilisation of wartime officers and enlisted men who were instructors made it a difficult and confused time and even the official history admits that ".. at a period of such transition a more complete record cannot be compiled nor, could it have been collected, would it have proved to be of much historical interest."

The Gunnery and Tank Driving Schools were the two major instructional establishments of the Central Schools, the others — reconnaissance, compass, camouflage, gas and smoke — had only a total establishment of 5 officers and 5 sergeants. The establishment of the Gunnery School was:

> *Commanding Officer - Major*
> *14 Officer Instructors*
> *12 Warrant Officer Instructors*
> *10 Sergeant Instructors*
> *27 Corporal Instructors*

In fact only one type of course was run in 1919 – a two month Gunnery Course. This course was split up as follows:

> *20 days on 6 pdr Hotchkiss QF Gun*
> *15 days on .303 Hotchkiss Light Automatic Gun*
> *3 days on .303 Lewis Light Machine Gun*
> *1 day on .303 Vickers Machine Gun*
> *1 day on German Maxim Gun*

At this time the **Mark V** and **Mark V*** were the tanks used for instruction. One course of interest was a tank gunnery course for 26 officers and 50 other ranks of the Russian White Army, who then went back to fight against the Bolsheviks.

1920 was devoted to training personnel of the Tank Corps and Armoured Car Companies which were being formed for duties overseas in Palestine, Mesopotamia and India. However the school did manage to get down to its normal duty, namely that of training unit instructors.

1921 saw the first Fire Power Demonstration. This comprised:

> 1 *Demonstration of Fire Power – MarkV and Medium C Tanks*
> 2 *Evacuation of Tank*
> 3 *Smoke cloud discharged from exhaust pipe of a tank*
> 4 *Demonstration of 6 pounder shooting, moving tank V moving tank*
> 5 *Tank crushing a path through wire entanglement.*

I don't think that they would have been at all worried by fishermen in Arish Mell gap!

A control tower was built and dug outs, made on A range and in 1920-21 moving targets were introduced. They consisted of canvas screens, to about three-quarters the size of a tank, constructed on light tree trunks, and were towed across the range by another tank. The procedure was as follows: The towing tank was set going and the crew than dismounted and went to ground in a dug-out. Shooting commenced at the target which moved at about 7 mph and was some 200 yards behind the towing tank. When the cease-fire was signalled the crew emerged from the dug-out and pursued their towing tank across country – nearly always overtaking it – and finally signalling up the shot holes! The towing tank was never hit and only once was the rope broken.

A great number of Instructors Courses were held in 1922 and a lot of progress made in the standardization of instruction. The Heavy and Light Gun Wings were abolished and every instructor had to be capable of teaching a student all the subjects on the course.

In 1923 the REs started work on the new revolver range and on a .303 machine gun classification range, and the Tank Park moved from the centre of the area to the north east corner of the Schools area. Naturally enough with all the different types of gun fire there were bound to be some casualties and in February 1923 a Staff Sergeant Instructor and a private soldier were taken to hospital suffering from perforated ear drums. This was caused during instruction, and was due to the intensive firing on the 6 pounder 1000 yards Standing Battery. Ear protectors were made compulsory as a result, and issued for all firing on that battery.

On the lighter side, in June, a bathing hut, for army personnel consisting of three dressing rooms, was built, and opened with great delight, at Lulworth Cove. As motor cars became more popular and appeared in camp in greater numbers, an order was issued that all owners of motor vehicles kept in camp were to be charged two shillings per month and the money was to be collected by the PMC.

All these changes and new buildings gave rise to much a sarcastic comment. This appeared in the Royal Tank Corps Journal:

"There is something seriously wrong at Lulworth! A feeling of grave unrest permeates the camp! There are goings on which have never been heard of before; should these happenings reach the ears of higher authorities there will be trouble - yes definite trouble. Strange men in queer garb with mysterious instruments may be seen creeping round the school muttering darkly. And what is the inner meaning of this strange activity? Wonders will never cease. The camp is actually being repaired and re-conditioned. The instructional huts will no longer sag in the middle; it will soon be almost impossible for Recruit Snooks to push Recruit Clarence through the wall during the first lesson on repair and adjustments. The barrack rooms will hardly know themselves; they now have almost complete floors and are the proud possessors of drains round them to take away the rain.

"As for our cook house! It has been so transformed that for the last month our cooks have been frequently lost either in the mixing room, the preparation room or the making-up room. So serious has the situation become at times, that the cook sergeant has, I am told, had to muster his staff once an hour and call the roll to see that nobody was lost."

Wool YMCA hut: the venue for concert parties.

Mr Glyn Evans recalls his arrival at Lulworth in 1925:

"I arrived at Lulworth at 1430 hrs from Wool Station and was met at the crossroads by the RSM – a giant of a gentleman, whose pastime was weight lifting. With him was the orderly sergeant who was ordered to march me off to my duties. I was told to go through a backdoor into a building and report to the Sgt there. It was the officers mess. So I started my life sentence in what I called 'The House of Lords' – The Sergeants Mess I called the House of Commons!

"Life in the mess was not all a piece of cake, sometimes being more Regimental than outside. We only had one half-day per week, from 1400hrs; if you were caught in the mess after 1400 on your half day you forfeited it. I was caught once and the penalty was to clean all the brass work in the mess all the doors had brass finger plates – all the taps in the toilet and cloakroom and all the doorknobs were brass!

"The Tin Shed was a primitive affair, a very old wooden structure. The kitchen contained a dilapidated range backed on to which was an old boiler for heating domestic water, as and when, in working order. If the wind was in the wrong direction as it often was, smoke blew all over the place, but everyone seemed to accept it! Coal was issued daily for Messes from the coal yard, the kitchen man had to go to the coal yard, get one of the two company handcarts and bring the ration back to Mess and dump this coal underneath the kitchen window. Very often coal dust used to blow through to the kitchen and mix with the flour, no one complained and to best of my knowledge on one suffered ill effects – Happy Days! For tea/coffee making on the range there reposed three very large, very old, cast iron kettles but, more often than not, the duty waiter used to draw off hot water from the domestic tap. Food rations were also drawn daily from the "Ration Stand" opposite the Mess Kitchen – we did not usually draw up all our entitlement of flour, choosing to draw in bulk at the end of the month. Afternoon tea in Mess was a sit down affair, with each officer having his own teapot of either Indian or China tea – cottage loaves were supplied daily, on payment, from Farrow's of Winfrith. These were placed on large, round, old fashioned bread boards and officers cut their own requirements – there were daily on the table various jams – gentlemen's relish, fish-meat pasties and home-made cakes.

"The man who was directly responsible for feeding the mess members was Charlie Whitlock – a truly great chef. He joined us in the Tin Shed Mess in 1932, coming from the RTC Depot Mess at Bovington – he had served his apprenticeship with the Cunard line. He remained in the House of Lords with me for 17 years.

"Catering in the Tin Shed Mess pre [1939] war had to be seen to be believed, the very best of foodstuffs was served. The messing rate for living-in members was 3s/3d per day, with 3d added if one partook of ½ grapefruit. The young officer's rate of pay was 10s8d per day. We only used to draw the weekly meat ration on Saturday, so that members could have at least one roast per week. The main ingredients especially at lunchtimes were in the form of bully beef or NAAFI sausages. These latter items were transformed by Whitlock into rissoles; toad in the hole; even curry; we used to have quite a lot of rabbit – poached on government property! We also had, from time to time, venison supplied by Heath Range W.O. As waiters we had three changes of clothing a day. Dinner was served every night except Saturday and Sunday when supper was served. Tuesdays were Guest Nights and the last Tuesday in the month was a Regimental Guest Night. In this we had the services of the Band from Bovington, nicknamed the 'Snakecharmers' – after dinner about a dozen of the band played in the Ante-Room for a while.

"Every officer, instructor or student, was issued with a book of mess rules. Fines were very much in evidence:

Warning out for dinner after 1800hrs – 1s6d NOT WARNING OUT – 2s6d. Request for sandwiches in lieu of dinner in – 1s6d [this was a perk for the chef!] *In finding a dog in the mess – 2s6d In dog urinating in Mess – 5s*

"Fines were shown on the members DAY SHEET in red ink.

"Attached to us from Depot was a major, a bachelor, who lived in a wooden single officers quarter, who had two dogs. It was a well known fact that the major was not popular with the 'Rank and file' mess staff. After a week I noted with alarm that there were many daily chits 'dogs in mess' – Major .... – these chits had to give the time, and be signed by, the member of staff 'who saw'. I discovered that whenever the major brought his dogs into the mess, the members of staff would witness a chit. I had to make out one day sheet for the major as the original, with fines on, looked as though a spider had fallen into the red inkwell and crawled all over the sheet!"

Lulworth Ranges: tanks and tents in the field, below the northern slope of Bindon Hill.

Lulworth Ranges: line-up of tanks facing east for a gunnery demonstration, on the edge of the Arish Mell valley with the woods of Lulworth Park on the skyline to the north.

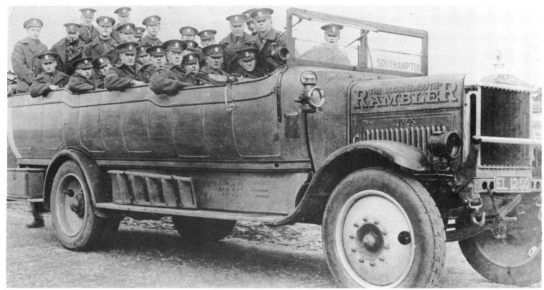

Bovington Camp: 'The Bournemouth Rambler No 4' joins the army.

The Bovington PRI charabanc

"THE CAMP charabanc — known as "Showboat" was driven by both Graham and Arthur Mansell; they were brothers, L/Corporals and also tank drivers. Every Wednesday, Saturday and Sunday the charabanc went to Bournemouth and Poole. It left from Lulworth Guard Room at 1400hrs and returned from Bournemouth at 2300hrs and Poole at Midnight. The return fair was 2s and was taken out of pay at source.

"The trouble was, that most of the soldiers were broke on Wednesdays, so the driver would report to the PRI and, on signature, was given a float of money. The driver then went round the huts at lunchtime, asking if anyone wanted to go on the bus. Those who wanted to go, but had no money, were given — again on signature — 2s for the fare and 2s for pocket money. This was stopped from their pay at the end of the month. The following day the driver returned any spare cash, and the signed up list of borrowers, to the PRI.

"The charabanc was also used to bring women from Poole — mainly from the Whitehouse Laundry — and Wareham, to the monthly all ranks dance held in the dining hall. The PRI did not charge for this service."[11]

Bovington Camp: the charabanc, known as the 'Showboat'.

Lulworth lettings

"MY FIRST engagement of 6 years was due for termination in August 1933 and my wife and I decided we would try our luck in civilian life. However we were thwarted in this plan by the Adjutant and PMC. I was an unpaid L/Cpl living first in Rose Cottage, West Lulworth and then The Forge, School Lane, Lulworth and was advised by the Adjutant and PMC that the job of Mess Paid L/Cpl was coming up and if I signed on for another 6 years I could have the job. There was also a WD letting in St Andrews Farm Cottages. These lettings were let through the Land Agent at Durrington Walls, Wiltshire, at a monthly rental of 3s6d! This was stopped out of your pay. These lettings were poor – no bath – just one room downstairs, with a small larder, and one upstairs. The stone floors were very uneven and the occupants used to place masses of newspapers under the lino in order to try and obtain a level surface. A small kitchen range, coal via a fatigue party from camp, cold water only by a tap utside each porch.

"The best part of the lettings was that they all had large gardens. As I was not 26 years of age I was not allowed to be on the Married Quarter list – but in 1936 I took over a beautifully kept, wooden married quarter from a staff sergeant and his wife, when they moved into the first brick built married quarters. In 1937 we moved into one of the next four, brick married quarters completed."[1 2]

Mr Glyn Evans, who is blessed by a very good memory and a clear mind's eye view of where things were in Lulworth, gives these further impressions of the camp:

"There were three entrances to the camp, West – near to the present entrance, North – where the plinth tank used to be, and East – which was never closed until the outbreak of the Second World War. Opposite the guardroom at the West gate, was the MI room (with no telephone) and next to that was a small post office run by NAAFI, where one could buy stamps and postal orders. If it was necessary to send a telegram one had to go to the post office in Lulworth Cove. Next to the NAAFI post office were three wooden huts which had been converted into married quarters, and after them came the Clothing Store, Tech Stores, and Barrack Stores (china, glass and hardware).

"Attached to the guardroom wall was the Detail Board – this was the main notice board for the camp and displayed Regimental Orders and other notices, it also showed the Dining Room menus for the week. This never changed except if it was rissoles on monday it would be replaced by liver/bacon and visa versa. The cook used to go into a huddle with the RQMS about the menu and one story claims that, when cook was asked if he could produce tapioca pudding, replied 'Oh no, I can't spell that, you'll have to have RISE!'"

Another man with many stories is Captain Edward Body, who spent many years at Lulworth in fact this total of 28 years, mainly on Gunnery Instruction, must surely be an army record for service in one station. He arrived in 1929, just before Lulworth Castle burned down, served under 19 different COs and knew all the old characters in the camp. One particular CO, a very fit man with a puckish sense of humour, who was "respected during the week and feared on Sunday," comes into one of Captain Body's memories:

"There was no church in Lulworth Camp in 1930, the nearest Church of England one was at West Lulworth and the Catholic Church was at East Lulworth so we were duly paraded on Sundays; some, indeed most, with hair like cavaliers (or so it appeared to me, fresh from the Depot) and wearing crossed and pocketed puttees meant to be wound parallel. We marched down the hill with the band playing and so into church to be relieved of our sins.

"Then the return (you know the hill!). Led by the CO at a spanking pace, the NCOs were soon too breathless to admonish us as we staggered up the hill. Some quarter of a mile up this seeming mountain, came the totally impossible order to march to attention! Invariably a puttee would become loose and unwind, and usually the poor unfortunate was in the middle of the column. You've probably never witnessed the hobbling havoc that this can cause to all within its ever widening radius, but this was not all, the band – even more physically distressed and out of breath than we were, then had to play a completely unrecognisable version of 'My Boy Willie' (minus most of its wind instruments!) – with the CO fired by the fanfare, going with the strides of a long–jumper, and the speed of a light infantryman, so that he seemed to be pushing the band and pulling the troops! No wonder, as it was probably the only time in the week that any of us had made the ascent without the 'Liquid Engineering' supplied by the Castle and Cove hotels!"

Another contemporary Lulworth character was RSM Hambley: "He was a huge man and a noted weight lifter. I shall never forget my first meeting with him. I was standing just inside the gateway to the camp, wondering where to go, when he came towards me. I stood rooted to the spot as a huge hand descended on my shoulders, and a deceptively gentle voice said 'any snags my boy'. I was to learn later that this had earned him the name of 'Snags' and was both his salutation and admonition. He once asked me if I had seen any fairies on the range, and anticipating a long strained silence he assured me that there were, and that they came out in the evenings, after firing was over. I learned that he really believed it! He was a man who would always invent an extenuating circumstance in your favour if you slipped up, and 'any snags' could be his most severe rebuke. It was just a question of voice inflection. Yet this same man, who, when a very noted boxer in our Corps became obstreperous and refused to leave the mess, called for a pack of cards and slowly tore them in half, then quietly said 'last show to-night gentlemen' – needless to say the mess emptied straight away,"[13]

Railway comes to Bovington

AS THE attractive stone bridge over the River Frome, at Woolbridge Manor, was continually being damaged by tanks – which were far too wide to safely use it – a spur from the main line station at Wool was planned, with a new bridge about 100 yards east of Woolbridge. Having crossed the bridge the line then crossed Bovington Lane, passed the revolver range and skirting the camp it came to an end at a siding near Workshops. It was opened for business in July 1919, having been built by the Prisoners of War who were marched daily from Lulworth to work.

"The Railway siding at Bovington Camp was opened for traffic in July 1919 and shortly afterwards derelict tanks from France began to arrive. There were some hundreds of tanks in all, in various stages of dilapidation, besides many train loads of stores. The tanks were towed off the train, away from the siding, and left at random in the Tank Repair Park. They had been entrained

Tank train: pushed by a saddle tank along the branch line from Wool to Bovington, about to cross the river.

Lulworth's Germans: prisoners of war built the railway bridge over the Frome and Bovington's workshops.

in France by personnel whose only thought had been demobilisation and they had been thoroughly rifled during their journey through France. Everything moveable had been taken as souvenirs, except mud, which had been lavished upon them."

The tanks were loaded on to rectanks for the journey: " The Rectank was a long, flat, open truck with a white line painted down the centre. It was shunted against an end-on ramp and the tank was then driven on to it, keeping the front shackle, situated exactly central between the horns, covering the white line. Although for height, when on the rectank, a tank comfortably met the requirements of the standard loading guage, I have seen as many as six attempts to satisfy the railway inspector regarding central alignment. He would take measurements to a fraction of an inch either side, rejecting the sligthtest overlap, so necessary was accuracy on account of the natural oscillation of the train in motion. There was no question of being able to adjust the alignment of the tank once on the rectank. A faulty drive on entailed a drive off and drive on again. With skilled drivers, loading and securing down was a quick operation, but with less skilled drivers it could prove an exasperating job, yet it never formed part of a driver's trade test."[14]

During 1919, a large number of **Mark IV** tanks had been sent out to various towns in Great Britain as War Trophies. These were rendered mobile and entrained at the Bovington Siding. When the tank arrived at its destination a small party of men from Workshops went to the town to unload the tank from the train and drive it to its resting place. All moveable objects were then removed and one sprocket taken out. This was done to prevent the possibility of its being used against the forces of Law and Order.

Bovington tank breakers: Cyril Roper and his gang. There were so many wartime tanks awaiting destruction that the work continued until about 1932.

Breaking up tanks

MR CYRIL ROPER of Wool, now in his eightieth year, was 14 when he left school in 1920 and went to work for the Sheffield Steel Breaking Company, one of the contractors engaged to dismantle derelict tanks. These had been brought to Bovington from France, on rectank wagons, and put at the northern end of the Tank Repair Park, near Clouds Hill: "They were all examined by a board

Bovington Camp: German prisoners of war building the Workshops.

Bovington Camp: the Workshops, with FX7770 stripped to the chassis.

of Workshop Officers during 1920, who classified them as to whether they were worth repairing or not. Some were overhauled and issued to the 5th Tank Battalion early in 1920, and to the 2nd Tank Battalion later in the same year. A large number have been broken up by the Slough Trading Company, to which Company they had been sold by the Disposal Board."

Mr Roper was first of all given the job of looking after the track of the narrow gauge railway, replacing ballast which had been washed away; then he worked for a short time in the blacksmiths shop, then finally he was given the job of breaking up the tanks. These were in the main **Mark Vs** and **Mark V**** engines. The work was done by gangs of four men, up to ten gangs employed at a time. It took four to five days to break up a tank, but as they were all on piece work, it was sometimes done considerably quicker than that – the record being two and a half days!

"The armour plates were removed by cutting the five-eighths inch diameter rivets by the use of sets and fourteen – pound sledge hammers, four or five blows being needed to cut out each rivet. There were flush rivets at the rear of the hull. If there happened to be any small arms ammo left in the tank, this added to the excitement! The sponsons and return run of the tracks were also removed, and when all the plates were off, the top of the frame was broken so that the side frames fell to the ground, allowing access to the engine and the rest of the works. The u-bolts securing the track rollers were levered off with crowbars, and the bronze brushes, each weighing 5lbs, were put into a shed for safe storage. The armour plate was taken to Bovington Station, and when there was sufficient for a train load, it was shipped off to Germany, apparently the only country with blast furnaces able to cope with this material. The mild steel and iron scrap was sent to British Furnaces each piece having to be smaller than 5ft 6in x 2ft x 1ft 6in, presumably to pass through the furnace doors."

Breaking up the tanks was not without its hazards as Cyril Roper explains, he was with another man, "breaking up a male sponson which had been removed from its tank. There were some rivets which could not be reached unless the sponson was turned over. When this was done, four live 6 pounder rounds fell out onto the ground. They must have been in the tank for some time and Cyril and his mate had been hammering out rivets with them close by. One of these rounds was shown to a group of officers who had driven out from Bovington and who promptly retreated to the Camp!"

Cyril also remembers other tanks being broken up at Worgret Camp. The last tanks to be dealt with by the Sheffield Company, was in 1928, and they were six **Mark Vs.**

In 1920 Central Workshops became the Tank Workshops Training Battalion, with 24 officers and 290 other ranks.

Trainees and Experimental Testing

REALISING THAT it would be difficult to recruit a sufficient number of properly qualified mechanics, it was decided to train boys for the job, and on 31 January 1920, the first batch of 40 boys were posted to Central Workshops from the 1st (Depot) Tank Battalion. During 1921 about 150 more were taken on, this meant that the boys exceeded the number of trained men.

So in June 1921 a Fitters Training shop was opened and all the boys learned to chip and file. Towards the end of the year it was decided to give the boys a more formal education, and those who passed the end of year exams were given an Army Certificate of Education (2nd Class).

"With a view to the better supervision of the boys, it was decided to transfer them all to one Company and to organise it wholly for their benefit. This was done on June 1st 1922 and all boys who, up to then, had been divided among the three companies, were transferred to 'A' Company. They were divided up into six squads for training and educational purposes; this was done primarily according to age, but owing to the poor education of some of the older ones, it was not wholly satisfactory. The intention was that boys should be admitted to the Tank Workshop Training Battalion at an age of less than 15 years, after an examination which would ensure that all could pass the 2nd Class Army Exam during their first year. After that their education would be primarily technical. A carefully worked out programme was drawn up allotting a certain proportion of their time to the Workshops, Education, Physical Training and Games.

"The boys were at first allotted to huts according to Squads, but later it was considered better to have them mixed up, and this was done in October. One boy in each hut was appointed Monitor and was given a gold stripe. All boys had 28 days leave during August and it was planned to close down the Works for that period so that the whole Battalion went on leave!"[15]

The scheme ended in 1924 when the Army Apprentice Schools were opened.

"During the early part of the 1920s the Central Workshops was kept busy maintaining the training tanks in full working order. They were also involved in some experimental work, including testing the **De Thoren Searchlight Tank,** and testing a **Peerless Armoured Car** on a 1,000 mile road test, and in the sand at Studland, and smoke tests on Tanks."[16]

They also helped in the "erection of machinery etc in the new machine Shops." and repaired Tanks for the other Schools and Units at the Centre.

"The new buildings included a machine shop measuring one hundred and fifty by sixty feet, with a capacity for rebushing and turning out twenty-four engines a week; repair bays fitted with two five-ton overhead travelling cranes and capable of accommodating twelve tanks of the largest type; repair sheds, made of galvanised iron and steel, which covered an area one hundred and eighty by one hundred and twenty feet, and a further large building, measuring three hundred by sixty feet, which contained a machine shop, an electricians shop, a coppersmith's shop, a wheeler's shop, a smithy and a laundry. These buildings were erected on the site of the original Tank Hangars."[17]

These permanent buildings were made of brick, steel and concrete – a complete contrast to the still wooden hutted "lines" – and one was dismantled and brought from Woolwich.

Special service detachments

THERE WAS a period of unrest at home and abroad, both in civilian and army life, demobilisation was being carried out rapidly but there was a limit, as there was a very large amount of work to be done and men had to be kept for that purpose.

"In the spring of 1919 there was a railway strike. Five Tank Sections were sent out from the 19th Tank Battalion, which was at the Training Centre. These were provided with **Mark V, Medium B** and **Medium C** tanks, all of which were overhauled by Central Workshops, and 1 officer and about 8 other ranks were attached from Central Workshops to each section. These sections were allotted to various Commands. Other sections were held in readiness at Bovington – one composed entirely of Central Workshops personnel, but it was never sent out."[18]

The railway strike only lasted for a few days but it was followed by others and threats of more so the Special Service Detachments did not return to Bovington until the end of that year.

In October 1920 there was a miners' strike and the Special Service Detachment was provided with **Peerless Armoured Cars** and sent out as before. However it was temporarily settled and the detachments returned to Bovington.

A much more worrying coal strike came in 1921, and in April, Special Armoured Car Sections were mobilised from among the units at the Training Centre. The drivers were mostly Instructors. One section of **Rolls Royce Armoured Cars** went to Edinburgh and one to Bulford. The four others had **Peerless Armoured Cars** and went to London, York, Shrewsbury and Bulford. They remained on duty in those areas until the strike was over – in June – and arrived back in Bovington in the first week of July.

"In January 1921 it was laid down that in war the Tank Workshops would be employed as Field Companies, while heavy repairs would be done by the Royal Army Ordnance Corps, and that in order that they might gain the necessary experience, a force of RAOC should be attached for duty to the Tank Workshop Training Battalion in peace time. About 80 NCOs and men, of the RAOC were accordingly attached to Workshops. These have been mixed indiscriminately with Tank Corps personnel for purposes of work, and the arrangement has been found to work well."[19]

Formation of 1st (Depot) Tank Battalion

THE 1ST (DEPOT) Tank Battalion was formed at Worgret Camp, a mile west of Wareham, on 28 July 1919. Up to that time recruits had been received by, and remained with, until posting, the Tank Corps Depot; but all fully attested recruits on the strength of the Tank Corps Depot were transferred to the Battalion, to which only finally approved and attested recruits were posted during the followng 12 months.

Worgret Camp, to the west of Wareham: glimpsed from the slope above the railway bridge.

On 17 January 1921 the Battalion moved from Worgret Camp to Bovington Camp and occupied F G and H Lines; subsequently termed "The Eighth of August Lines".

The majority of recruits came from the ranks of the unemployed and many of them considered that joining the Tank Corps was a way of continuing their trade or learning one which would be of value when they left the army. The recruiting poster of this period "Let Professor Tank teach you a Trade" had made a great impression. The Depot's history records:

"During 1920 and the first half of 1921 Tank Corps recruits were trained in exactly the same manner as infantry recruits; the course lasted 14 weeks and included no instruction in the weapons with which the Tank Corps is armed, nor in the mechanism of the Tank itself. Education was not included in the syllabus.

"In February 1921, it was decided to re-organise the training and to re-introduce into the recruits course, instruction in the Tank, 303 Hotchkiss Light Gun, 6 pdr Hotchkiss gun and revolver, education also being made a compulsory part of the curriculum.

"The length of the course was increased from 14 to sixteen weeks and by 1922 this was increased again to 18 weeks.

"Recruits under Depot training formed only a small part of the strength of the Battalion. At the end of their training anyone with previous engineering experience was tested and if suitable, was accepted into the Tank Workshop Training Battalion. Those who failed the test joined those with no previous engineering skill and after their Depot Training went on to train at the Central Schools and went to serve with Armoured Car or Tank Units."[20]

Those who had completed their Depot Training and who were not selected for posting to the Tank Workshop Training Battalion had to be considered from two different points of view – age and length of service.

"Boys who had enlisted between the ages 17 and 18 would not be available for foreign service until a year to eighteen months after completing their training. Others who were on short service of 2 to 4 years would only be chosen for foreign service for there was a manpower shortage.

"Both the trained recruits, and also men who had served several years with the Tank Corps and now had only two years service left, were considered available for either of the two purposes: They could be posted to units serving in the UK – including being posted to the permanent staff of Depot Tank Battalion itself – or they could be used at the Depot for Garrison duties or attached to the Central Schools, which was 60% short of the number of men required.

"As the permanent establishment of the Depot was unable to provide sufficient men for its own needs it was therefore unable to provide the 100 or 50 men needed for extra regimental duties. So those recruits too young for immediate foreign service and those in their last two years of service, were used for extra regimental duties.

Worgret Camp: the 1st (Depot) Tank Battalion was formed here on 28 July 1919.

Recruitment poster: 'Let Professor Tank teach you a trade.'

"All recruits were very anxious to join Armoured Car Units abroad and they were very discontented when recruits who had just completed their Depot Training were sent abroad rather than those who had completed training some time before but who were being used on Regimental and extra regimental Guards and Fatigues."[21]

The scheme designed for the re-organisation was as follows:-

It was found that posting of all Recruits on arrival to A Company was just causing unnecessary clerical work on pay, clothing, transfer accounts and messing. So recruits were to be posted direct to Companies – each company receiving the men until 4 squads were formed.

Postings to the Tank Workshop Training Battalion decreased. Men who enlisted as trained artificers went directly to Tank Workshop Training Battalion (and from 1922 Boys training as artificers also went there direct) instead of going through the Depot. Classification of recruits according to the amount of training they had done, was dropped.

Squad sheets containing the name of every private soldier on the strength of the Battalion – except those in their last two years of service – proved to be of great value in selecting men for drafts. As squads were numbered successively according to the date they were formed, it was possible to check each sheet to make sure that no man was overlooked.

The 1st (Depot) Battalion considered itself quite successful in the sporting field. Football was always well supported and the team always took part in the Army Cup and Inter Unit competition. Boxing was very popular and the Battalion team won the Corps Boxing Championships four years in succession. Its crowning achievement being the winning of the Army Team Championship and thus winning the Kings Trophy. Hockey, Cross-Country running and Athletics were also played and with reasonable success, but cricket was always poorly supported as was Rugby. A Swimming team was formed in 1922 but was hampered by lack of facilities for practice.

With few exceptions, all officers on courses at Bovington, were attached to the Mess. In 1922 their numbers were so great that other accommodation had to be found and for six months Clouds Hill Camp was used. In 1925 the new brick officers mess was completed and became the Garrison Officers Mess.

Towards the end of 1921, a grant was made for the purchase of books and it was decided to choose a building to be used as a Library and Reading Room. The Old Sergeants Mess in F Lines, having been used variously as a temporary Officers Mess and as the Shoemakers Shop, was converted to the Library. Chairs, tables, linoleum, pictures and curtains were acquired and it was opened in 1922: "The bar, lined with shelves, housed the books, and the old ante-room became the writing room; whilst the larger room on the west of the building was adapted as the general reading room, in which men could read the daily newspapers, play indoor games (bagatelle, chess, draughts etc), or amuse themselves according to their bent. In addition to books, the library fund provides for a number of monthly magazines, which are an added attraction."[22]

Bovington Camp: hut in Elles Road, chosen for conversion to married quarters. The contemporary drawing opposite was captioned 'The House of Dreams' and shows such a hut after conversion.

Bovington trader: C.W. Payne, himself ex Tank Corps, was the haircutter.

The Battalion band had great difficulty in remaining functional because of lack of funds. In spite of this lack, the band still managed to play at all social occasions in the camp, and the appointment of a Bandmaster in 1922, gave official recognition to this institution.

The camp had its own piggeries. Foot and Mouth disease was widespread during the early part of 1922 but towards the middle of the year pigs were bought and put into the sties built near to the stables. They proved to be a sound financial investment and provided a splendid feast for the men's Christmas lunch.

An Entertainment Committee was formed with the CO as President, to organise activities especially for the winter months when sport was curtailed. They promoted whist drives, dances, dancing classes and band concerts, one of these entertainments being selected for two evenings a week.

A new parade ground was completed, north of F lines in 1922, which provided a drill ground for the Instructors. A building on the east side was adapted for use as a tank shed in which instruction in Tank Mechanism was taught. A new Sergeants mess just ready for completion had its roof blown off in December 1922.

Permanent quarters for Officers were constructed and a number of "Officers Lettings" were constructed on the western side of the camp, for married officers.

A "diary" written by an officer's wife in the Tank Corps Journal, shows the anxiety and frustrations that wives and families faced when trying to accompanying their husbands to new postings, particulars at camps without any, or few married quarters:

"Tuesday – Went to see Mrs Tanner the wife of a local confectioner, the owner of six cheaply furnished houses in the district. Endured a long history of her newly-married girl, who is selecting the best furniture from each house for her home. Ascertained after much difficulty that all the houses were let, but found we might put down our names on her long waiting list. Felt this was a huge privilege. Mrs Tanner explained that she felt she had 'done her bit' through the war, by buying up these houses and letting them to officers. She was bursting with satisfaction over her patriotic record. Having heard about the rents she charged, I did not feel obliged to offer congratulations. Later met Mrs Murphy, a corporal's wife I knew at Aldershot. She is living with her husband and babies in two rooms here, for which she pays a guinea a room, without attendance. They can't afford it (who can wonder?), so she is going back reluctantly to her mother in Ireland. She asked me, in her pretty brogue, with tears in her eyes, whether the War Office didn't understand that husbands and wives wanted to be together after the war? I went on, feeling troubled. What about all these rows of empty huts I have seen standing in camps all over the country?

"Visited the house-agent, who smiled at me with pity and amusement when I asked for a list of furnished houses. There are none, and will apparently never be any. He would not promise to let me know if anything did turn up as 'it would hardly be worth my while, as I have so many scores of applicants.'

"So it continued, with a tumbledown cottage being about all that was on offer, and tears closing discussions on alternatives such as a caravan, old railway carriage or a houseboat:

"A month later – Still waiting and hoping. Nothing to report."

Certainly accommodation was very basic, the huts built in the war were still being used and had seen better days having been occupied by thousands of men who had done their training at Bovington.

The War Office finally managed to get Government approval for a building programme in the Camp. In the Army Estimates for 1923-24 account was taken of the need for new accommodation for married families: "... the redistribution of troops after the war, and the creation of new units, such as those of the Tank Corps, have necessitated the use of hutted camps, erected during the war and designed only for the occupation by single men. A very considerable sum will be devoted in 1923 to 1924 to the construction of quarters for married officers and other ranks in these camps, which is one of the most urgent military necessities. The provision of these quarters will have the further advantage of releasing accommodation for the civilian population in the vicinity of the camps."

In order to build these new quarters the War Office Land Department had to purchase more land. In March 1924 the War Office paid £4,318 to the Frampton estate for a piece of land to the west and south of the camp; this did not include Tintown.

In fact the army had already been using this strip of land for some considerable time. The large military hospital and all the playing fields were on part of it.

An article from the Royal Tank Corps Journal gives a light-hearted glimpse of life at the Depot in 1923-24 for the newly joined subaltern:

"In those days, after two years of intense physical activity, both on and off parade, mixed with a little mental exercise, the newly commissioned subaltern went straight to the Depot at Bovington. There he found a number of things about his new life which shook him to the foundations. Generally, newly joined subalterns were known as 'Warts,' a wart being an unpleasant excrescence on the face of the Regiment!

"On arrival at Bovington the newly joined were immediately put on the 'Square,' and there drilled by drill instructors who knew far less about drill than they did. But there were two honourable exceptions to this. One was the Regimental Sergeant Major who was known as 'Tisshup' due to the perculiar noises he occasioned by clearing the phlegm from his throat before giving a command. The other was a Quartermaster Sergeant of the Household Cavalry, who, when one of his charges made a mistake, would project his 6ft 4ins on to the square in an attitude of prayer, and on his knees with eyes turned to heaven, would address the offender in far from biblical terms. One of our favourite amusements was to feign collective deafness as a squad, and continue to march smartly off the square into the moorland beyond it while the instructor got redder in the face and hoarser in the voice. This worked well until one day when the squad was well off the course and into the rough, they heard close behind them, the dreaded "Tisshup"! There followed an agonizing twenty minutes of doubling over the very rough countryside. After that the squad remained on the square.

"Our accommodation had to be seen to be believed. We were housed in a collection of huts known as "Siberia". They were neither draft proof or rain proof. The only way to sleep in comfort was to hoist an umbrella or waterproof sheet above the bed, and to buy a large dog to act as a mobile hot water bottle. Nor did the present mess exist. The mess was a series of interlocking huts, but they were waterproof.

"After completing our period on the square we proceeded to do our elementary D and M courses at what was then known as the Central Schools, and at Lulworth. The courses lasted two months each ... The amount of instruction one imbibed depended on one's instructor's personality to a very great extent, and on one's own respectivity. At Bovington our instructor was an excellent wielder of the crowbar and sledge hammer, but during periods of theory, which he learnt by heart, rather after the manner of a museum guide, it was quite possible to steer him on the dirty stories after the first ten minutes of the period, these stories getting bluer and bluer as the period progressed to its salacious end. On the other hand at Lulworth our instructor was so good that one could not help learning from him."

Tank Corps becomes 'Royal'

1923 SAW a change in the nomenclature of the Tank Corps. A Royal Warrant dated 18 October 1923 [Army Order No 369 of 1923] stated: "Whereas we have noted with great satisfaction the splendid work that has been performed by our Tank Corps during the Great War, our will and pleasure is that this Corps shall enjoy the distinction of 'Royal' and shall henceforth be known as our 'Royal Tank Corps'

Another change was made in 1923 – the cap badge was changed to a tank encircled by a wreath of laurel and surmounted by the Imperial Crown and the motto 'Fear Naught' in a scroll under the tank. Gilt buttons with the interwoven monogram RTC surmounted by a crown also became regulation uniform pattern.

The beret appears, 1925

IN 1925 the name of the 1st (Depot) Battalion, Royal Tank Corps was changed to the Royal Tank Corps Depot. An alteration was made in the uniform too – Army Council Instruction No 113 of 1925 stated that "a black headdress with a white metal badge (silver for officers) in substitution of the Service Dress Cap, to be worn in all orders of dress".

The first time the beret was worn in public was at a Levée held on 10 March 1925 and brought comment from the daily press. The Royal Tank Corps Journal noted: "Perhaps the most

THE ROYAL TANK CORPS UNIFORM.
ANOTHER UNFORTUNATE JUXTAPOSITION.

The Royal Tank Corps beret: it faced a degree of stick.

OPPOSITE: The King at Lulworth – George V's visit in April 1928.

discussed topic in the canteen nowadays is the expected advent of our friend 'Beret'. Some are quite undaunted in fact almost unconcerned about the matter; others, grim stern-visaged veterans who pride themselves on their masculine dignity, deeply resent the somewhat effeminate appearance they may present to the public gaze. Certainly the prospect of a self conscious soldier hastening along a crowded thoroughfare, followed by the derisive howl of 'Queenie' from a crowd of elated urchins, is hardly an enticing one, but this is mere speculation, so sufficient unto the day is the evil thereof."

Tune for the Corps March unfit for the King

DURING 1925 a representative committee of senior officers of the Royal Tank Corps was convened at Bovington to choose a suitable tune for the corps march, in a competition to be decided by a free vote of the committee and the bandsmen. Several tunes were played, including some folk tunes, specially arranged by the bandmaster. It was eventually decided to accept two tunes, coupled together to form a contrast. Those were *My boy Willie* and *Whistle Daughter, Whistle* taken from the *English Folk Songs* colected by Cecil Sharp.

Permission to use the tunes was obtained from the publishers and the literary executors of the late Cecil Sharp. A military band score was prepared, forwarded to HQ RTC Centre, to the War Office and finally to the Commandant, Royal Military School of Music, for approval. It was pointed out that the proposed march should have the approval of His Majesty King George V, as Colonel in Chief of the Corps, before being officially sanctioned.

During its course through the departments of the War Office, it was pointed out that the Army Council would have to consider whether the words of *Whistle Daughter, Whistle* were suitable for the troops; it was eventually decided that they could not be submitted to His Majesty. For a time the matter was in abeyance, and the Band President was instructed to find some other suitable tune. Finally, in February 1927, he removed the second tune from the score and

reduced it to *My boy Willie.*

The March was finally approved by His Majesty the King, and appeared in Army Order No 351 of 1927, as the official march of the Royal Tank Corps.

The Twenties at Bovington

IN SPITE of all the precautions taken against disease, in particular the inoculation of troops, in December 1926 an epidemic of influenza hit Bovington Camp and lasted from January to March. Seventy-two were admitted to hospital and the rest were treated in huts set aside as medical wards. This was followed not long afterwards by a particularly severe outbreak of measles, when 250 soldiers were isolated for several weeks.

In 1927-28 many improvements in the camp to the roads, gardens and buildings, made a big difference to the look of the place. Avenues of trees were planted; lawns laid down; colourful plants placed in beds in front of messes and main buildings. Roads and houses were named after battles and bases occupied during the First World War and for the tank's pioneers. The ten houses built for senior officers between 1926 and 1928 were called Bermicourt, Bourlon, Cambrai, Elveden, Flers, Hamel, Moreuil, St Quentin, Swinton and Wailly and all of them are still occupied today.

Improvements were also made to the Revolver range. It was levelled and drained, new butts were constructed and better accommodation provided for the range warden and the men using the butts.

A Gas Chamber in G lines was completed and training in anti-gas procedures was put on the training syllabus.

Visitors to the Centre included His Majesty King Amanullah of Afghanistan, on 20 March 1928 to watch a tank demonstration at the Gunnery School; followed in April by a visit of His Majesty King George V.

The winter of 1927-28 was one of the most severe in the area for several decades. There were many very heavy falls of snow and long periods of thick frosts. Freezing east winds caused huge snow drifts, which gave the camp a Christmas card look but caused a great deal of hardship to the troops.

Bovington Camp: the Royal Tank Corps Depôt's guard of honour, which formed up twice in 1928, for the visits of Kings Amanullah of Afghanistan and Britain's George V.

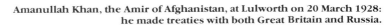

Amanullah Khan, the Amir of Afghanistan, at Lulworth on 20 March 1928: he made treaties with both Great Britain and Russia.

Crawley feted as the hero: on his return to Bovington with the European Amateur Middleweight Cup.

Boxing honours for Sergeant F.P. Crawley

SERGEANT CRAWLEY was one of the prominent sportsmen of the Corps, and was associated with every branch of sport. However his main sport was boxing:-

> 1919 – *runner up in Corps Middleweight Championship*
> 1920 – *runner up in Corps Welter Weight Championship*
> 1921 – *Won Southern Command Welterweight Championship*
>   – *runner up in Army Open Individual Welterweight Championship*
> 1922 – *Won Army Open Individual Welterweight Championship*
> 1924 – *Won Army Open Individual Welterweight Championship*
>   – *Won Army Middleweight Amateur Championship*
>   – *Won ISBA Amateur Championship*
>   – *Selected as first reserve for the Olympic team.*
> 1925 – *Retained Army Open Individual Welterweight Championship*
>   – *Retained ISBA Amateur Championship*

Sgt Crawley represented the Army on many occasions and more than justified his selection as Britain's leading Middleweight, by winning the European Middleweight Amateur Championship of 1925. His opponents were Christensen of Norway, Krippel of Germany and Hans Holdt of Denmark all of whom he beat with brilliant performances.

Fox hunting over the heath

A MEET of the South Dorset Hounds took place at the Royal Tank Corps Centre Mess: "Luckily we had a fine day and the home coverts held a stout dog fox. The first draw was the bog by the railway line and a fox was soon viewed away from the thick patch under the revolver range. He led us over Woolbridge Heath, leaving Longthorns on the left, through Hethfelton and across Stokeford Heath with a very bare scent. Then we crossed the Wareham Rd, past Budden's Farm, and ran up the valley to Trigon mill. Here he funked crossing the flooded river and turned along the meadows towards Hyde, crossing the river Piddle between Trigon and Hyde. Here the field had to crawl under a fallen tree and then ford or swim, the river, into the deer park, according to the size of their horses. Some turned back and were not seen again. Hounds were held up by the wire boundary fence but soon got on terms with their fox and hunted him well through the rhododendrons out on Hyde Heath. Here he went to ground in a rabbit burrow, after providing a good wild hunt of 1 hour and 20 minutes. We hope he may give us another gallop before the season is over."[23]

Lawrence of Arabia at Bovington: in 1923 he enlisted in the Tank Corps as T.E. Shaw.

Clouds Hill: temporary camp by the roadside at the point where Lawrence would have his death crash in 1935.

A famous recruit

ARGUABLY THE most famous person ever to enlist into the Tank Corps was TE Lawrence – "Lawrence of Arabia" as he was known to millions of people all over the world. His exploits in the Middle East during the Great War had, by the Twenties, become almost legendary, however, Lawrence found the utmost difficulty in living directly in the public eye. Having been forced to resign from the Royal Air Force, still hounded by reporters wherever he went, he sought refuge in the anonimity of the ranks of the British Army. He had to use all his influence with friends at the War Office to get permission to do this, but finally received a letter from the Adjutant General saying: "... I have received this morning a letter from Elles who is prepared to consider your proposal ... . He asks you to write to him at HQ Tank Training Centre, Bovington Camp, marked personal ..."

Thus, on 12 March 1923, under the name of TE Shaw, one of the country's most famous soldiers, enlisted into the Tank Corps at Bovington Camp, and was posted to 'B' Company, Depot Battalion, being allocated a bed in Hut 12. He made one or two friends during his brief sojurn in the Corps the quieter men who read and listened to music – Privates Russell and Palmer (always referred to as 'Posh Palmer') being his two main companions. He found the rest abhorent and wrote to his friend Edward Garnett: "... I've really struck bed-rock or base material this time. The army is unspeakable: more solidly animal than I believed Englishmen could be, I hate them, and the life here ..."

While he was stationed at Bovington Lawrence rented from a relative, a small almost derelict cottage called 'Clouds Hill', for the princely sum of 2 shillings and sixpence a week. Sergeant Knowles, who lived in another cottage opposite 'Clouds Hill', helped TE to renovate the building, and whenever he could Lawrence, either alone or with friends would escape to this peaceful refuge, to write, read, or listen to his records. In a letter to AE Chambers (3 August 1924) he wrote: "... Wool is the Station, the cottage is alone in a dip in the moor, very quiet, very lonely, very bare. A mile from camp. Furnished with a bed, a bicycle, three chairs, 100 books, a gramophone of parts, a table. Many windows, oak trees, an ilex, birch, firs, rhododendrons, laurel, heather. Dorsetshire to look at. No food, except what a grocer and the camp shops and canteens provide. Milk, wood fuel for the picking up. I don't sleep here, but come out 4.30pm until 9pm nearly every evening, and dream, or write or read by the fire, or play Beethoven and Mozart to myself on the box. Sometimes one or two Tank Corps slaves arrive and listen with me ... but few care for such abstract things."

Some years later (1st September 1938) EM Forster wrote in an article published in The Listener, about 'Clouds Hill' in Lawrence's time: "In those days the two bottom rooms were full of firewood and lumber. We lived upstairs, and the sitting room there looks now much as did then, though the gramophone and the books have gone, and the fender with its bent ironwork has been remodelled. It was, and it is, a brownish room — wooden beams and ceiling, leather-covered settee. Here we talked, played Beethoven's symphonies, ate and drank. We drank water only or tea – no alcohol ever entered Clouds Hill ... and we ate – this sounds less romantic – out of tins. TE always laid in a stock of tinned dainties for his guests ... TE slept in camp, coming out when he could during the day as did the rest of the troops."

Not knowing who TE was, one of the Sergeant Instructors at the Tank Corps Depot reported to an officer that one of his squad was making notes of his lectures in Greek! Actually Lawrence, bored with the elementary lectures, was writing in Arabic. Basic training completed, TE was put into 'A' Company stores. As it was not an onerous job he managed to do quite a lot of work on his book: *"Seven Pillars of Wisdom"*.

After two years in the Tank Corps, getting steadily more depressed – almost to a suicidal pitch according to one source – his influential friends began a campaign to get him back into the RAF, even writing to the Prime Minister, Stanley Baldwin, to plead his case. Eventually, on 21 August 1925, two years and five months after he had enlisted into the Tank Corps, Lawrence was readmitted into the RAF. He spent a relatively happy time for the next ten years, until 26

Final journey from Bovington: Lawrence's coffin leaves for his funeral at Moreton.

February 1935, when, Aircraftsmen Shaw, as he was then called finally left the services.

He returned to 'Clouds Hill', which he had been preparing for his retirement, with the idea of writing another book, to be called: "Confessions of Faith". Until the idea for the book came to him TE had been worried about his coming retirement, not being to happy to: "... potter about like any other retired Colonel."

However, his retirement was not as trouble-free as he had hoped and once again he was continually besieged by reporters, eager to know what the famous man was going to do next. Before he, or they, could decide, fate stepped in and, on 13th May 1935, a mere ten weeks after returning to 'Clouds Hill', Lawrence was critically inured in a motorcycle accident very near his cottage, when he swerved to avoid a young cyclist. He was taken to the Bovington Camp Medical Centre, but died six days later. His grave in Moreton Churchyard is now, like 'Clouds Hill' a popular tourist attraction, but that apart, Lawrence has had little impact upon Bovington Camp or upon the daily life of the Depot, or the Training Centre.

Married quarters and schools

THE FIRST married quarters were modified huts in A lines. The troops were gradually moved to lines eastwards as more of their huts were turned into quarters for the families. They were divided, with breize blocks, into family accommodation – with bedrooms to suit the number in the family.

One family who moved into a converted hut in 1921 were the Carpenter family – RSM and Mrs Carpenter and their two daughters – Peggy aged six and Vera aged four. In 1985, the "Carpenter girls" revisited Bovington Camp, whilst they were on holiday in Dorset, and came to the Tank Museum to donate their photographs. They were photographed in front of one of the old huts still standing in the camp, by our photographer.

There had been a steady increase in the number of children in camp – it was said that by 1921 there were over five hundred. Dorset County Council paid to take some of them to school in nearby villages and even as far away as Poole. There was a long, protracted argument between the War Office and the County Council's Finance Committee as to which of them should provide a school at Bovington. A year later the problem was getting desperate and so the army agreed to convert a military building for use as a school.

Bovington Camp: Peggy and Vera Carpenter in 1921, and on their return to the camp in 1985.

One of Bovington's old residents says it "was made of corrugated iron, with wooden partitions and floors and backed on to one of the old parade grounds, which was used as a playground. The Headmaster was a Mr E G Walking and there were three other teachers. The building was quite large and there were nearly a hundred children there when it opened in 1923. When there was a sports day or concert – for example on Empire Day – the Commandant and his wife used to attend. A lot of parents came too. We also did a play called *Abou Hassan* which was a great success.

"When the Commandant made his thank you speech in 1924 he said 'We all know what they were like before you cam and we appreciate the work that has brought them to the standard they are today.'

"The teachers, children and camp authorites pulled together and made the classrooms bright and cheerful places to work in and soon the pupils were showing great improvement in their work. The army resurfaced the playground, provided desks and chairs, supplied fuel for the stoves – and delivered it – provided transport for school outings and even housed the Headmaster. Later they built some teachers quarters opposite the school.

"By 1925 another class room was added to the school for the older pupils, a hut with woodwork benches and a garden area for the gardening classes were also added.

"Domestic Science and woodwork were popular additional classes and some of the older boys were given evening classes in mechanics by instructors from Central Schools. Of course the ordinary range of subjects were taught too and the Bovington School developed a good reputation.

"We felt that we could do with a great many more headmasters and teachers of the type to be found at Bovington. If all schools were run on these lines we do not think there would be much fear for the future of the country.

"With the coming of wives and children the camp lost the attractive backwoods atmosphere which had tickled my imagination in the far off days of 1917, Respectibility and smugness were now the order of the day. Soon we became used to seeing perambulators, well-fed women and overdressed children on roads and paths that had once been sacred to the prancings of athletes. So Bovington ceased to be a community and became a garrison; and when the domestic background had been filled in to the last cat and clothes line the officers wives took their places as leaders of military society. We of the huts saw very little of the commissioned ladies, but we heard tales of their frequent duty visits to the married mens quarters where it was a pleasure to inspect all newly–arrived babies. Headed by the Colonel's wife, they made a brave show at such officially approved entertainments as the Regimental Dance, cricket matches of the deckchair and cold buffet class, and the annual sports meeting. Accompanied by pedigree terriers and carrying shooting–sticks, they turned out frequently to encourage the gentlemen of the rugby fifteen, but I do not remember that they ever showed much interest in soccer."[24]

So wrote Alex Dixon in *Tinned Soldier*. Not everyone would agree with him – especially the families who have spent long periods separated from their soldier husbands because they were "subject to the exigencies of the service". It was a term many of the army wives would come to hate.

Mr Cooper, a Bovington resident since 1925, has many memories:

"I started my working life, at the age of 15, apprenticed to the boot repair civilian contractor down in D lines. The workshop was an Army hut – partitioned – with the Regimental tailor, Bert Cox, on one side and our Workshop on the other. It was sited approximately where the NAAFI club is now, near the Sandhurst block. The name of my boss was Dick Tongay, an old soldier and a real character. he wore breeches and leggings and a tartan waistcoat (he had bandy legs and looked a little like Harry Lauder) but I heard someone remark that the only connection he had with the Scottish race, was out of a bottle! He said he knew T.E. Shaw [Lawrence of Arabia] when he was a company storeman – but did not know his backgound at the time. When the facts leaked out in 1925 Shaw was eventually posted, I started to work for Tongay a few months later. Tongay did obtain a copy of the *Revolt in the Desert* through Herbert Smith. They were a bit rare in those days and expensive –£5, a lot of money at that time – 1926. It seemed that Shaw sought refuge from the noise of the barrack room to write his abridged version of the *Seven Pillars of Wisdom*. He had many friends in Bovington. One of them was a Mr Forse, a barber in Fish Street. The story is that Mr Forse let Shaw use the small back room of his business premises, to write in peace. But this happened before I came to Bovington of course. The Forses lived in a wooden army type hut opposite Woodside Cafe. It burned down in the 1930s and I can remember stories that most of the valuable papers of Lawrence's — contained in a tea-chest, were destroyed."

"Another person of note in the camp was Garrison Sergeant Major Sutherland who sometimes played the part of MC at different functions. At inter-service Boxing tournaments (held in the Garrison Hall), he introduced the contestants and was also judge, referee etc. He was a commanding figure and much respected and lived in a quarter at the end of Arras Rd next to the old school. He was the proud possessor of a Douglas Motor Cycle and sidecar. There were very few motor cars around at that time and a motor cycle was a bit of a luxury.

"Sergeant Dan Crawley was another sporting character. He had the reputation of being rather clumsy — especially at social events. However his performances in any sporting event was very different. His most successful sport was of course boxing. I can remember seeing a cartoon by Tom Webster in the sports page of a 1926 News of the World, showing Crawley astride a scaled — down tank moving forward, indicating his intention to crush all opposition in ABA competitions at the Albert Hall! His record proved it right with many trophies! He was Amateur Middleweight Champion of Europe [1925]."

The Garrison Theatre: Bovington's superior picture house.

Cinema and concerts

WHEN HE came to Bovington as a boy of 14, in 1925, Mr Cooper says: "What I particularly noticed was the number of ex-railway carriages — less wheels of course — in use by civilians in the 'civilians only' parts of camp. I later learned that these carriages could be purchased for £20, and £20 extra for transport to any suitable site not too far away. They served as cheap homes for ex-servicemen mainly. Quite a few of them were situated in the village, as we called it. The only street for the civilians was Fish Street.

"There were the small traders and craftsmen that served the wants of the local Service personnel, tailors, barbers, cobblers and last but not least Collins laundry. Also in Fish Street was a photographer, cycle shop, butchers, a general store, lock-up garages, two cafes and a fish and chip parlour.

"There were also two cinemas at that time. One was built during World War One and the other after the war. The first, and older, cinema was civilian owned and was a big barn-like wooden building, very draughty and cold during the winter days, but 'heated' by coal-fired combustion stoves and on a cold night it was 'overcoat order'. There was a change of film every three days and the cost of admission was 2½d. The 'Garrison' up the road was a bit superior, charging 3d and had radiators which sometimes did not work. The Garrison changed their films every 2 days. There was plenty of selection between the two! The seats 'down front' were wooden forms in both places but they were well patronized for all that. The floor boards, I recall were in a bad state. Sometimes one would be seated where the floor boards would be broken and the soil beneath could be felt with the foot. The music was provided 'down front' by piano forte played by a small, thin Irish lady called Mrs Coglam and usually, whilst playing, a Woodbine cigarette was hanging from her mouth. She could play very well but a scanty repertoire. Her favourite tune being "Down in sunny Havana". She would play this repeatedly even if there was a gale blowing outside! There was a silent film made around that time of Hardy's "Tess of the D'Urbervilles". It was filmed in Dorset, in Puddletown and roundabout the district. It was shown in the old cinema and the story opens showing a labourer – Tess's father – saying 'Oh what a lovely summer's day in Dorset'. There was much raucous laughter, with much stamping of feet on the already weathered floor boards, as there was snow on the ground outside! Sometimes the projectionist would make a mistake in the change over of the reels, and the screen would be showered with peanuts and orange peel.

"An enormous amount of peanuts were consumed, also oranges,which were very cheap. A large bag of nuts was 2d and oranges were 1d each – it made the cleaner's job a difficult one. These refreshments were obtained from the NAAFI kiosk within the cinema – served by a Mr Christmas. He also put up the posters of forthcoming films. The assistant projectionist doubled up as the cleaner, having to clean up the nut shells and orange peel. Admission 3d; bag of nuts 2d; an orange 1d; and a small packet of 5 Woodbines 2d – grand total of 8d.

"There was no trouble at the Garrison cinema as there was a camp Police Sergeant present. Rats would come out from under the floor boards and consume the peanuts that had dropped. One night something happened that was not at all amusing. One misguided soldier fired a starting pistol during a western. Mrs Bugg, wife of the proprietor, had a miscarriage and this was to have been their first child. If Bill Bugg could have caught the fellow it would have been a bad day for him.

"There was an amusing incident that happened prior to the opening of the new post office in 1934. The old one was sited where the bus shelter is now – at the end of Swinton Avenue. The old Post Office was wood and lay alongside the Garrison cinema – about nine feet separating the two. One night 2 soldiers removed some timber from the back wall of the building, unbolted the safe from the floor – put it on a military handcart and wheeled it past Guardroom cells in the early hours of the morning. Sgt 'Tiddler' Ede of the Garrison Police (weight 16 stone) who was having '40 winks' on one of the cell beds, later remembered that he heard the rumble of a cart go by the barred window but did not suspect anything at the time. The safe was taken up on the heath and opened from the back but contained only a few Postal Orders and stamps. It was rumoured that both the culprits were 'drummed' out of the army."

From the very beginning of the camp, entertainment was provided in many ways. The first items to appear, were the band concerts and concert party shows, with local artists, in the YMCA huts both at Bovington and Wool. Obviously concert parties were popular, as is shown by the following heart-felt letter in the Tank Corps Journal of 1921:

"As the winter months are now upon us we hope that some effort will be made to organise a concert party for the men at Bovington Camp. Cinemas have their attraction, and billiards and snooker are a mild form of dissipation to some; but nothing can compete with a good concert party for a real swing. Surely there must be a great deal of talent amongst the units here, and a combined garrison sing-song party would help to pass the long winter evenings. An

Entertainment Committee should be formed, and if they worked in conjunction with the Tank Corps Compassionate Fund and Association the result would no doubt prove beneficial to both."

The Garrison Theatre which was at the corner of Swinton Avenue, doubled up as a Music Hall as well as a Cinema. Nine parties of Imperial Players (NAAFI Concert Parties) toured remote areas that leading music hall artists would not visit. The entrance to the NAAFI Buffet Bar was to the left of the Garrison Theatre and was sometimes better patronised!

As time went on there was more and more sport. Inter-Battalion sports included football, hockey, swimming, cross country running and boxing. All were popular, as were darts, billiards and indoor board games. Of course then, as now, the soldier's favourite pastime was drinking tea and having a 'wad' and there gradually became more and more places in which he could indulge this habit.

Camp followers

DURING THE war a number of traders sensed an obvious need and moved into Bovington. They erected a variety of wooden huts, tin shacks and old railway carriages at the southern edge of the Camp. There were a number of old railway carriages – brought from the railway for £20 and a £20 delivery charge. They were used in many ways probably the most surprising use being that of housing the piano belonging to a woman who gave piano lessons from her carriage!

Among the first civilian traders to move in, were George Keene and Herbert Smith. The former visited the camp on Sunday afternoons bringing his wares in a suitcase from his tobacco and sweet shop in Poole High Street. The latter began his family business by cycling round the camp selling the Daily Express and earning fifty shillings a week from the newspaper proprietors. Later they opened small adjacent shops in huts on the corner of what is now Swinton Avenue.

Herbert Smith expanded his business rapidly, opening a fancy goods shop on a site opposite his newspaper shop. This building was the original row of cottages which was used by the Purchase Brothers as a general shop and post office. The Smiths built a glass covered verandah

Bovington: Keene's Stores and a column of Rolls-Royce Armoured Cars.

Bovington traders: Purchase Bros became H. Smith's Handy Stores – Herbert Smith is on the left.

front to the shop – Smiths Handy Stores – and lived in the other part of the cottages. Later, 1921, an extension was added. This took the form of a large galvanised-iron building which was used as a cafe and billiard saloon.

By the early twenties, "Tintown" – as Bovington civilian area came to be known – was quite a large area. There were hairdressers, barbers, cobblers, chemists, tailors, grocers, blacksmiths and butchers as well as five cafes, two billiard saloons, two cinemas, two cycle shops, a fish and chip shop, garage and laundry .

Bovington: the bus stop.

Bovington trader: cheerful Fred Smith took over George Keene's corner shop.

Mr Cooper remembers the shopkeepers of "Tintown" and has this to say about them:
"Mr Smith's paper shop was a lock-up wooden building and as well as selling newspapers he sold cigarettes, magazines, lighters and watches. The premises were sometimes broken into and stock taken – the thieves getting in through the sky-light. One day Mr Smith decided to leave a large unleashed dog inside the shop, to guard his property. The next morning, on opening the shop, he was greeted by a wagging tail and the dog with a large bone in its mouth – and a lot of his stock missing!"

The Elite Cafe was managed by a Mr Gordon Smith (no relation to the above) who was in business from the twenties until the fifties and Mr Cooper says "I was served with a cup of tea in 1954, by the same gentleman, so I would say he had a good innings serving the troops with tea of NAAFI canteen potency, for all those years. The blacksmith not far from the Elite was also owned by a Mr Smith (again no relation) who had the nickname of 'Shooey'.

"The tailor 'Tich' Leigh, nicknamed 'Tich' because he was only 5ft in height, had served with the Motor Machine Gun Corps. He had been trained in London originally but on demob he had remained in Bovington. He plied his trade in a very small way doing alterations, sewing stripes on tunics, in order to supplement his meagre dole payment. He lived in one of the railway carriages, which were dotted around Bovington, and in spite of all his difficulties remained a cheerful and witty character, always dressed smartly in pin striped, pressed trousers, collar and tie, a black jacket and highly polished shoes."

The Thirties at Bovington

1931 WAS a year of high unemployment and world depression. Applicants exceeded vacancies. This also applied to the army and as a result standards were high and recruiting centres were selective.

Mr R W Munns, gives a vivid picture of what it was like to join the Royal Tank Corps at the age of 19 in 1931. He had never heard of the Corps and had only a driving licence as a qualification:

"I was given two days pay with ration money which amounted to about six shillings, and told to report again to the Recruiting Office in two days time when I would be despatched to the RTC Depot in Bovington. It was quite an experience to be put on the train for London, as I had never previously been further than 20 miles from Liverpool. Being late November it was dark and cold when I finally reached Bovington and reported to the Guard Room. I was tired, hungry and cold as I climbed the steps, knocked on the door and entered into a warm, well-lit room. The members of the Guard were sitting at a wooden table on which were plates of food and mugs of tea, and I was invited to sit down and give some details of myself. Finally I was asked if I had eaten and when I said not since Waterloo, I was offered some of their food and a mug of hot tea, poured out of a bucket and told it was too late to get any food from the dining room. I was then taken to the recruits hut, where I was handed over to the NCO in charge of recruits.

"There was little time for introductions that evening 23 November 1931, and I was happy to get some sleep, after being shown how to make an Army bed, with 3 mattresses or biscuits filled with coir, sheets like sandpaper, and a pillow of the same material, filled with straw. I heard my first Reveille at 6.30 am the following morning. I washed and shaved along with the others, in the cold water of the annexe between the recruits hut and the next one, and then had my first army breakfast. As I remember it was a piece of bacon with a fried egg which had a kind of plastic skin over it, two pieces of bread with a pat of margarine and a mug of tea.

"During the following few weeks sufficient recruits arrived to make up a squad of 24. We soon became accustomed to army life – marching to the dining room for meals; making beds; cleaning the barrack room each morning, by each recruit tidying his own bedspace; and sweeping and scrubbing the floors. Cleaning utensils such as brooms and dry scrubbers were laid out on the floor after being washed with soap and water, table tops and forms scrubbed white, personal kit boxes left tidy in front of made beds with mug, knife and fork and spoon laid out on top; fireplaces cleaned with blacklead and whitewash; windows cleaned; wash bowls and toilets cleaned in the annexe and a last minute dusting before being inspected.

"We were issued with the regulation kit from the RQMS stores:

> *2 uniforms – one for best and one for every day use, including RTC shoulder badges, small silver coloured collar 'dogs' (badges);*
> *2 black berets with RTC cap badges;*
> *2 prs heavy army boots, which had to be 'boned' to produce a high polish;*
> *2 of all underwear including the rough army shirts;*
> *A "housewife" – a small linen pouch with needles, cotton etc for repairing clothes;*
> *A mug, knife, fork, spoon, toothbrush, shaving brush, razor, comb, hair brush, brass button stick, great coat, woollen gloves, a short case with a silver knob on which was engraved the RTC crest; and most important of all 2 pairs of brown overalls or dungarees, which we wore daily.*

"Each day we were detailed for a 'fatigue', which usually started at 0730 and continued until late afternoon. The two popular ones were the sergeants mess and officers mess, as there was spare food to be had, and this was important to a growing 19-year-old. The jobs were mainly washing up after breakfast, morning tea, lunch and tea at 4 pm; but occasionally one had to return in the evening to help out with the dinner and again this meant left-over food. The worst fatigue was in the depot cookhouse and we tried desperately to avoid this. Not only were there dishes to be washed but also the cooking tins, and some of these were so large that they would have to be placed on the floor, filled with hot water and soap and cleaned with an ordinary bass broom. The large coppers in which vegetables were cooked (the lids were lifted by a weighted chain) one had to climb inside to clean these monsters.

"The recruits were permanently hungry as their last official meal was at 4.30 pm and consisted of a cup of tea and 3 pieces of bread, margarine and jam. It was a long time till breakfast.

Sometimes if food had been left over from the mid day meal it was made into soup, poured into a galvanised bath and left in the dining room. At 7 pm the duty trumpeter would sound "cookhouse" and those brave (and hungry) enough to tackle this concoction, would take their mugs and dip into the bath, arriving back at the hut with a mug of glutinous substance. Many couldn't stomach it but it kept the wolf from the door.

"Of course there was the NAAFI canteen, and several other cafes within the camp, but money was scarce and wages were soon spent. All recruits were paid 14 shillings a week, 4 shillings of which was deducted to cover the cost of haircuts, washing, items of clothing. Of the 10 shillings left each week 5s was sent home, the other five bought toiletries, white and khaki blanco; 'bluebell' polish for buttons and other brasses; boot polish and other small items, the balance, which was not a lot, could be spent on food.

"The Elite Cafe was a favourite haunt and usually filled with hungry recruits on Friday and Saturday. Bread pudding squares known as 'train wreckers' were the best value money could buy and on Fridays and Saturdays at least, we had full stomachs, but on Monday we were back to the soup – if it was available. A few enterprising recruits managed to save a shilling out of their wages and would buy 'train wreckers,' and other such belly fillers, during the week when most recruits had no money; these would be auctioned off in the barrack room to the highest bidder and many a hungry man promised to pay a shilling out of his pay the following Friday for something which cost a penny or so.

One of the reasons why they were permanently hungry was the fact that they were all fit young men doing a lot of physical work.

Once the Squad was formed they had a daily time table:

8 – 9 am	PT in the gymnasium
9 – 10 am	Regimental History and general education
10 – 12.30	Drill on the square
12.30 – 1.30	Main meal
1.30 – 3.30	Drill on the square
4.30 pm	Tea
9.30 pm	Roll Call – standing by ones bed whilst the Orderly Sgt checked that everyone was present.
10.15 pm	Lights out.

Any spare time between tea and Roll Call was spent cleaning personal equipment ready for the following days parades."

After the 21st week the training at the Depot was complete and recruits moved over to Lulworth to do a 9 week Gunnery Course. This course was not without its funny but, at the time, hair raising occurrences, as Mr Munns relates:

"I suppose there was an element of danger in teaching young recruits to fire a 3 pounder shell from a moving tank. The 3 pounder was fired from a tank on four sides of a square run, each side being about 1/2 mile long. The first side ran from north to south away from the camp, towards Bindon Hill, where the shells were supposed to finish up. At the end of this 1/2 mile run, the tank turned left – an angle of 90° for the next leg of the run, and the gunner traversed his gun 90° to the right to keep the gun pointed down range. Unfortunately this recruit got mixed up and traversed 90° to the left – the gun was now pointing directly towards the camp! Worse still he fired – the shell screamed over the range and into the camp, thudding into the Officers Mess gardens, just as most officers were taking morning tea. There is no record of the comments made by the officers! The recruit concerned was taken to task and duly reprimanded."

Having been brought up in a city Mr Munns had seen little of rural life and he came to have a great affection for country walks: "A walk to the summit of Rings Hill was for me a great pleasure. I particularly liked walking over Bindon Hill and down to Mupe Bay, where I learned to swim. Being summer, I did a great deal of walking over the ranges. So after 9 weeks of gunnery we returned to Bovington having got through our exams with various grades. We did a short period on Medium tanks at the D & M Schools, and our training was considered complete when we had done a 24 hour guard at the same guard room that I had approached so apprehensively nearly 12 months previously. So ended my training at the Royal Tank Corps Depot, which must have been similar to hundreds of other recruits who joined in 1931 – a year I look back on with happy memories."

The Officer Commanding the Depot in 1931 initiated a scheme for panelling the interior walls of the ante-room and hall of the RTC Centre Mess. The construction was done by a local family of wood-carvers, who had been practising their craft for generations.

The panelling in the ante-room — up to four and a half feet from the floor, had the crest or initials of the donors carved in the centre of the panels. The work was done in oak, and the iron tie-rods in the roof were covered with wood casing to give the effect of oak beams. In the centre of each 'beam' was a carving of one of the armoured fighting vehicles with which the Corps was armed — the **Mark V, Medium C, Mark II Medium Tank, Rolls Royce Armoured Car** being represented. The cornices displayed the national emblems of England, Scotland, Ireland and Wales.

Work on the Mess-room started in April 1932 and was finished by June 1933. The panelling style was identical to that in the ante-room but the material used was Honduras mahogany. The screen which separated the serving alcove from the rest of the room was a striking piece of carved wood.

Swing doors for the main entrance from the hall, were presented by ten of the twelve first direct entrants from Sandhurst into the Corps, who were known as "The Twelve Apostles".

The hall was small and rather out of proportion to the rest of the building, so to minimise the height the walls were panelled from floor to ceiling cornices, with small oak Tudor style panelling with the letter racks, notice boards and post boxes being part of the integral plan. The majority of this work was paid for by donations from individual mess members, the shortfall being made up from mess funds.

This mess, built in 1924, approximately on the site today occupied by HQ RAC Centre, was pulled down in 1969 when the new mess — known as the Bovington Hilton — was ready for use.

1934 and 1935 were very dry summers and the swimming pool, which had been sited to the east of the camp, on a level with the revolver range, was used as often as possible. Funds for improving the pool were allotted and work began in fitting a new type of filter which was incorporated into the water system on the inlet side. The water in the pool had been only partly filtered up to this time and looked rather dirty and had a brackish taste. A chlorination tank was also built and a surface drainage system. Rows of pines and rhododendrons were planted to form a wind break and to create a more attractive setting. There were regular swimming competitions between the schools during the summer months.

At the same time as the work was being carried out on the pool, four hard tennis courts for the soldiers, were resurfaced, the hockey pitch was levelled and drained and the clay pit at the southern end of Higher Wood was gradually filled in, levelled and sown with grass. The clay from this pit had been removed and taken to Moreton brick works, beside Moreton Station, and made into bricks for local buildings.

The Sergeants Mess, north of the barrack square, had two new red tennis courts made on a site adjoining the two grass courts and all four were enclosed in wire, and the sloping sides surrounding the courts was turfed.

Bovington's main street, mid-1930s: Smith's general store, C.E. Way's shoe shop, the butcher's, Speed's hardware store, Red garage, Payne's — and the Post Office opposite.

Bovington Camp: armoured car gun-carriage for a funeral in the 1930s passing Smith's Restaurant.

1937-39 – the years of change

THE DECADE prior to the outbreak of World War Two saw the slow expansion of British armoured forces which was to culminate in 1939, with the formation of the Royal Armoured Corps (RAC), bringing together the newly mechanised Regiments of the Cavalry with the existing Battalions of the Royal Tank Corps. At its peak the RAC would comprise some 190 regular, territorial and war-formed units, however, the initial melding and mechanisation did not happen either easily or quickly, so the effects upon Bovington and Lulworth were gradual. This book is not the place in which to catalogue the thorny progress towards mechanisation, except as it directly affected the RTC Training Centre and Depot.

These effects were almost minimal until 1937, despite the fact that mechanisation of the first Cavalry units had begun as early as 1927, when the 11th Hussars and the 12th Royal Lancers exchanged their horses for armoured cars with considerable success. Unfortunately their achievements did not immediately herald a general change of heart, indeed, it was not until 1935 that the next cautious step was taken. Even when the mechanisation began in earnest, most of the initial conversion training was carried out within units so did not affect Bovington apart from the provision of instructors. Expansion of the RTC also did not properly get under way until 1937, everything being bedevilled by lack of finance as well as by a powerful body of opinion which still saw horsed Cavalry as the main "arm of decision" on the modern battle field.

1937 was undoubtedly a turning point, but, as the RTC Depot historical records explained, there were problems: "The year 1937-38 was one of great difficulty in the RTC Depot. The process of re-organisation which affected the RTC as a whole, affected the Depot in a marked degree. In accordance with a policy adopted by the War Office, a very heavy strain was thrown upon the RTC as regards resources of Officers and NCOs in the capacity of instructors for other arms. At home, Units were extremely short. This shortage was brought about by: (a) Attachment of large numbers of NCO instructors to the RTC Depot to deal with the inordinate numbers of recruits who were accepted for the Royal Tank Corps. (b) The numbers of Officers and NCOs who were ordered to act as instructors to Cavalry units which had been reorganised on a light tank basis and (c) Officers and NCOs employed in a similar capacity as in India ... The trouble is likely to be aggravated by the fact that the 8th Bn RTC is due to be formed early in the year 1938/39. The number of recruits, namely 1450, which were posted to Field Units during the year 1937/38, was far in excess of any number that had passed through the RTC Depot since the end of the Great War."

At this time the RTC Depot was still organised basically into two companies – Recruit Coy and Administrative Coy, but with a new peace-time establishment (wef 17 June 37) of 32 Officers and 1210 Other Ranks. A new Recruit Vehicle Wing was also included for the training of recruits in driving and maintenance, while a QM (Technical) was authorised to take charge of all the necessary additional equipment for this training. The expansion led to the RASC lines in Bovington being handed over, in March 1937, to the RTC Depot, as garages and MT Stores for the new recruit D & M Wing.

Army Armoured Fighting Vehicles School

1937 ALSO saw the establishing of the Army Armoured Fighting Vehicles School at Bovington and Lulworth on 1st April 1937, to replace the RTC Central Schools. The new establishment comprised D & M and Wireless Wings at Bovington and a Gunnery Wing at Lulworth, and took on the training of instructors for the mechanising Cavalry Group, as well as an RTC Group. The general training pattern which emerged was governed by the fact that, while the RTC units manned the heavily armoured "I" tanks, for infantry support, and the medium tanks, for the medium tank brigades, the Cavalry crewed the simpler armoured cars, light tanks and six wheeled trucks, for use in the reconnaissance and protection roles.

Glyn Evans remembers the first conversion courses for cavalry officers which began in April 1937: "Among the students were Maj Dollar and Maj Harvey 10H, Maj Clements 4H, Capt Lord Grenville 10H, who was the Gold Stick in Waiting at the Coronation of Their Majesties King George VI and Queen Elizabeth that year, and Capt Willie Turner of the Bays who later became one of our wartime Commandants. These officers were so pleased with life in the 'Tin Shed' mess at Lulworth, they asked for permission to remain there for their entire course. Permission was granted and the form was that every morning at 0800hrs a couple of Rolls Royce Armoured Cars used to draw up outside the mess and return them in the evening. Happy Days! We also had the 11th Hussars from Tidworth for annual firing around this time and attached to them from 10H was HRH The Duke of Gloucester.

"The only formality connected with his stay was that he wished to be addressed as 'Sir' by everyone and for all officers in the anteroom to stand up when he entered before dinner each evening. He brought his own civilian valet, who dined with my mess staff and slept in the same block as HRH. HRH signed his bar chits 'Henry' and without exception asked for two fried eggs on toast for breakfast every morning. His valet used to bring in a large tin of tea which was marked: 'Especially for the Royal Family' and was packed by a firm in Tunbridge Wells. The tea leaves turned to a shade of green I remember".

Glyn had his own memento of the Coronation in the shape of the Coronation Medal, two only having been allocated to the Gunnery School, the other went to QMSI Parrish (later Major). Col Tilley from HQ Bovington came to present the medals together with other awards. The staff and students paraded in a hollow square on the soccer pitch and fortunately an old Cambrai veteran friend of Glyn's had given him some advice about the ceremony: "He explained that as a rule the officer presenting the medals had great difficulty finding the small khaki loop on the Service Dress of the recipient. He advised me to get a large safety pin, insert it on the inside of my tunic and press outwards. It certainly proved a success! The parade was formed up by MSM Ernie Hayward, DCM, MM as Parade Marshal. Col Tilley gave his address: "The first medal I have to present is to S Sgt Highfield RTC and it is the Indian North West Frontier Medal. I want you all on parade to know that S Sgt Highfield did not earn his medal hanging around Piccadilly Circus!" The next two medals he presented were Long Service & Good Conduct Medals – one to QMS (Tiffey) Cooper, RAOC, the School armourer and the other to S Sgt Jimmy Hargreaves, RTC adding his comments on how these medals were earned. Next he came to the two Coronations Medals, saying that Mr Parrish and I had earned them through loyalty and hard work over many years. As he pinned on each medal he shook the hand of the recipient and said 'I am proud to present you with this medal.' I was the last in line and he put his hand on my shoulder and he said 'Cpl Evans, you have damned well earned it!' I think at the time I thought more of that remark than of the medal itself! Then Mr Hayward said: 'Recipients right turn quick march', we did so and the four medals of the four in the front of me all fell off! Mine – Thank God! – 'Stood Fast'!"

The Sandhurst Block: Bovington's largest building began construction in 1937 and was completed in 1939 – it provided quarters for 650 men.

Wireless Wing
and the accommodation crisis

FROM 1 April 36, 1 Offr, 2 Sgts and 2 Cpls of the Royal Signals had been authorised to be attached to the RTC Central School to form a Wireless Wing. They had run three courses a year, each of three months duration. From 1938 the Wing was a Major's command, all instruction was given by R Sigs personnel and wireless sets studied were the WS 9 and WS 11, while the vehicles used were 15cwt trucks and some assorted light tanks.

The expansion of the school highlighted the extremely bad accommodation and lack of amenities in both Bovington and Lulworth as the camps had remained virtually unchanged since the end of the Great War. To quote the Depot history again: "The extremely bad accommodation, shortage of Officers and lack of amenities generally in Bovington Camp, led to repercussions in a number of directions. The lowering of the standard to the recruit accepted for the Corps led to an inevitable increase of crime and in the number of General and District Courts Martial. The number of these, as a result of this, was considerably in excess of anything that had happen in previous years. Numerous representations as a result of this state of affairs culminated in a special visit to Bovington Camp by a senior staff officer of Southern Command, at the direct direction of the Secretary of State for War".

The result of the Southern Command inspection, was that in November 1937 it was decided to considerably enlarge both the Regimental Institute and the dining halls and to make "certain improvements" to the existing hutted accommodation. However, the most important building projects to begin in 1937 were permanent brick buildings, namely; the Sandhurst Block, designed to accommodate 650 men, on the Old Depot Parade Ground (8th August Square), which it was anticipated would be completed in 1939; 40 brick married quarters in the vicinity of the Garrison Recreation Room, to be ready for occupation by the end of May 1938; and a new gymnasium in the NE corner of the camp immediately behind the offices of the Recruit D & M Wing. At Lulworth, the foundations of a new brick Officers' Mess were laid in 1938 on what had been the camp soccer pitch.

The shortage of accommodation at the RTC Depot and the need to provide more trained personnel for the new army tank battalions had led to the War Office giving authority (on 7th January 1937) to reduce the existing training syllabus for recruits from 35 weeks to 27 weeks, broken down as follows:-

Elementary Drill, etc	—	5 weeks
D & M Training	—	14 weeks (but including one week's leave)
Gunnery Training	—	6 weeks
Final Training	—	2 weeks

On 6 March 1938, instructions were received from the War Office to put up a proposal to train Cavalry recruits at the RTC Depot. However, as the Depot history puts it: "Consequent to a policy of procrastination the question of establishing a Depot for the Cavalry Recruits did not receive consideration, and when the Cavalry Regiments of the Mobile Division were converted onto a light tank basis, it was found that units concerned had neither NCOs nor instructional facilities to deal with their training."

A compromise was eventually reached, based on the premises that by August 1938, all field units of the RTC would be up to full peace establishment, so the intake of recruits for the RTC could be restricted to 9 a week, and the difference between the small numbers of RTC recruits needed and the Depot Peace Establishment, could be made up of recruits for Cavalry units of the Mobile Division. This system took effect on 7 April 1938. It was agreed that Cavalry recruits would arrive in their second week of service and complete the same 27 weeks course of training as for RTC recruits, except that the six weeks Gunnery course at Lulworth would be modified to give more time to machine gun instruction (.303 and .50). This was achieved by eliminating all 3 pounder instruction, as this weapon was only found on vehicles which the RTC crewed, ie: medium tanks.

What was it like to be a recruit at Bovington in those days? George Stimpson of Kidderminster arrived at Bovington on the evening of 22nd April 1938 and left to join the 5th Battalion RTC at the end of November. He writes: "The overall time spent in training for a few squads including mine (No 549) that year was two weeks longer than normal, due to training at Lulworth being suspended while we dug trenches and constructed air raid shelters in anticipation for the impending war which was infact still over a year away.

"Recruits were first accommodated in huts F8 and F9 in 'F' Lines, when our squad was formed we moved to two adjoining huts in 'D' Lines, we had a squad sergeant and a corporal as supernumerary. After about six weeks when our drill was not up to standard the sergeant was relieved and another one took over.

"The first six weeks of training consisted of drill, drill and more drill, with some PT, education and mechanical theory, then a few days leave followed by twelve weeks mechanical theory and practical maintenance, such as fault finding, etc, and lorry driving. There was still some more advanced drill (pistol and guard mounting), PT and education, we may have had a bit more leave, I'm not sure, but then it was over to Lulworth for Gunnery training. This was the only time we had anything to do with tanks until we joined the Battalion, then back to Bovington to do an HQ Guard and a spell of fatigues, including a couple of days at the piggery. At the end was one last parade in second best uniform (the one we had used every day) for the CO to inspect us, then posting to the Battalion, in our case we all went to the Fifth, I think 28 started with the squad but only about 20 ended the course.

"While training we had to do our share of duties such as fire picquet which also included spud bashing, a hefty job in those days! It would also be fair to say that during the summer months there were always a couple of heath fires which recruits had to put out, and for the first six weeks we were confined to camp."

Formation of the Royal Armoured Corps

ON TUESDAY, 4th April 1939, Mr Leslie Hore-Belisha, the Secretary of State for War, announced in the House that the newly mechanised regiments of the Cavalry were to combine with the RTC battalions to create a single Corps, to be known as the Royal Armoured Corps (RAC), with precidence immediately before the Royal Artillery. The RAC would deliberately be far more an "association" than an "amalgamation", so as not to offend anyone. It was, as Liddell Hart called it in his history of the Royal Tank Regiment, "a characteristically British compromise that was designed to cause the least possible disturbance of regimental feelings and traditions, even though it complicated organization."

For the time being only the 18 Cavalry regiments and 8 Yeomanry Regiments which were already mechanised or were about to be mechanised, would be included, together with the 8 regular RTC battalions and their seven Territorial battalions. All units of the RTC would keep a corporate existence within the new Corps, becoming Battalions (later changed to the Cavalry nomenclature of Regiments) of the Royal Tank Regiment and His Majesty was graciously pleased to become their Colonel-in-Chief.

All RAC recruits would have a common uniform and cap badge, which they would wear in training until posted to their units. A new Pay and Records office would be established, so personnel would eventually be interchangeable between units, however, this process would not be rushed. Regimental identities would be preserved and all units of the RAC would keep their old designations, distinctions and badges.

The RTC Journal summed up the news thus: "Whether this 'marriage of convenience' will, as we must all hope, develop into a love match, rests in the hands of the parties now joined together. A sentimental regret for the loss of the Royal Tank Corps cannot but be tempered by the new position of the regiment at the Right of the Line."

The change at Bovington was probably more lasting than anyone imagined, when, in April 1939, the RTC Depot ceased to exist and became the Royal Armoured Corps Depot. As we shall see, the new unit did not remain in existence very long before changing its title to 52nd (Heavy) Training Regiment RAC, though an RTR Depot was never again to reform even after the war had ended.

**Bovington Camp: Peter Franklin stands guard with his father's rifle.
Trooper J Franklin was in charge of the stables and batman to Colonel Symes.**

4   WORLD WAR TWO

New buildings

"NEARLY £1.25 MILLIONS to be spent on armaments in Dorset," read the headline to the leading article in the *Dorset County Chronicle* on 23 March 1939. The article then explained that this expenditure was part of a much larger sum (£6 million) which had been earmarked by the Government for new Army buildings countrywide, the aim being to replace many of the older barracks with more modern, purpose-built accommodation. As far as Dorset was concerned this included:

BOVINGTON	LULWORTH
£200,000 for a new army training school	£350,000 for the replacement of hutments
£550,000 for a new army depot	
£140,000 for a new military hospital	

The article went on: "The immensity of the sums is of course due to the fact that permanent buildings are replacing wooden structures, especially at the Armoured Fighting Vehicles School, West Lulworth. Bovington has been a very large hutment camp since early war days. Huts there have done very good service for a quarter of a century but are no longer serviceable."

It is not all that easy to pin down the building that was actually financed with this money. Certainly at Bovington it must have included the completion of the Sandhurst Block, although it is not clear if finance for this had already been included in the Army Estimates for 1938-39 as work had of course begun some two years earlier. Presumably the "new army training school" was Allenby Barracks into which the D & M Wing and Wireless Wing of the Army AFV School moved. Although this was mainly new wooden buildings, some of considerable size, there were also brick structures, such as the tank hangar and vehicle instuctional bays. There is no evidence that the new military hospital was ever started, the Nursing Sisters Mess having been completed in 1935, while the old hospital buildings remained in use until well after the WW2 era.

At Lulworth it is easier to list, namely completion of Officers' Mess started in 1939, the Other Ranks accommodation block and the extensive instructional wings and indoor range areas. Not long after the war had started additional new wooden hutted accommodation was built in both camps – Stanley Barracks at Bovington and Park Camp Lulworth, just to the north of the main camp area.

More of these later, but first back to the Dorset County Chronicle for an article which appeared in the local paper shortly after the war had begun and gives a stirring account of a day their reporter spent with a tank training unit "somewhere in Wessex" (clearly in Bovington!) which appeared under the headline "Leave it to the Tanks":

"The day started with an address from the Officer Commanding who began with a witty reference to the comparative power of pen and sword which, perhaps out of respect for his guests ended decidely in favour of the pen. He then explained that 34 militiamen came to them every week to be prepared to take their places in armoured car and light tank regiments. The course they took lasted 24 weeks and the object was to turn out men sufficiently trained in the various trades of the Royal Armoured Corps to enable them to take their places in field units in battle. Men are trained as drivers, gunners, wireless operators, driver mechanics, fitters, electricians, clerks, storemen, in proportions laid down by the War Office.

"During the first eight weeks, they are given general military training, which includes physical training, revolver, musketry, gas, elementary tactics and the introductory lessons to driving and maintenance. At the end of this period they are earmarked in various trades, due regard being paid to their experience in civil life and the aptitude they have shown since enlistment. Before starting to specialise in their trades they are given three more weeks in driving and maintaining wheeled vehicles, and a similar period in doing elementary gunnery. The idea is that everyone, no matter what his trade, can at a pinch, do a job in a tank crew. Drivers then do six more weeks and learn tracked work, gunners do six weeks advanced gunnery and the remainder go to their respective trades.

"The last four weeks of the course are devoted to collective training, in which they are taught by lectures, sand table exercises and out-door schemes, the functions and handling of the units of the Royal Armoured Corps. At the end of this each man should be able to command a troop and also have a sound knowledge of the function of a squadron and battalion.

"The Commandant explained that each man did an average of 44 hours a week. They were divided into four companies – 'A' was administrative staff and training; 'B' and 'C', recruits; and 'D' collective training. When they came in they were in charge of a senior sergeant and a junior corporal. "Frequently" said the CO, "they are very homesick, but it doesn't take them long to get over that phase." The first week of their new life was devoted to squadding, getting their uniforms (cap, overalls, uniform), inoculations and various other essential preliminaries.

"They had four good meals a day, and a break in the morning when they could have cocoa or soup. They were provided with 1lb bread, ¾lb meat, 1½oz sugar, ⅜oz tea, per day and out of their cash allowance of 10d per day they could buy milk, butter, eggs, fruit, potatoes and cheese. This was actually done by the Messing Officer who had something like £50 a day to play about with to feed 1,150 men. Working hours were 8am-12.30; 1.45-4.30 (Saturdays 12.30). They had organised games on Saturday and Sunday, and each man paid 6d towards grounds and sports equipment. There was a Garrison Cinema and theatre, and NAAFI concert parties came down at least once a month – usually more frequently – and a grand pantomime was being staged after Christmas. Good recreational facilities in the shape of billiard tables, wireless sets, etc, are provided in spacious huts at the camp where also writing facilities and a library are available.

"After this survey of the work and play of the men at the camp came a visit to the Sandhurst Block one of Mr Leslie Hore-Belisha's innovations in the shape of a luxurious building intended to house the men in pre-war days with every modern convenience, including all electric kitchens, dining halls, small dormitories and so on. Then came physical training in the spacious gym and a visit to the training cadre where the principles of the petrol engine were laid bare by working models which only the most unmechanically minded could fail to understand. Wireless instruction with the familiar, "Cornelian B calling, calling, Over Cornelian B!" noises and everyone with headphones playing with complicated pieces of machinery which (we were told) replace the sets found in the modern tanks. Then to foot drill then to pistol drill, map reading, and actual tank driving on the driving ground which is two feet thick in mud with light tanks racing around the heavier models and movie cameramen lying on their stomachs to get shots of these monsters raising their snouts and plunging down precipitous slopes.

"After lunch the party moved to the firing range where men were trained first indoors in the use of various tank guns. Aiming at moving targets with an artificially caused swaying movement similar to that operating inside the tank and pellet firing at toy tanks moving across a sandy country side were particularly fascinating. More spectacular of course was the actual firing on the range with pink tracer bullets shooting like stars on to the hillside from rapidly moving tanks rushing agitatedly, but yet in perfect formation, towards the enemy.

"Thus ended a day in which one of the less publicised units of the British Army in training, showed its mettle and gave one a comfortable feeling that even the coldness of the day could not dispel. May one add a word of praise for the unexampled and unfading courtesy of the officers and men of this unit in entertaining the eyes and ears of the British people – Britain's secret weapon!"

Training machine gets underway

THE DEVELOPMENT of the RAC training organisation was based upon five major principles: (a) the need to have initial training regiments in which a recruit from civilian life would be trained right up to the point when he could be accepted by a unit in the field as an operational reinforcement; (b) that there must be the minimum time-lag between completing this training and posting to a field unit, with continuation training available during any interval; (c) close liaison between the training organisation and the personnel branch in the War Office; (d) the development of initial training on scientific lines for economy in instructional staff and material; (e) the absolute necessity of co-ordinating training from a control body – the War Office.

When compulsory military service was introduced in 1939, each regular unit of the Cavalry and Royal Tank Regiment in the UK formed a Militia Training Squadron and received periodical intakes of conscripts. These Militia Training Squadrons became the nucleus of the RAC Training

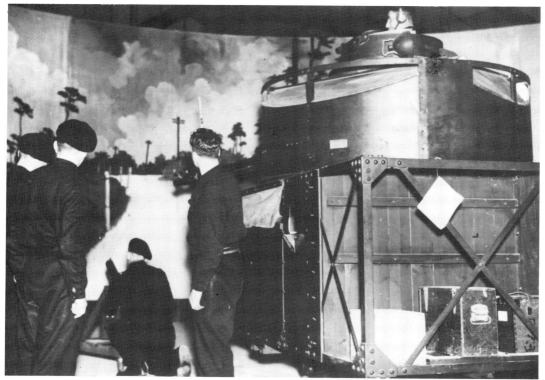

Lulworth Camp: Dorset pines on the painted backdrop to the simulated firing procedure at the Gunnery School.

Regiments which were formed on the outbreak of war. There were eleven of these Regiments formed in the first year of the war, two of them being located at Bovington – the 52nd and the 58th.

52nd Heavy Training Regiment

THE OPENING entry in the War Diary of the 52nd explains how, on 11th September 1939, the Royal Armoured Corps Depot (Bovington Wing) was disbanded and the 52nd Heavy Training Regiment, Royal Armoured Corps, formed in its place. All ranks on strength of the RAC Depot were posted across to the new unit. It was then commanded by Lt Col G Stevenson, RTR, and had a total establishment strength of 1,175 (21 Officers, 61 WOs and Sgts, 75 Cpls and 1,018 Troopers). In addition to the RAC personnel there were other attached troops one of the earliest elements to arrive being a party of 48 girls of the 1st Dorsetshire ATS. They were attached for employment as clerks, cooks mess orderlies etc. and were billeted in the newly completed married quarters in Higher Wood.

One of this initial little group of intrepid ATS girls, braving "a man's world" was Mrs Sylvia Wood (nee Dood). She joined the ATS in 1939, served at Bovington as a telephone operator in the camp exchange, met her husband-to-be there and had numerous midnight chats with Winston Churchill! Recalling those early days she told me: "I was posted from the Nothe Fort, Weymouth, to Bovington in 1939 soon after the declaration of the war. I had quite a send-off, even some advice from one old soldier about life in the trenches. I remember getting off the train at Wool, seeing a staff car and having been told that I would be met, going up to the driver and telling him to take me to Bovington. I found out afterwards that he had just brought a senior officer to catch the train I got off and that one didn't do that sort of thing, but at least I arrived in style!

"I was, with a handful of others, the first to occupy the just completed married quarters at Higher Wood. There were some well-known local names among these early arrivals – we were all known by our surnames of course – I was called 'Dodd'; there was Weld, known as 'Weldy'

Lulworth Camp: 'stoppages' – an instructor explains the workings of the Besa 7.92 mm machine gun.

from Lulworth Castle; Hunt, called 'Hunty' who came with her horse, and later Churchill's daughter, who was cook to our house for a short while. I remember that she couldn't cook and said so, also that she came down to breakfast in a negligée. Having been allocated a room with two others in the house, drawn up a bed, paliasse and some rough brown blankets, we were told to settle in. Someone asked for a pillow and we were told to use our tin helmets with our day clothes inside. It was very cold that first winter, I had chilblains on my feet and hands, but wouldn't have dreamed of complaining. No heating, no means of hot water, we had to break the ice for washing. When I got short leave I'd have a bath at home in Weymouth but have no idea what the others did.

"I didn't want to be seen in Weymouth at first after my 'leaving for France'. However, I soon returned with some sheets and one or two other comforts and eventually over the years got my own room, having reached the dizzy heights of Lance Corporal – with even a bedside table and mat!"

More from Sylvia later. First, however, some reminisences from another early wartime arrival at Bovington, who remembers that winter all too well. Major (Retired) Chris Gray, late RTR, was one of the last Gentlemen Cadets at the Royal Military College, Sandhurst, just before it became the wartime OCTU for the Royal Armoured Corps. In Mid-December 1939, he and some dozen others were due for their Special to Arm training at Bovington and decided to make the journey down by road:

"Four of us rashly decided to make the trip by motorcycle. By the time we had got to Winchester we were frozen to the marrow and so took on considerable quantities of anti-freeze in the form of rum. The effect of this had hardly worn off by the time we arrived at the entrance to Bovington which, in 1939, was up Cologne Road. Traces of the old, much more winding road can still be seen near the entrance to the present school. It was this winding bit, still with some icy snow on it, which caused the leader of our little convoy to slide and end up in the ditch. The rest of us were so busy laughing that, in the end, all of us came off our bikes. It was thus a rather scruffy and still slightly merry quartet which reported to the guardroom at the top of the road.

"It was here that the laughing stopped.

"Our troop of former Gentlemen Cadets of GCs (not to be confused with other officer cadets who wore the ordinary type of white hat bands and collar patches) were following at a respectful distance of about six weeks (or 3 troops) the troop of GCs who had been our senior term at the Royal Military College. Unbeknown to us innocents, our much revered seniors had apparently created a high degree of animosity between the staff and themselves, so the sight of more of the same breed brought forth from certain time-served sergeants shouts of: 'Stand to attention! Double March!" and other equally pungent remarks. We had arrived before the train party and our cause was not helped by a suggestion to the Orderly Sergeant that he provide us with some wood to light the stove in our freezing hut (E 15) on the edge of Amiens Square. After the comparative luxury of the Royal Military College, this aged hut with its outside ablutions was indeed a rude introduction to basic soldiering.

"D and M instruction for the first two weeks was indoors in the West Wing (now swallowed up in the Base Workshop complex). The cook-house, which managed to provide quite inedible food was in G-lines, more or less where the SW corner of the main square is today. Indeed, after the first couple of days. I don't think we went near it again. Most of our eating was done in the Elite Cafe. This Cafe occupied the gravel space which is now car park to the West of HQ DRAC/Headquarters RAC Centre building. This was a most comradely spot where steaming hot mugs of tea and ample portions of eggs and chips could be consumed at almost any hour. With the outside temperature at or below freezing and the inside one at about 80 degrees Farenheit it soon got the blood circulating.

"After some two weeks of this arctic living we were sent on a fortnight's Christmas leave and told to report to Stanley Barracks when we returned. This break marked the opening of Allenby Barracks as the D and M Wing and Stanley Barracks, for the time being, as spare accommodation. The changeover was sheer bliss as the newly completed wooden huts were centrally heated and we were given our own Cadets' Canteen in what was to become a Sergeants' Mess a year later. Indoor instruction was carried out in the big wooden 'Cathedral' in Allenby Barracks which is now the only surviving wooden building apart from the re-built NAAFI canteen which is now the Garrison Church. Instruction on the vehicles (in our case the Mk VIb Light and the MKI Infantry tank) was in the Tank Hangar which is now the Tank Museum. What are now the stables were instructional bays containing running engines, hence the pipes still sticking out of the walls on some of them.

"At the end of January 1940 our brief spell of soft living came to an abrupt end when we transferred to the Gunnery Wing at Lulworth to be housed once again in an aged, freezing cold hut with outside permanently frozen ablutions. As I recall, for most of the six week course we hardly ever took our clothes off. It was usually a case of putting even more on at night. Once a week on Friday evening, we went down to one of the hotels in the village to have a bath and put on a change of clothes, so as to be clean and properly dressed for the terrifying inspection of our barrack room on Saturday morning by the Adjutant, whose favourite joke was to drop on the floor, accidently of course, any mug, china, one pint, which had the slightest blemish on it. We did, however, have a Cadet's canteen. This was the room that in later years became the main Lulworth conference room and Tactical School model room. Saturday evening were the camp's social high-spots when there was All Ranks dance to which bus loads of nurses from Poole and Bournemouth used to come, presumably knowing all too well how isolated and lonely were the 'brutal and licentious' soldiers.

"One occasion when I incurred the wrath of our instructor (S/Sgt Wilf Firmstone) when it was my turn to collect the "prepared for firing" machine-guns from the old wooden instructional huts (later the Tactical School) and take them to the firing point. This little chore consisted of putting the four Vickers guns on a sledge and towing them behind a light tank. Unfortunately I omitted to secure the tarpaulin which covered them and, on arrival at the firing point, two of the guns were under inches of frozen mud thrown up by the tracks. I spent nearly a whole night re-cleaning and preparing those guns for the next day's firing.

"And so at the beginning of March 1940, back to the Royal Military College for the remainder of our training. Our visit to the AFV School had been untroubled by the war which at that time was smouldering away in what was called the 'Phoney War'. However, when I returned only four months later, things were a bit different."

Arish ·Mell Gap: dragon's teeth anti-invasion defences supplemented with an old medium tank from Lulworth Camp to help block the expected landings of the enemy's panzers.

Invasion scares and worse

WITH THE fall of France and the evacuation of the BEF from Dunkirk in May 1940, the situation became steadily more serious. Bovington and Lulworth were affected in three main ways: firstly with the reception and rehabilitation of BEF personnel from France; secondly in anti-invasion plans and thirdly, by the ever-increasing number of German air-raids as the enemy tried to batter Great Britain into submission. The effects of the first of these is perhaps best illustrated by this extract from an Appendix to the War Diary of the 52nd which reads:

"At the end of May, 1940, instructions were received that approximately six thousand ex-BEF personnel would be arriving at Bovington Camp, pending disposal instructions. These personnel were to be accomodated etc, by the 52nd Heavy Training Regt RAC, the D & M Wing AFV School and the Gunnery Wing AFV School. Arrangements were made for the reception of these personnel and the question of accommodation presented no mean problem as this was already scarce prior to the arrival of the BEF personnel. Batches of BEF personnel then began to arrive in groups of two to three hundred at a time, usually composed of men from various Regiments. On arrival, each man's particulars were taken down and these were sorted out and nominal rolls forwarded to the Officers I/C Records concerned. The men were then sorted out into their respective Regiments and despatched to join units on receipt of disposal instructions. During this period of reception, several Officers and Other Ranks of the French Army were accommodated. The RAC personnel who had returned from France were attached to this unit pending the reformation of their repective units at Bovington Camp. Owing to the severe strain placed on this unit during the period of reception and disposal of ex-BEF personnel, it was found necessary to temporarily suspend Recruit Training for several days."

At Lulworth, the first inhabitants of the new Officers' Mess were some of the Dunkirk survivors. Glyn Evans was by then the Mess Steward and recalls those days thus: "The Mess was not yet completed, so these officers had to sleep on straw palliasses on the floor of the bedrooms. Blackout was a nightmare, as blinds had not been properly fitted, in fact this was still a problem when we did move in en bloc about September 1940 .... The mess had 58 bedrooms, over 12 bathrooms I think, plus public rooms which were a vast cry from the Tin Shed Mess, although many officers quoted to me that they preferred the latter! Eight of the Officers' rooms were singles for senior staff officers in three old wooden married quarters opposite the mess and more in the old officers quarters near the old mess. If at times the Commandant did not wish to live in Merlincourt House near the East gate, then we used to house twelve senior student officers.

"After taking over the Mess, the Commandant (Col Rex Rimmington) said that he would like myself and my family to live in the mess. At the time we were firmly entrenched in brick married quarters B5, but move we had to! We took over three officers rooms over the Mess Kitchen, plus two servants rooms, one of which was fitted with a cooking range for us. In the original plans there was to have been a bungalow for the Mess Steward near Havrincourt House, but it was never built.

"I had a total of 46 ATS staff, 12 of whom were employed in the kitchen – 6 on shift from 0700 hrs to 1400 hrs, and 6 from noon to 2100 hrs. The kitchen was very large and modern ... during the war years if we had less than 150 for lunch daily we were quiet!"

Another wartime member of Lulworth Garrison was Edward Body, who was still an instructor there. He writes: "I think that the first real impact I remember was the poignant return of the Dunkirk Army. We had to vacate the instructional rooms to accommodate some of them. Loads of straw were strewn on the floors and all instruction and places of work were hastily reprogrammed, improvised areas, corners, alcoves etc, inside and out were alloted to us in lieu. This had its funny side that I remember best. You had to decode your programme, for instance, if it said Classroom 3 for Period 4, it meant the SW corner of the Pellet Range outside if fine, or inside the Tank shelter on the hard standing if wet. You couldn't use the SW corner inside because another class was already in there because it was wet! Since each period was only forty minutes long and there were many classes interchanging between the numerous places of work, there was a traffic problem too! These improvised areas of work were far apart and gun kit had to be drawn and handed in during the 10 minutes interval between periods, so much water was turned into wine! But it happened and within limits it worked well.

"Then there was our local ARP. Whatever happened the show must go on, not a minute of instruction must be lost or the initiative would pass to the enemy! This thinking sometimes had a dramatic and historic insistence which ignored the reality of possibility, but with hindsight can be forgiven. ... A long trench was laboriously dug by staff and students together, which ran the length of the Instructional Wing, some 15 to 20 yards in front of and parallel to it, on the Bindon side [ie. to the south]. The usual "Do's and DONT's" were issued in connection with its use – you know, no natural or procreative functions to be exercised therein and that sort of thing! But of course the elements didn't receive a copy and insisted on dropping in continuously. A few zealots maintained that, although the air raid alarm necessitated a quick change of accommodation, ie: a sprint from classroom to trench; parts of weapons and tools etc, could be carried – notwithstanding the precipitous leap into the trench – and the lesson resumed. What practical naivety! Can you imagine the instructor leading the charge, lock spring (Vickers) in one hand and pins-split-bush-axis-side-lever-head (the smallest part with the longest name) in the other, making a forced landing into a muddy trench a la Mons or Arras, and dropping either or both (the parts not the places!) with a screaming siren, negating all silence for miles, blasting his ears, first checking his flock (this was a strict must) and then continuing imperturbably: 'Now which part do we remove next?' But under the auspices of some of the more tenacious, this somewhat tentative suggestion created the most hilarious situations, further complicated by the fact that noisy, thrilling 'dog fights' were going on overhead. I can still see the CO, binoculars in hand, perched precariously on the parapet, surveying the scene.

"And then there were the Inns of Court cadets, solicitors and lawyers to a man who were later to officer and command tanks so well and bravely. I had several classes of them and dreaded every session. I was grilled and cross-examined relentlessly. If I split an infinitive, changed a tense, used a double superlative, or said 'impinged on' instead of 'struck', I would be in the dock, with a prosecutor, defence and a judge who had grown his own wig! I learned a lot about the law, I can only hope they did about gunnery.

"Can you imagine PT I and II Orders having a highly coloured "Page 3 of the SUN" sort of heading? Yes, even that happened! Somehow an artist, I think his name was RC Sheriffs, infiltrated the Orderly Room or somewhere as a clerk, and persuaded the top brass that our attention would be riveted to these mundane scripts if they were topped by a scantily veiled nude or some such visual attraction. This sacrilege bore the inscription: 'She's worth looking at – so are these!'"

Bovington Camp: Sylvia Wood at work in the telephone exchange, where she had nightime chats with Winston Churchill.

Bovington Camp: Amazons of the ATS, in silk stockings for the duration of the war, practice bayonet fighting outside the telephone exchange.

Once you had read orders and discovered you were on guard duty things were not always as straightforward as one might imagine as Glyn Evans told me: "Two identical episodes but with very different results. One Commandant who had been out of camp in his car, returned, stopped at the barrier at the Guard Room, but the sentry raised it immediately and waved the CO on. Did not ask for his ID card, etc. Both the CO and the sentry had served together pre-war in the same unit at Lulworth and knew each other well. CO asked the sentry why he had not demanded to see his ID card etc. Sentry said: 'Well Sir I know you, etc'. Sentry was put under close arrest – 28 days detention next day. Another Commandant who had been out with his wife and returned with no ID etc, and was refused admittance by sentry. CO said: But you know who I am, sentry said: 'Yes Sir, but I have my orders, no ID no admittance!' CO said: 'fetch the Guard Commander' and told him to tell the sentry to report on COs Orders next morning. Result – sentry up in front of CO who made him a Lance Corporal for his extreme diligence!"

Sylvia Dodd had a frosty reception from the civilians at the Bovington Camp exchange who were so incensed that the ATS were "coming to take their jobs away" that they gave the girls no instruction on how to work the equipment, the ATS just had to learn the hard way. Quite soon after their arrival they had an air-raid: "we sat in a slit trench with our feet in water, singing led by a Welsh girl. We did it only once, infact I never did get into an air-raid shelter all the war. One day a call came from the Home Guard at Lulworth that the Germans were landing. I rang HQ with the message and later the OC rang saying that they were preparing to evacuate the camp and that we had to stay and do the best we could and to check if we had a gun in the exchange. I explained that there was one there, but that we had no ammunition, so he sent some along. A sergeant who later came to mend my electric fire (I married him later) pointed out that the ammo was the wrong calibre! Fortunately the "invasion" turned out to be just a drifting landing craft."

Not only were the Germans expected to land from the sea but from the sky as well, as the War Diary of the 52nd explained: "It is estimated that Germany has 4,000 trained parachutists who might be used to capture some vital point such as an aerodrome near a port. Germany can also carry 15,000 men in civil aircraft." If an invasion were planned, it is thought that these air carried troops, in conjunction with a heavy air offensive would be used to seize a port, where the remainder of the invading force would be disembarked.

Mobile Columns

TO MEET these threats from air and sea Mobile Columns were organised in both Bovington and Lulworth Camps. The 52nd's War Diary outlines the task and organisation of BOVCOL, the Mobile Column for the Bovington Area. Its task was to be ready to move rapidly and at short notice from any point within 45 miles of Bovington to attack any enemy concentration. It consisted of a light tank troop, and medium tank troop, two motorised troops and a Camp reserve troop, all under command of a Column HQ. The original Operation Order specifying their tasks was dated 10 May 1940. Just two months later BOVCOL was altered in name, composition and task, to become the Support Group for the new REXFORCE which comprised:

One troop of 'T' tanks	)	
Three troops of light tanks	)	provided by other units in Bovington and
two motorcycles	)	Lulworth
two troops of medium tanks	)	
two troops of carriers	)	
one motorised troop	)	provided by 52nd HTR
two companies of riflemen	)	

The reason for this change was that operational control for the area had been taken over by 50th Northumbrian Infantry Division, so the main roles of the troops in Bovington and Lulworth Garrisons were to be acting in support of part of 50 Div, or to act as divisional reserve. However, they still had to be prepared to revert to their original four groups:

REXFORCE (Comd. Col Rimmington): area — *exclusive Osmington Mills; inclusive Poxwell, Warmwell, Puddletown, Bere Regis, Wareham, Wareham Channel round south side of Brownsea Island to entrance to Poole Harbour.*
ROFORCE (Comd. Col Roberts); *area — Poole*
RESERVE GROUP (Comd. Maj Wilcox)
W TROOP (Comd. 2/Lt Scarborough); *Warmwell Aerodrome protection.*

Although none of these forces ever had to fire a shot in anger they all took their jobs extremely seriously. I was fortunate enough to find two excellent descriptions of their tasks, the first, written by Mr CT Witherby.[25] He was attending an Officers D & M Course at Bovington in May 1940 and wrote: "On the Tuesday, 21st May, we had our classes normally in the morning, but after lunch, I was walking past one of the huts when i saw a crowd of men I knew, mostly officer students, digging trenches. Someone said: 'They expect German gliders and aircraft to land here at any moment." I got a pickaxe and joined in the digging until dark. These were not weapon pits, but the kind of air-raid trenches which one had seen in London since 1938. While this was going on the Permanent Staff were driving and towing tanks, old vehicles and tree trunks, out onto the Sports Ground and surrounding fields, to serve as obstacles for aircraft trying to land. Even the mild steel Matilda was so used. There were quite a number of private cars at Bovington then and anyone who had a car drove it out onto the fields to help block them.

"Next day there were no classes and the School was closed. Men whose courses were ending and whose units were close by were sent home. The men in my class were just starting and their units were far off. In the afternoon I went out with one or two others on a recce as we were told that a Mobile Column was to be formed. We drove to Wareham and also went over the hills to the Blue Pool and on to Studland, having a very pleasant pre-war style afternoon tea in a hotel at Corfe Castle. There was still a peacetime atmosphere.

"The Dutch had had to admit defeat and on Thursday, 23rd May, the Belgians ceased to fight. In the morning I met my Infantry Platoon, which consisted of 32 RAC sergeants. These men were mostly from the armoured brigade fighting in Belgium and so could not be sent back to their units. They were older men, regular soldiers, so they took the situation calmly. Each sergeant had been issued with a rifle and five rounds of ammunition. I was platoon commander and another officer — a much more capable man — was second in command (he was a week or two my junior).

"We had been told little about what we were supposed to do, but the scare about gliders at

Bovington seemed to be fading. Everyone felt that scattered parachutists might land to commit sabotage. After the platoon had been enrolled by the senior sergeant, we had a discussion and then went on a route march. We also practised an attack on a wood where parachutists were supposed to be hiding. ... On Saturday, 25th May, the entire Bovington Mobile Column formed up and set off on an exercise. There were at least three platoons of sergeant-infantry in lorries, a Besa machine gun carried in a truck, and an Infantry tank Mark I (Matilda I), crew one driver and one gunner with a water cooled machine gun. This military formation made its way to Wareham, crossed the causeway, turned left at Stoborough and went across the heath to a point on the edge of Poole Harbour, where we had a discussion on the beach defences.

"One could not help feeling sympathy for the Commandant at Bovington in his situation of suddenly finding himself on his own in command of a strange infantry force where nearly all the officers were beginners and not one of the personnel had any infantry training, where weapons were lacking, yet being about to grapple with one of the most formidable armies of modern history .... In Bovington, with our ludicrous force we seemed entirely on our own. There were no other soldiers about and except for the RAF at Warmwell, I never remember seeing any other Servicemen at all at this time."

Mr Witherby then goes on to tell of the arrival of the first stragglers from Dunkirk and recalls how worried everyone was that the heavy surf on the Dunkirk beaches would prevent a proper embarkation and thus the majority of the BEF would be lost. However, this did not happen and he goes on: "On 31st May and 1st June 1940, floods of men began pouring into Bovington. There were French as well as British, many of them wounded. Most had rifles and a few Bren guns. They bivouacked all over the playing fields, almost hiding the cars, lorries and tree trunks that had been put there a few days before. All these men were processed and soon went off. It must have been a huge adminstrative problem. We were still on our Mobile Column task, for which we were quite well suited. After 4th June, the Dunkirk evacuation ceased and those men who remained were authorised to surrender." At Bovington, the Mobile Column stood down and classes re-started. As to what the Mobile Columns achieved, Mr Witherby concludes: "On 25th May as we went through Wareham, members of the public must have been impressed. The sergeants looked tough. No one knew that they only had five bullets each. Certainly the column, and its sister columns throughout Britain, must have prevented panic during the terrible days before the evacuation from Dunkirk was complete."

Bovington Air Raids and Decoys

ANOTHER MEMBER of a Mobile Column was Chris Gray, who had, as we have seen, left Bovington in March 1940, to return to the Royal Military College to finish his training as an officer. He returned four months later and recalls his return thus:

"The atmosphere in Bovington in the middle of July 1940 was one of purposeful determination; training would go on but if Hitler decided to invade then he would find veritable hornets nest awaiting him in this part of Dorset. For my second visit I had arrived as an officer of all of two months standing to attend an instructors course at the AFV School, Wireless Wing.

"Even allowing for the fact that it was now high summer, the quality of life was far removed from the basic conditions of seven months ago. I had a reasonably comfortable room in N-Block which was one of three corrugated iron huts on the top of Cologne Road, and the AFV School Officer's Mess. However there wasn't much time for gracious living because, superimposed on the life of the student, was ones part in the 'Defence of Realm'.

"A measure of how serious it had all become occured only a day or two after my arrival when the Prime Minister, Winston Churchill, and General Alan Brooke, soon to be C & C Home Forces, visited the South Coast Defence area and had a meal in the Officers' Mess prior to catching their special train back to London. Round the area there were many defence posts including static AFVs of various kinds such as the 'Independent' from the Museum which were manned by a combination of subunits of 69 Infantry Brigade with its headquarters in Bovington and soldiers of the AFV School, RAC Depot and 52nd Training Regiment. As a very junior officer one was on some sort of duty practically every night whether it was sleeping in an orderly officers room, visiting outlying pickets or, particularly for wireless students, manning various communication centres either in a dug-out or mounted in trucks. Just to add to the realism was the air war which during the day raged overhead as the squadrons from Warmwell (609 and 152 Sqns) got among the raiders seeking to bomb Portland or Poole, or shipping in the Channel. Several aircraft fell out of the sky not far from Bovington and to this day I still have a souvenir bit from a ME 110 which crashed in a vertical dive from about 12000 ft onto Creech Hill, east of Lulworth.

"Air activity was not confined to the daytime alone. Even on a rare free night an already hazardous journey back from the Seven Stars Pub across the footbridge could be transformed into sheer farce with people falling on their faces into the various ditches and dykes along the route back to camp. The only bombs I remember actually falling on the camp area at this time were some oil-filled incendiaries with whistles on their fins which fell about quarter of a mile north of the camp on the driving ground, but which sounded as though they were coming down on one's head. I remember diving into a ditch beside my quarters as these came down and then feeling somewhat silly when I realised how far away they had actually fallen. On the same night several sticks of ordinary incendiaries fell into the rough ground just to the east of H-Lines. Only one hut in H-Lines was actually hit and that was a paint store which burned fiercely until the fire brigade doused it. The Storeman who lived in that hut had a lucky escape as he was out at the time. One incendiary bomb had gone right through his bed.

"As my course progressed so the tension surrounding the expectation of an invasion increased. This culminated in the great 'Stand-To' of the 7th September when training did actually stop, I think, on the issue of the code word 'Cromwell' from the War Office. All the defence posts were manned throughout the South Coast area. When nothing happened, we went back on to normal schedules after some 24 hours or so. However, the 'Stand Down' eventually came on the 19th September which, ironically was the day my course ended and I then returned to Warminster.

"My third tour of Bovington started only some 6 weeks after my last departure. However, in that short time the atmosphere had again changed. Now that the threat of invasion had receded, training was going ahead at full speed. The enemy threat had now changed to one of bombing and the possibility of air drops on strategic targets. I was sent down in the beginning of November as OC Wireless Wing of the 58th Training Regiment which was to form in Stanley Barracks under the command of Lt Col EJ (Squeek) O'Connor. Due to the restricted size of the barracks both the Gunnery and Wireless Wings were housed in the married quarters of Andover Green. These had been hurriedly evacuated but not without a certain amount of dissension according to other historical sources.

"The Warrant Officers and Sergeants had their mess in the building that, on my first visit to Stanley Barracks, had been the Cadet's canteen. [The OCTUS now had their own training wings and so cadets no longer came to Bovington.] The officers of 52nd and 58th Training Regiments together with those of the RAC Depot all shared the old RTC Depot mess. This didn't really lead to overcrowding as the actual accommodation was spread around the various blocks in the area, although the 52nd had pinched the best, including "Scandal Mansion" the two storey building beside the mess. My own room was in some converted huts in F-Lines, roughly were the band practice building now stands.

"Training equipment came through slowly but training eventually got going at the beginning of December. In the Wireless Wing we instructed on No. 9 and No. 11 sets and all operators were taught morse. In addition to the training schedule there were air defence posts, fire pickets and security schemes to keep one occupied in those still anxious times; consequently it was not often possible to go further afield than the Officers Club in Elles Road for light entertainment. However, there was a reasonable supply of nurses and FANYs to brighten the evenings. On Saturdays there was usually a dance in one of the four Sergeant's Messes to which WRAFs from Warmwell came to supplement the local talent. The camp's ATS were housed at the Higher Wood married quarters and their guardroom was the first quarter on the right.

"Although I had, of course, missed the bombing of Sherborne on the 30th September when it received 300 bombs in three minutes which were originally meant for Bristol, but were unloaded when the local fighters got at the bombers, there was still enough air activity along the South Coast to keep us on our toes during the day and awake at night.

"The enemy raids were mostly on the airfields such as Warmwell, Hurn and Christchurch. Moreton Church had been wrecked by a bomb on the 8th October. However, its re-building gave it some very fine new glass by Lawrence Whistler which is well worth a visit. There were two raids on Bournemouth, on the 15th November 1940 and the 11th April 1941. I got rather too close to the second one as I was going through the square when Woolworths was hit by a stick of incendiaries. I am afraid my little old Morris made one of its quickest-ever trips back to camp that night. On the 1st April 1941 a day time raid on Warmwell by three Heinkel 111s killed about 10 people (and made a great deal of noise in Bovington). It was a day of low cloud and the airfield's ack-ack guns were clearly not expecting trouble as the planes were over Bovington and heading for the coast by the time they started shooting. The camp's machine-gun ack-ack posts were noticeably ineffective against the HE 111s as they climbed back into the clouds!

"All Training Regiments, not just those at Bovington, had some sort of operational commitment and the task given to the 58th Training Regiment was the defence of Warmwell airfield against airborne attack, working of course in conjunction with the RAF's own defence and the local Home Guard. To carry out this task a small force was organised from the permanent staff called "Comforce" after the CO who commanded it. The force consisted of four Mk II light tanks (refugees from the Dutch Army), two 3-tonner personnel carriers, each carrying about 25 men and their ammunition etc, six motorcyclists (for communication back to Bovington) and an HQ. Light tanks were commanded by instructors from the Gunnery Wing who were the only people likely to be able to work the Vickers machine-guns (most tanks were now converted to BESA machine guns).

"We used to have turnouts every so often when this little army set forth along the lanes past the Seven Stars to take up positions around the airfield. The HQ used to be in Warmwell House which was occupied by WRAF who let us have a downstairs room. The resemblance to Dad's Army of TV fame was uncanny so far as the Home Guard was concerned. Most of the turnouts were during the day but some were at night and on one particularly dark and wet night the force accounted for its first Spitfire, when one of the tanks removed the aircraft's tail by putting a track over it. The plane shouldn't have been where it was but, no more night exercises were held after that incident.

"In order to try and deceive the enemy raiders there were two "decoys" in the area. One was at Arne to protect the Holton Heath factory and the other was at Winfrith (where the Atomic Energy Establishment now stands) to simulate Warmwell airfield. Both sites were, I believe, quite successful. Certainly the open ground at Winfrith got more than its fair share of bombs, although it made life at Bovington rather noisy at night. The decoy consisted, among other things, of light moving across the ground to represent aircraft taking off. When the authorities came to build the Atomic Energy buildings they were very surprised to find a considerable number of bombs in the ground. Had they asked in the right quarter, they would have been told what to expect!

"As 1941 wore on the local air raids became more scattered during the day time and fairly normal recreational pastimes took place although the ack-ack posts were still manned. In the 58th Training Regiment I became Officer in charge of Hockey and we mustered a remarkably good team made up mostly from old sweats who had learned their hockey in India before the war. Among other venues where we played away games was RAF Warmwell where we played the administrative staff (while the pilots and ground crew were busy getting on with the war). Then after tea we repaired to their messes for some excellent parties with the now relaxing air crews. On one such occasion, just as it was getting dark, the station commander was called to the phone and then informed us that a damaged Hurricane from some distant airfield was coming in. When the pilot duly arrived in the mess he turned out to a chap I had been at school with and so that was an extra excuse for more celebrations.

"The movement of AFVs between Bovington and Lulworth had not so far presented any problem as the largest of them had been the **Medium,** the **A9** and the **A10.**However, the advent of the **Churchill** presented problems at Wool bridge. Three out of four of these AFVs touched some part of the bridge parapet and pushed it into the river. The authorities therefore decided to dismantle both parapets and put up scaffolding in such a way that there was planking and a handrail for the pedestrians and on either side of the bridge, while at the same time giving the tanks an extra 6ft of room. This arrangement actually lasted until well after the war was over. The bridge parapets were then re-built and now you can hardly see the join!

"All AFVs were (and still are) routed to Lulworth via Holme where a Bailey Bridge and then a new bridge were built. The inhabitants of the East Stoke have always been rather less than happy with this arrangement as AFVs have got progressively larger and noisier!

"In 1940 HQs AFV School was in Elles Road in a hut located conveniently close to the Officer's Club. As a student officer doing Garrison Duty Officer one took one's camp bed and slept fitfully in the Brigadier's office. Most nights the telephone would ring and the operator would say: 'Air Raid – Red', whereupon one had to get up and operate an enormous red handle to sound the sirens. This, of course, had to be repeated for the 'All Clear'.

"By 1942 the HQ had moved to Cambrai House. For a few weeks, while awaiting a posting order after handing over my wireless wing to Eric Richardson (Afterwards Colonel, RAOC) I was a tempory GSO 3 in the HQ and had a small office in what was probably a box room. As I recall my main job was to keep the war map in the Brigadier's office up to date."

Lulworth's air raids

MENTION IS made above to the air raids which took place in 1940-42. Those at Lulworth were probably the most serious and are well documented in the War Diary of the Gunnery Wing AFV School, which mobilised on 1st September 1939 and continued to fulfil its normal role, namely that the training AFV Gunnery instructors, but now on a war basis. A permanent blackout of the camp was immediately ordered and window screens prepared. All were supposedly in position by nightfall, 2 September 1939. As Glyn Evans has already told us, however, this was far from true. The first air raid warning message was received on 3 June 1940, however, the first bombs were not dropped until 9 July, when a low flying enemy light bomber dropped two 50lb bombs from a height of about 1200ft. no material damage was done as the bombs landed in a field Southwest of the 30 yard range. Details of air activity over Lulworth shown later in this chapter, however, three of the most serious raids occurred on 23 August 1940, when two men were killed and 7 wounded; on 10 November 1940 when the Tank Park was raided and two people, including one ATS, were wounded and finally, on 14 December 1942 when one man was killed and three wounded. The first of these raids saw an act of gallantry performed by Sgt J Thompson which was recorded in Southern Command Orders thus:-

"During an enemy raid at Lulworth Camp on Friday, 23rd August 1940, the above NCO was working in the detachment stores when the "All Clear" was sounded. Several minutes later an enemy plane was noticed flying low over camp. Realising that recruits under instruction at Lulworth Camp were doing infantry training nearby, he immediately left the stores and went to ensure that the men had taken proper cover, moving around shouting to the men to lay down and keep still. During this period the plane dropped several bombs, killing two men and wounding seven. Sgt Thompson himself received severe leg wounds. It is considered that had it not been for the courage and initiative displayed by this NCO, regardless of his own safety, a great number of casualties would have occurred. By his courage and devotion to duty he set a very fine example."

The second of these two raids is well remembered by Glyn Evans, as the ATS girl wounded was one of his Mess Staff. He writes: "Jerry decided to pay us an afternoon visit, his target being the Tank Park. Also, we were told later, the soccer pitch in the woods in the Castle* grounds where a soccer match was in progress. Jerry did some harm, wounding Sgt 'Squiffy' Asquith RTR, the young Pay Sgt, who was courting an excellent ATS waitress of my staff – Megan Jenkins. They were walking past the Tank Park intending to see the soccer match when Jerry struck. Asquith got some leg wounds – not too serious, but Megan was more seriously wounded and I remember Col RAH Walker RTR, telling me that he had visited them both in Shaftesbury Military Hospital and was amazed at her courage, saying that she was a very brave young lady."

The third of these raids was not until two years later although there had been quite a lot of enemy activity in between as the annex explains. SSM(I) Stan Robinson recalled this one in an article he wrote recently for the Tank magazine: "On a peaceful Wednesday afternoon in late October 1942 a German fighter bomber – without bombs – flew through Arish Mell Gap towards the Tank Park; after firing a burst of small arms the pilot banked sharply to the left and flew low over the concrete road leading to the Camp. Being disturbed by the firing, the range being closed, and hearing the approach of the plane I moved quickly to the back door of my office hut to observe what it was up to. On reaching the nearby junction of the concrete and tar sealed roads it climbed over the Camp, banked left and presumably returned to base.

"The RAC Gunnery Experimental Wing occupied seven of nine large huts. From their front doors was a clear view of C Range and Bindon Hill. No 1. hut, the furthest hut from the School

Lulworth Camp: quad Besa anti-aircraft guns – the Mark II model of February 1942. Its predecessor had been hastily improvised at the Gunnery School in 1940 and manned during air raids. Stan Robinson was the designer.

entrance, was EW HQ. No 9. hut, nearest the School and flanked by the small EW hangar was the Barrack Wardens' Store, No 8. was the EW Workshop, whilst no 7 held my office, situated and enclosed, left centre of the hut. At the back of these huts ran a narrow footpath with a sparse hedgerow on the far side. There was an opening opposite the back door of the Workshops. Looking half left from this opening towards the Camp, one saw some 150 yds away the back of the Officers Mess. The open ground between the messes and the line of huts was intersected, some 20 to 30 yds from the back of the huts by a tar sealed road terminating at EW HQ. Opposite the back of hut No 3. was the junction of the two roads. I went back to my office and, thinking about the plane incident, decided it was a Recce exercise. But for what? It was a long time since we had seen or heard a plane. Baffling! Now to the raid.

"The quiet afternoon of 14 December was cool with no wind. The active war was a long way away, but our work went on hard and unrelenting. I once again sat at my desk, forever writing. The tranquility was shattered by the sound of an enemy aircraft approaching from the Tank Park. I ran to the door in time to see a familiar 'new fighter/bomber' climbing fast over the Camp. I returned to my writing. Then followed the flight of a second aircraft but with a stunning difference. The ground and hut shook with the force of a large bomb landing, which fortunately did not explode. The plane, a similar one to the first leader then turned sharply left and opened fire with MG's and 20mm at our huts. I crouched under my desk. The gunfire passed over my roof into the Workshop and Barrack Store. Had the pilot opened fire a second earlier I doubt I would be writing this account. I went out in time to see the plane disappearing towards the Cove.

"The Workshop was shambles. Full of smoke and dust and Sgt Jack Stevens our welder, lying on his back in the middle of the huts. Running to turn off his gas 'bottles' I saw he had been hit at the base of his skull. Sgt Hansen was losing blood in spurts from his arm. I applied a tourniquet and sat him in the ditch outside. SSgt Bill Holliday has lost a finger and was badly hurt having, as he later told my 83 pieces of shrapnel embedded, head to foot, in his left side, while SSgt Freddie Angliss was dazed, having only just escaped being killed. He dropped on his knees at the first burst, and there was a bullet groove in the jaw of his vice. I shouted to him 'Call for an ambulance'.

"I went to check on the Bk Warden. He sat transfixed at his desk and the match boarding which enclosed his was on each side of him peppered with bullet holes. I am sure the pilot took on the wrong hut. It should have been mine. I sent my splendid soldiers to their barrack rooms.

"Two of the MRS doctors were quickly on the spot, being joined by Major Kelly the MO. I asked them about Jack Stevens, they shook their heads. The ambulance took the injured to Bovington Military Hospital. Jack died in the early hours next morning. After a military funeral he was buried in West Lulworth churchyard.

"Next morning we moved out. I went and had a look at the bomb. The 2 to 3 foot circular top was three feet deep in the concrete at the junction of the roads. The 'tail' was very big being at least five feet long. Thankfully it was an 1800 kg dud. On the second day the Bomb Disposal Officer came. I asked him what damage would have followed had it exploded. 'The Messes would have suffered badly, the front of the School would have been battered.' I asked about the line of huts and the old brick power station 'Demolished' he said.

"Reflections on the raid, I am aware that in relation to the Blitz and the Desert War our small affair was insignificant but the shock was total. Why a Recce prior to the attack? Indeed, why the attack? Why drop a bomb on a largely open space? Had the bomb been dropped about 200yds further on and exploded it could have been the magazines that also went up. Exit a large part of Lulworth Camp. It leaves a large question unanswered."

Bovington had its share of air raids, but not as many as Lulworth. Sylvia Wood vividly recalled one particular night when a big ration store near the telephone exchange where she worked, was hit and much time was spent in and around the burning building looking for a cat with kittens, which were eventually saved although everything else was badly damaged: "We drank smokey tea for ages afterwards". Another night after a heavy raid they pulled back the metal sliding doors in the roof over the switchboards and "to our amazement found two butterfly bombs caught in the wire netting. The Officer's Mess next to the exchange had disappeared and there were more butterfly bombs on the roadway and in the trees. One soldier at least lost a foot by kicking one."

East Lulworth: Mark VIB light tanks move out from the park (third glimpsed behind the lodge roof) and into the lane.

Summary of Lulworth's air war, 1940-42

Date	Location	Type of Action	Result
9 Jul 40	Field SW of 30 x range	Light bomber raid	two bombs dropped no damage
11 Jul	Povington Heath	ME 110 shot down by RAF fighters	
27 Jul	road between E Lulworth and searchlight post	Light bomber raid	two bombs dropped, no damage
11 Aug	C Range	Hurricane fighter of 213 Sqn	made forced landing on C Range
13 Aug	¾ml E of Kimmeridge lookout	Me 110 crashed in flames	crew baled out and were captured
23 Aug	Sportsfield, St Andrews Fm and ranges	bombing raid 8 bombs dropped	two killed and seven injured (see account)
25 Aug	Air battle over coast with a number of aircraft (reported in newspaper as 24) shot down.		
11 Sep	North of Burngate Farm	Bombing raid	two bombs dropped but did not explode
27 Sep	General camp area	Me 110 flew low over camp	Camp AA MGs opened up and plane crashed some 1000x from shore
7 Oct	large formation of 60 to 70 enemy aircraft observed approaching coast at 1545 hrs, engaged by a heavy AA barrage then fighter aircraft (15). Just before 1600, the enemy returned directly over camp and one Me 110 crashed into sea 2000x from Arish Mell Gap. Another enemy aircraft shot down near Owermoigne. Raid ended at 1637 hrs.		
10 Nov	Tank Park	raid by enemy aircraft – three groups of two Me 110s protected by three Me 109s.	damage to buildings (including Tech stores fitters shop, Oil store and Battery Charging Room), two tanks superficially damaged two wounded (one ATS) (see account)
1 Apr 41	Lulworth Cove	Machine gun raid by lone aircraft	Attacked Signal Station and Cove, generally; no casualties.
21 Apr 41	Camp area	enemy plane flew over camp	engaged by camp MGs.
4 May	Winfrith Heath	Ju 88 shot down by AA fire	crew baled out and were captured
9 Jun	Coast near camp	two groups of three Me 109s	engaged by Spitfire and dispersed
10 Sept	'B' Range firing pt	Spitfire made forced landing and turned upside down but was only superficially damaged and was recovered.	
21 Oct	Bindon Hill South slope	FW 190 crashed into Bindon Hill and pilot was killed	
14 Dec 42	Tank Park	bombing raid on Workshop one killed, three injured, considerable damage (see account)	

Flying bombs – tanks to the seafront

BEFORE LEAVING the subject of air raids, it is interesting to note a connection between the AFV Schools and the combatting of the flying bombs sent against London and the Home Counties in 1944. An Anti Aircraft (A/A) Section had been formed at Lulworth early in 1942, when it became apparent that the A/A gunner must be an expert at his job, early spotting and quick recognition of aircraft for example, giving him the opportunity to build up a volume of fire against all types of air attack.

Even earlier in the war various types of light machine gun mountings had been evolved, one of the most successful being a light tank mounting a quadruple BESA MG which was used "in anger" in the defence of Lulworth Camp. From 1943, proper training got underway at Lulworth the first course being trained on the Crusader 40mm Bofors A/A tank. An A/A Dome Trainer was set up and proved extremely useful in teaching 'Eye Shooting' technique.

During the early part of 1944, all the A/A Troops of 21st Army Group were trained – nearly 3000 students in all. Then, in early June 1944, orders were received to move to Kent to combat the flying bomb menace. Tanks were loaded up and within 48 hrs were in position on the sea front at Hastings, and in Dymchurch and Littlestone.

They were all subsequently moved to the Hythe area and performed their task admirably and even carried on their training to boot, their students being the only ones in the Army who had real targets to shoot at!

Lulworth Ranges: a line-up of Cruiser tanks, on the flat ground south-east of Lulworth Camp, and Comets firing southwards from the same area – towards Bindon Hill with the Purbeck Hills in the background.

Bovington Camp: Covenanter goes into a deep puddle in the training area – which was as close as this type of tank would come to the war. Covenanters suffered a series of mechanical defects and were never sent into battle.

OPPOSITE – Bovington Camp: words of defiance from Lance Corporal H. Rayner with drawings by Trooper J. Haddock express the John Bull spirit of the days when the island's 'fullest fury' was 'yet to launch'.

PREVIOUS PAGE –
Lulworth Ranges: Churchill inspects his Churchills, 6 April 1942. The new tanks bearing the Prime Minister's name had arrived in the winter of 1941. It was a stony-faced Churchill. The Japanese had taken Singapore in February and the Germans were advancing towards Egypt. The Churchill would be first used in action by the Canadians on their disastrous Dieppe raid in August 1942, but it would make its real debut in the close, hilly country of Tunisia in January 1943 – and go on to prove itself as the best British tank of World War Two.

Lulworth Camp: instructor Arthur English of the Gunnery Wing became 'The Wide Boy' of wartime stage and wireless:
'I don't have to run to Wool to catch the Passion Wagon to Poole anymore and it seems a long time since I had a pint in the Castle.'

US

England at war by fate's decree,
Count not the odds you men so free,
Unite yourselves, resolve and stand
To arms for your great glorious land.

'Tis not a time to loathe, abhor,
The cursed uselessness of war
Or ask oneself the reasons why
Death rains incessant from the skies.

Look round you, men of British breed,
On this fair isle of ours, and heed
The threat which hangs o'er Britain fair
From land and sea and in the air.

Look once again at country fields,
Streams and valleys, lanes and wealds,
Nature's glory, radiant, rife
With beauty, freedom, joys of life.

Freedom, a word that does convey
To man the right to think and say
Just what he thinks in home or street
To neighbour, stranger he may meet.

To have a home, humble or bold,
In city, village, town or wold,
'Round which he may build his life,
Content, in peace, with folks and wife.

This England gives us such a life
As best she can, free from all strife,
But now dark forces rise in rage
Against us and our heritage.

These evil slaves of Satan's mould
Would smash us and all we uphold
If they could but discern that we
Dared not to fight for liberty.

Gaze fondly once again I pray
On sights beloved, and come what may
Commit yourself to their defence,
From barbarous hordes of hate intense.

Our island stands, though scarred yet
          staunch,
Its fullest fury yet to launch
On those whose stupid folly vain
Prompts them our hallowed shores to gain.

H. Rayner, L/Cpl.

Illustrated by J. Haddock, Tpr.

58th Training Regiment

THE OTHER Training Regiment which Chris Gray came back to help form, in early November 1941 at Stanley Barracks, was the 58th. This was a somewhat specialised training organisation as it concentrated on volunteers, who were chosen for their potential as future NCO crew commanders and officers. Instead of the normal training cycle as practised at the 52nd, the 58th gave the volunteers an exacting six months course, which covered all three crew trades – driving, gunnery and wireless – and culminated in an intensive period of collective training and crew commanding. Lt Col (Retd) Tony Blad, MBE, late RTR, was trained at the 58th Training Regiment in 1943 and he told me:

"I joined the Army on 20th May 1943, travelling from Hampton Court via Waterloo to Wool by train, accompanied by Roy Hayward who I had known for some years and who was later to be severely wounded in Normandy. The buildings on Wool Railway Station were at this time, and for many years to come, extremely rudimentary – most of them consisting of disused goods wagons. We were met by the truck and taken to 30th Primary Training Wing which was housed in a series of wooden huts in the area between the present Education Centre (Anderson House) and the road adjacent to the RAC Memorial Hall. Soon we were issued with uniform and our civilian clothes were packed away in parcels and sent home. The intake consisted of over eighty recruits and we were divided into a number of different platoons. We all wore berets with the badge of the General Service Corps, made of a brown plastic substance.

"The huts, as I remember, were joined together in pairs with a corridor running between them containing the washing facilities. The outside of the barrack rooms was sandbagged. The huts were scrupulously clean inside. We slept on double-tier bunks, reveille was at 0545, washing and shaving was in cold water. The furniture in the barrack room consisted of a six-foot trestle table and two wooden benches which were cleaned by scraping the surfaces with a razor blade until they were white. There was a stirrup-pump and fire-blanket, also a coal bucket but as all these items had to be kept clean and smart they were never used. Nobody ever contemplated lighting the round stove which would otherwise have heated the premises.

"The keen young soldiers spent the next six weeks learning the basic skills of military training, drill, the rifle, the Mills grenade and the Bren gun. We were also taught the Boyes Anti-tank gun which was by then obsolescent, if not obsolete. There were lessons on gas which given by a Sergeant who was known as 'Phosgene Pete'. Knowledge of chlorine and mustard gas did not seem to have engendered a sense of humour in this otherwise efficient instructor and we treated him with considerable respect.

"The platoon sergeant who occupied the Non-Commissioned Officer's bunk at the entrance of the hut was a quiet, smart, well spoken Infantryman who had fought in France and returned via Dunkirk having, at one time, been posted missing. He was well liked but firm and it was almost wholly due to him that in six weeks we became reasonably turned out and presentable. The officer in charge of the whole intake was also popular. It was rumoured that he had been an actor before joining the Army and at a concert in the barracks he achieved special recognition when he sang a very amusing song: *She had to go and lose it at the Astor.* At the end of the six weeks the majority of the intake moved down to the 58th Training Regiment at Stanley Barracks. The Regiment was responsible for training recruits for the Royal Armoured Corps in the skills needed by tank crews and it was said to be particularly geared to the training of potential NCOs and Officers. The first three weeks were spent in General Military Training which was an extension of the work at 30 PTW but we now wore the RAC Badge. Then began our 'proper' training with five weeks of Driving and Maintenance.

"It was an extremely good course which included basic instruction on vehicles followed by wheeled vehicle driving, classroom instruction in tank details and tank driving. The wheeled vehicle driving instructor was a somewhat stout Corporal who played the saxophone and had a much better sense of humour then the majority of Corporals who we had contacted so far in our training. Driving a **Crusader** tank made one feel a bit special even if there was only a qualified "f good" on ones training report.

"The accommodation was in the familiar wooden spider blocks' where the same high standards of cleanliness were maintained as had been instilled in the Primary Training Wing. Bedding was folded and 'blocked' each day and a complete set of webbing was blancoed, polished and laid out. All clothing had to be marked with ones Army Number and occasionally there was a full kit check with every item of equipment presented and displayed in accordance with time honoured custom and in the correct order 'knife, fork, spoon, razor and lather brush'.

"By today's standards the discipline was extremely strict. Troopers stood to attention when speaking to NCOs and only high standards and turnout were accepted. Everyone leaving barracks reported to the Guardroom and was inspected before 'booking out' and it was not unknown for men to be told to return to their barrack room and clean their buttons, brasses or beret. A great deal of time was spent in ironing knife-edge creases in our battle dresses. Those who did leave the barracks had to book in at the Guardroom on their return and present themselves to the Guard Commander who, one hoped, would write 'SPD (sober and properly dressed)' against the appropriate name in the book with the time of return beside it to confirm that one was not late. As the nearest pub was 2½ miles away, the pay extremely low and there was no transport, it was most unlikely that anyone returning to camp would be drunk. There were two Provost Sergeants, one rather smooth and cultured (there was a rumour that he had been an assistant to the Archbishop of Canterbury and this was widely believed despite its improbability). The other was less sophisticated and neither were at all popular with those who were undergoing training. There was an occasion when one of them produced a bag of apples and handed it around to those of us who were on guard. We were sure that some dastardly trick was involved but felt that it unwise to refuse the offer. In fact, the apples were quite nice.

"Part of the four-week gunnery training was completed in Bovington but the firing took place in the Lulworth Ranges and it was during this time that the trainees were housed and fed in Park Camp. It was a fairly scruffy collection of huts and fortunately there was a compensating reduction in the need for spit and polish. The cookhouse was run chiefly by the ATS who were roused for the breakfast meal with an early call by members of the guard. One enthusiastic early caller, in imitation of the method used to arouse the trainees, flung open the door of their hut and marched up and down the barrack room shouting 'Rise and shine' and 'Show a leg'. We were told later by the Troop Officer that the instructions to the guard would be amended to avoid the neccessity for the members of the guard entering the ATS quarters – chuckle, chuckle. On the ranges, we fired the two-pounder gun mounted in **Valentines.** This was at the time nearly, if not quite, obsolete. We also fired the six-pounder and, amongst the machine guns, a Bren gun mounted on the turret with a system of springs intended as an anti-aircraft weapon. We fired on Bindon Hill against an aeroplane silhouette which moved in a straight line on the moving target track – even so, it was extremely difficul to hit.

"Four weeks were spent in Wireless Training wrestling with phonetic alphabets, radio procedure, the Morse Code and the Number 19 Wireless Set. It was a change to be away from the dirty jobs associated with the tank park and, to a lesser extent, the Gunnery Wing. Those who learned about the 19 set were special for it needed constant attention to keep it working properly, tuning and retuning using the "penny screws" and readjusting the variometer. The morse test was at eight words a minute – although it was never entirely clear, then or later on, why the subject was taught.

"Throughout the course there was plenty of drill and PT. The physical training staff were not over-popular especially one of the more senior ones who inspected the troop for cleanliness before training and on occasions carried a cotton wool pad dipped into methylated spirits which he applied to the necks of those he deemed to have not washed. The PT itself was active and energetic and we were all extremely fit.

"The final part of the course was Collective Training which consisted of a tactical exercise with carriers, simulating tanks, each carrier with a crew of four. There was also a fifty mile "bash", a sort of old fashioned "yomping". The troop was divided up into sections and taken to some forgotten place fifty miles away and set off with maps, kit and food with the aim of returning to Bovington within forty-eight hours. There were occasional tactical incidents on route but the main task was to complete the journey. The arrangements at night were to be at our own initiative. At one village we stopped and asked whether they had a place where we could shelter and before long permission had been given for the local chapel to be opened and, moreover, the boiler was lit. When you are young, fit and tired, there is no better place to sleep than under a chapel pew with ones back against warm pipes.

"The troop eventually dispersed early in 1944. Those who had attended and passed the War Office Selection Board at Winchester were made unpaid Lance-Corporals, a doubtful distinction which meant that former friends tended to disown one. Later, the potential officers were formed into a squad in a separate barrack room where their interest were looked after by a small, wiry and witty pre-war Sergeant who acted as guardian and friend. It was he, I think, who master-minded the final kit check when every item of kit on each bed was immaculately prepared and lined up. It was he, too, who as we marched towards the square for the last time called out "left, right, left, right, one, two, buckle my shoe". Shortly afterwards we left Bovington for the Pre-Octu at Blackdown.

"If occasionally the adminstration was less than perfect and the discipline over-strict, more good and little harm was the result. Certainly the standard of training was extremely high and the majority of the troop were posted to Regiments. Many must have fought in Normandy in 1944-45."

58th Training Regiment moved out of Stanley Barracks in 1944 to Farnborough, Hants.

Alterations to the training machine for first American tanks

ALTHOUGH THERE were no more significant alterations to the basic structure of the two camps of camp buildings once Stanley Barracks was completed, the training machine which they contained was in a constant state of flux. Initially, as we have seen, it was a matter of making do with whatever resources were available. Men like Major TA Lakeman, RTR, did sterling work producing inexpensive, simple training equipment from 1939 onwards. This equipment proved invaluable during the years that followed, because nothing more suitable was produced through "normal channels". Lakeman's Weapon Training Workshops was moved from Warminster to Lulworth in 1943, and continued there, designing and constructing many valuable items of training equipment until the formation of the RAC School Training Equipment section in 1945.

In the spring of 1941 a series of special courses were run in preparation for the arrival of the first American tank to serve in the British Army, the **M2A4 Honey,** which was the first of the **Stuart** light tank series. In June that year the first students from the Guards Armoured Division arrived for training, to be followed later by Canadians Czech and Poles. In July, the American

Lulworth Ranges: British raider, a Yeovil-built Westland Lysander, practising on a Sherman tank beneath the Purbeck Hills.

forces started to arrive in Southern Command and, although Bovington was unaffected, most of the Training Regiments had to move up to Northern Command to make room for them (52nd, 55th and 58th remained in situ). About the same time there was a specialisation of recruits and instructors onto specific types of tanks and other AFVs – hardly surprising when one realises that a rough count in 1944 showed that the RAC was equipped with no less than 42 different AFVs! A selection system was developed that earmarked a man for a particular type of AFV before starting training, then ensured that he was trained exclusively on that AFV and finally, that he was posted to a unit so equipped. This did produce some problems, especially as some AFVs, most notably the **Sherman** and **Cromwell** tanks, were not immediately made available to the training organisation. However, it was proved time and time again, that if a soldier had been thoroughly trained basically, conversions to other equipments were easily accommodated.

From 1943 onwards, the main task of the training machine was to help get the invasion force ready for D Day. It was a rush job not made any easier by cuts in training manpower in order to make up field force units and by the withdrawal of training instructors from the School for continuation and specialised training in units. The AFV School was undoubtedly the most important part of the RAC training machine. It was described as the "the birthplace of doctrine for training" by Maj Gen ED Fanshawe, CBE then Major General, Armoured Training and Commander Trg Establishment RAC at an Inter-Allied and RAC Schools Armoured Training Conference, held in July 1944. He said it had been decided that the School would, in future, get any new equipment first, so that they could formulate the doctrine and disseminate it to everyone else, because they were so well equipped with both trained personnel and proper facilities.

In summary, as he explained, the AFV School supplied doctrinal pamphlets and diagrams, etc, and trained Officer and NCO instructors, not only for all RAC units, but also for a large number of units for the Dominions, the Allies and the course, for the Guards Armoured Division. It also trained instructors in AFV recognition for all arms and for the RN, RAF and the US Air Force. To cope with this workload, the School had expanded to almost three times its pre-war size. From 1941 it had also taken on the training of all RAC specialists tradesmen (electricians, vehicle mechanics and gunnery mechanics) for their post basic courses (ie: their training on actual AFVs in the field).

The Ranges – expanded into Tyneham

AS THE war progressed more and more land had to be taken over by the War Office for training. One of the main reasons for this was a requirement to meet the ever changing needs for larger calibre main armaments in AFVs. In 1939, Bindon Range at Lulworth was the only fully equipped AFV range in the UK. Not only did all students at the AFV School use this range, but also field force units of the RTR and converted Cavalry fired their annual courses. The facilities available were: Maximum distance for firing – 1500 yds. Sea Danger area adequate only for the 2pdr gun, 3 inch howitzer, 3.7 inch mortar, and all small arms. There were four ranges complete with dug-outs, broadside moving targets and adequate safety areas for all weapons quoted above. The total area was much too small to attempt any fire and movement exercises, except for a very short run for a single troop of tanks. There appeared to be little possibility of expansion, indeed pressure from outside had been exercised for years to try to get the range closed, so that the area could be freed for public use. However, this pressure was effectively dealt with and the range became firmly established.

Of course with the wartime expansion of the RAC, the urgency for a major increase in range space was paramount, to cope with the training of additional units, the introduction of larger weapons, the urgent necessity of battle training with firing and providing extra range requirements for American armour and other foreign nations. Another major factor was the introduction of HE shooting which included firing at ranges previously unheard of in tank gunnery. All this led to the establishing of ranges all over the country at places as far afield as Castlemartin, Minehead, Warcop and Kircudbright.

At Lulworth, Heath Range was taken into use and the sea danger area suitably extended to cover all RAC weapons. Heath allowed for shooting at a maximum range of 4500 yds approximately. There were four firing points. On two it was impossible to engage targets at ranges between 1000 and 2000 yds due to "dead ground"* but from the other two points targets could be engaged at any range up to 4000 yds. One firing point could only be used for low velocity weapons due to the restricted width of the danger area. The original ambitious construction plan for facilities at Heath Ranges was not completed and finally shelved at the end of the war, so the range had no dugouts or moving targets, only a few roads and a Control Tower were completed. Tank movement on the Heath was difficult as two-thirds of the area was natural bog, while great care had been exercised in order to prevent damage to buildings, historical landmarks, etc.

Perhaps the most emotive range area to be taken over was Tyneham Valley, where all the villagers and some fishermen's families in Worbarrow Bay, were moved out just before Christmas in December 1943, so that the area could be used for fire and movement exercises. At the time it was anticipated that the valley would be given back after the war, however, as we shall explain later, this was not to be. The eviction orders, signed by Maj Gen C H Miller of Southern Command, contained the words: "the Government appreciate that this is no small sacrifice which you are asked to make, but they are sure you will give this further help towards winning the war with a good heart." The total area to be evacuated was inside the square formed by East Lulworth – East Stoke – East Holme – Kimmeridge.

Mess Life – porridge to a stopwatch

OF COURSE a great deal of the small amount of leisure time available was spent by the officers and sergeants in their respective messes. Glyn Evans recounted the following andecdotes on mess life at Lulworth during the war: "When war was declared various schemes were put into operation, yes even domestic! We collected a lot of Shiphams potted meat jars to be used for holding each member's sugar ration for the day. The carpenter knocked up two trays with spaces to hold the jars which were numbered with sticky paper. Then along came a certain officer of the permanent staff who noted that quite a number of the jars still had sugar in them at the end of the day, because officers were out on training or had not used up their entire ration. Arming himself with an old style Smiths Crisps tin he used to wait until the dining room was empty and pour the remains from the pots therein. Then he would depart to the mess cellar, sit on a beer crate and 'score' loads of sloes (which he had got young officers to collect for him from the region of Arish Mell Gap). His tool for this operation was a Star razor blade. He then popped the sloes into half full bottles of Burnett's White Satin gin. They stayed in the cellar until he was satisfied with the colour, etc and then took them up to his room – I well remember he had about eighteen bottles on show! Some time later, he sent for me one evening and asked me to look at his bottles and I noticed that the colour was weak and sickly and I told him so. 'Yes' he said, 'that so and so batman of mine (a real little crafty cockney!) has been drinking them and topping them up with water!' I thought that the batman was really for the high jump, but as his home had been doodlebugged and he was awaiting a compassionate discharge, he was forgiven!"

The use of the Mess Suggestions Book had its amusing side too as Glyn told me: "One officer who was on a course wrote: 'Now that student officers have to carry out nightly Duty Officers visit to the outpost at Arish Mell Gap, it is suggested that luminous tape be laid from the back door of the mess bar to Arish Mell, so that we can find our way back to the bar!' The PMC replied: 'Judging by the time I note you spend in the mess bar I am sure you can easily find your way back unaided day or night from the outpost you quote!' Another entry read: 'That the vast amount of ironware be removed from the settees and armchairs in the anteroom so that those of us involved in the War Effort can be afforded a little comfort!"

For some officers however, time was not to be wasted nor standards be allowed to drop in wartime: "One senior officer who stayed in the mess, stationed himself at the bottom of the staircase, an imposing figure in battledress, complete with ammo boots. He watched everyone descending and had a word with them re dress, etc. At nearly 0900 hrs down came the then Range Officer, wearing on his feet as was his wont, a pair of very loud carpet slippers. I happened to be nearby putting up the officer's morning mail – my God did the General go to town! Made the unfortunate officer go back upstairs to change properly and then no breakfast – just report to your duty! One Commandant we had, a fine gentleman, used to come into breakfast at 0700 hrs sharp every morning, just to take a plate of porridge nothing else, and sit eating it with a very large sort of railwayman's watch in front of him. I asked him one day about it and he said: 'Mr Evans, eating time is a waste of fighting time!"

Entertainment

THE NONSTOPS Troop Show was typical of the many concert parties formed all over the UK to help entertain the troops. Run by Bettina Hockey of Christchurch, it did a great deal to help keep up the Forces morale in the Southern Command area, giving over a 1,000 voluntary shows and travelling everywhere within a 40 mile radius of Bournemouth. They played to audiences in garrisons with fully equipped theatres, right down to small units under canvas and wallowing in mud, stationed in the New Forest just before D Day.

Performing four or five nights a week, in addition to their full-time day jobs, this small concert party really did its bit during the war. There were sixteen artistes, singers, comedians, musicians and dancers, viz: Peggy the soprano who was an officer in the American Red Cross; Sandy an old fisherman, sleight of hand; Billy the comedian, who ran a transport café; Dippy, a soldier stationed in Bournemouth; Gus a cartoon artist; Pat, baritone was in the building trade; Iris and Norman, a husband and wife act on vibes and accordian; Nellie, a Nellie Wallace type comedienne; Betty, principal dancer doing the Can-can, Hula, Seven Veils etc; Peggy on the piano; Mac, the electrician and finally, three dancers Monica, Pat and Babs.

The concerty party visited Bovington and Lulworth on many occasions as Betty recalled to me: "Bovington and Lulworth Camps will always be remembered with great fondness and happy memories of the wartime days when I visited them frequently. One night at Bovington, half-way through the show there was a Red Alert. The Concert Party, still dressed in costume, were rushed off the camp by bus which had to drive through the country lanes without lights as was the law in those days. It turned out that we had a lucky escape, as a bomb hit the building next to the theatre. True to traditional fashion, we returned after the raid and the show went on!

"Lulworth has a favourite spot in my heart, coupled with our compere Ken. He was a much loved man who had only one kidney at that time, yet bravely carried on fighting against all odds. He died shortly after the war ended but will always be remembered for one memorable incident at Lulworth. Dressed in an evening suit, topped by a hunting pink jacket and sporting a monocle, he strode onto the stage. Gazing down at the front row of officers he saw that the CO was also wearing a monocle. For a few brief moments there was silence as they gazed at each other 'monocle to monocle', then they both dropped them simultaneously. A laugh went up among the troops and the party settled down to a very happy show!"

Bovington Camp actually had its own concert party, aptly named the "Black Berets" and I have come across numerous references to performances they gave in Dorchester and elsewhere, in the Dorset County Chronicle. Sylvia Dodd was a member and recalls how she first took over a Dutch dance, being dressed and pushed onto the stage: "I was told to follow what the others did, having not the foggiest idea what was going on! I made the biggest mess of it that you could imagine, mind you, they still clapped like anything at the end. I was in the chorus from then on, our dresses came from Drury Lane, London, via ENSA, who sent someone down to turn us all into ballet dancers overnight."

Concert parties and ENSA shows were the entertainment 'highspots', normal day to day amusement was more mundane, as Tony Blad recalls: "During the weekdays at Lulworth there was very little relaxation other that tea and buns or weak beer from the NAAFI. Occasionally there was an outing to the cinema which occupied a hut in the area of the Medical Reception Station. The cinema was noted less for the quality of the films and more for the audience participation. Comments, often witty, were directed at the screen and the not unusual breakdown of the film was always greeted with hearty cheers. At weekends, it was sometimes possible to get a thirty-six hour pass but mostly the time was spent in barracks or occasionally fare for soldiers to these two towns at the rate of sixpence return.

Inevitably there were some who used these tickets to travel to Waterloo where they jumped the barriers when the train arrived in London. To combat this on the return journey, the railway staff assisted by the Military Police sometimes stopped the train a mile or so outside Wool station to check the tickets, but this only resulted in the guilty leaving the train early and making their way back to barracks on foot. Weymouth was probably the more popular place to for a few hours of relaxation and there was a good, cheerful Salvation Army canteen near the station although at times the splendid canteen staff began services of praise and thanksgiving which was not always how their customers had intended to pass the time.

There was sport to be had on Saturdays for those who were interested and few in the troop will forget the call: 'Anyone want to go for a swim?' on a hot summer's day which resulted in the majority marching from Bovington to Lulworth and back in order to swim in PT shorts in Lulworth Cove, avoiding the barbed wire and anti-tank obstacles which were placed along the shore to deter the invader,"

Introduction of main vehicles to AFV Schools, 1939 – 45

1939

Apr	–	A13
Jul	–	A11
Sep	–	A9
Nov	–	**Matilda**

1940

Aug	–	**Valentine**
Nov	–	**Tetrach**

1941

Jan	–	**Covenanter**
Feb	–	**Crusader**
May	–	**Humber Armoured Car**
Jun	–	**M2A4 Honey** *1
Jul	–	**Daimler Armoured Car**
		Daimler Scout Car
Sep	–	**Churchill**
Dec	–	**M3 Medium Lee** *1

Bovington Camp: a view of Allenby Barracks at the end of the war. The Headquarters of the Driving and Maintenance Wing of the Armoured Fighting Vehicles School is on the left and the brick-built vehicle instruction sheds lie beyond, to the east.

Lulworth Ranges: a German visitor. This Pz Kpfe III Ausf J, mounting a 5 cm gun – the ninth of thirteen Marks it would go through in its long production run – was captured in France and brought to the Purbeck Hills for test firings in 1944.

1942

Jan	–	**Covenanter Bridge Layer**
Mar	–	**Ram** *2
Sep	–	**Valentine Bridge Layer**

1943

Jan	–	**Sherman V** *1
Feb	–	**Cromwell**
Mar	–	**Centurion**
Apr	–	**Cavalier**
Jul	–	**Harry Hopkins**
		Sherman III *1
Aug	–	**Staghound Armoured Car** *1
Dec	–	**Stuart V** *1

1944

Feb	–	**Churchill Bridge Layer**
Apr	–	**Sherman I** *1
		Stuart VI *1
		Locust *1
Sep	–	**Coventry Armoured Car**
Nov	–	**Comet**

1945

Feb	–	**Chaffee** *1
Apr	–	**Churchill Crocodile**
Jun	–	**Alecto**
Sep	–	**Adder**

TOTAL: 35

*1 US Eqpt
*2 Canadian Eqpt
(Source: Desk Diary for 1946, printed and published by AFV Publications Section, AFV School).

5 POST WAR 1945-69:
THE UNEASY DAYS OF PEACE

Victory!

"ON MAY 5th 1945 the war in Europe ended. I sent my soldiers away early, tidied up and at midday, made for the Sergeants Mess. It was practically deserted, in fact the whole camp was very quiet, so I went home to East Lulworth. The end of the war was for us a traumatic experience, but the pressure had been so great for years that I believe peace was an anti-climax. How the instructors had gone on year after year, teaching the same lengthy and advanced syllabus I do not know, but they were splendid."

So wrote SSM (I) Stan Robinson, when I asked him to recall his feelings on VE Day. VJ Day three months later was a similar anti-climax. It was a time for quiet satisfaction on a job well done, rather than for the noisy celebrations of the towns and cities. Most soldiers looked forward to getting out of uniform as quickly as possible and back to their loved ones. However, although there was a fairly rapid run down of men and resources, there was still a need for armour in the garrisons all over Europe and the British Empire, so the training machine still had to be kept going.

It would take at least two years for the RAC to run down to its initial peacetime size of 20 Cavalry and 8 RTR Regiments. The RAC Territorial Army units were similarly reduced to peacetime levels, while the converted infantry battalions and the Guards Armoured Division converted back to their pre-war roles or were disbanded. During the same period the training machine slimmed down and some of the remaining units, as we shall see, were repositioned.

RAC Conferences

THE FIRST of the regular yearly postwar RAC conferences took place in November 1945. One of its major topics was "unification" of the Corps. "Under Major General R Briggs, then DRAC, a proposal to invite HM King George VI to become Colonel-in-Chief was put forward, along with a suggestion to create Cavalry and RTR Wings – The Cavalry having five Colonels Commandant and the RTR two".[26]

This proposal came to naught and the 'marriage of convenience' continued much as it had done throughout the war, with, as Macksey puts it "the members of Regiments invariably putting the RAC last in their list of loyalties, seeing in it only an agency to carry out those complex functions which were beyond simple regimental means". Matters would come to a head again a couple years hence.

Major Blueblood's Daughters

"THERE CAME to live in married quarters Major Blueblood's pretty daughters. Officers soon called to woo them, but away Blueblood would shoo them. Two pretty girls would stand and sigh, while would-be suitors passed them by.

"Now Blueblood, though very martial, to alcohol was very partial. On this assumption two young Subs took him on tour round all the pubs, from 'Plough' to 'Swan' they led him on, until in drink he was far gone.

"At closing time they heard him mutter, 'think I'll kip down in the gutter.' Gleefully they left him there and went to seek his daughters fair. But when they got to his domain they found their plans had been in vain.

"The accident had happened thus: Another subaltern (called 'Gus') pretending in the mess to dream, had heard the two discuss their scheme and while they led Papa astray Gus whipped the daughters far away!"[27]

Getting back to normal

ONE OF the main ways in which peace-time soldiering returned to Bovington was an influx of families. Although new quarters would not be built until later, some of the old WWI huts were converted into married quarters. The huts were old and sub-standard, but after years of separation a little discomfort was a small price to pay for being together again.

AND NOW, TO THE GREEN FIELDS BEYOND

Major (Retd) Bert Starr, MBE and his wife Rhona, took over one of the old WWI huts in Lulworth Camp in 1946 – Hut B3 immediately opposite the Officer's Mess. Bert was a Staff Sergeant Gunnery Instructor at the time and told me that conditions were "very spartan". Heating was just the old iron coke stove in the middle of the hut, with a Valor paraffin stove or a primus for cooking. Furniture included two army single beds with "biscuits" instead of mattresses. He recalled that the furniture synopsis included such strange items as "stools wooden-headed sergeants"! They stayed until the end of the year and, despite the spartan conditions, they still have very happy memories of that year in Hut B3.

The civilian population of Bovington was also not forgotten. In his handover notes Brig (later Maj Gen) Nigel Duncan, who was the Commander, RAC Centre from 1947-49, explained how he had 24 houses built for civilians in Cologne Road and that the Ministry of Health had promised a further 44. He goes on: "Negotiations for the sale of land for this batch are in hand and the Wareham and Purbeck Rural District Council are prepared to develop this new site as a proper housing estate and to get away from the ribbon development which has taken place so far. The houses will provide accomodation for those civilians who are living in married quarters in the Camp by the virtue of the fact that they are working for the War Department either with the Army or the Workshops."

Gen Duncan did a great deal towards trying to develop Bovington on logical lines as he explained: "In 1938 a detailed plan for the Camp was drawn out. This covered realignment of the roads, siting of new barracks, a new church, new Headquarters etc, and proved of the greatest value in camp work during the war years. Since the original plan was drawn up Bovington had rather changed its scope and the training regiments who were to have been located here are now in Catterick.

"It is therefore obvious that the 1938 plan is no longer applicable in its entirety. I have therefore convened a Zoning Board and I have re-zoned Bovington for future development. Up to date my efforts to get a Town Planning Board to locate individual buildings and to draw out their sites in relation of one to the other have failed. I am having one last shot at South Western District and I think that it is a thing that you might well pursue since without it you will find it difficult to put up various structures in the camp without going across ultimate development."

He was understandably scathing about the remnants of "Tin Town" which still remained viz: "This is a horror, nasty little wooden shacks without sanitation or water which never should have been allowed to grow up. The War Department are prepared to buy this land after the District Council have made demolition orders for the worst of the properties. These demolition orders will not be issued until alternative accommodation is available i.e. 44 houses to which I have already referred. I am afraid that you will have to accept the range of brick buildings from Smiths Shop down to the Garage and the zoning plan to which I have referred provides for their incorporation in the area reserved as a civilian shopping centre."

Bovington Camp: Italian PoWs laying sewer pipes in the making of George V road into the garrison – seen at the point where it now joins the southern end of Cologne Road.

School for the children

"THE ORIGINAL building was old and I am sure it must have been taken over in the 1920s." So wrote Mr R E Morley of Cologne Road Bovington who first taught at the Bovington County School in 1947. He recalled his arrival at Bovington: "It was in early 1947 that I first arrived at Bovington Camp, with a rucksack on my back, to take up my first teaching appointment. 18 months previously I have been released from a German War Camp – I was captured during the

Lulworth Camp: German PoWs built eight houses at The Oval – the old Medium 'A' (Whippet) is now safely inside Bovington Tank Museum.

Battle of Arnhem. Now, after a year at Teaching College I was standing amongst rows of wooden huts, a complete stranger to Bovington, wondering where to go. I waited, looking around, hoping to catch sight of someone. The wooden huts seemed to mesmerise me, my thoughts went back to similar wooden huts in the POW Camp in Germany and the events that had happened there.

"I looked around to reassure myself that this was indeed England. There were no high fences of barbed wire or look-out towers, no harsh voices bawling out at you in a guttural language. Suddenly a quiet voice brought me back to reality: 'Hello Mr Morley, I'm glad I have found you. May I welcome you to Bovington Camp, come with me to the Sergeants Mess.' It was the voice of RSM Kitchen."

Mr Morley went on to describe the school, where he and 17 other teachers (six of whom were straight from "demob" – 1 Navy, 2 RAF and 3 Army) worked under the headmaster, Mr R Day: "It was infact a wood and galvanised iron building with a few small rooms as classrooms and a larger one for the hall. The toilets were four cubicles in the centre of the playground. The heating was the old type, an iron stove burning wood and coal, with its chimney to the roof.

"A delapidated board on the outside of the building told the passer-by that this was the Bovington County School. The addition of the word 'County' meant it was run by the County of Dorset, and was not entirely an Army School, although we were much attached to the Army with the Brigadier as a member of the Governors. It was an all-age school, 5 to 14 years, and later to 15 years, but the building itself was far too small and we had to extend outwards to two married quarters – one in St Julian Road, and the other in Elles Road. Generally speaking, the infants and juniors were confined to the old school and all the senior pupils to the married quarters. Within a few years the number of pupils had risen to bursting point, but the authorities had already foreseen the birth explosion and had planned another school to replace the present one."

More from Mr Morley later, but first some reminisences from another teacher Mr F Hunter, of Wool who joined the staff in 1948. He walked up from Wool railway station to the school in

Swinton Avenue and vividly recalls the scene: "I remember walking up the road past the Tank Museum and thinking I had walked into a film set for a 'Western' movie – the outline of the buildings gave that impression – and on past the old post office and the C of E canteen, both wood-built structures, on the corner of Swinton Avenue. On the opposite corner was the Garrison Engineers yard which still I believe, held the pumping system which brought up water from the artesian well which had supplied the camp with water in the early days. Behind this was the old Garrison Theatre – a corrugated iron building and nearby, the NAAFI shop and bakery, also of corrugated iron, if I remember rightly. In those days most of the camp buildings seemed to be of either wood or corrugated iron structure.

"On my way to the school I passed down Swinton Avenue. On the left were cottages and a little Garrison church (long since demolished) beyond the church the road opened out onto a carpark in front of the old Garrison hall. I was to know this hall fairly well, for during those years we produced and presented school pantomimes there, aided in this by one of the Tank Corps regimental bands.

"When I arrived in this area I looked in vain for any building remotely resembling a traditional school building. But what I did see opposite the carpark was a long, low corrugated iron building with windows at intervals and a door at about the centre.

"Across the frontage of the building from right to left were 3 classrooms with joining doors, a very small room for the Headmaster and another for his secretary. Beyond was a further classroom and then a bigger room used as an assembly hall. Only a section of the school could assemble at one time. At midday it became the dining hall in which the children sat in relays. Beyond was a kitchen where, inspite of the conditions, Mrs Briggs and her assistant cooks produced some excellent meals. There was no staff room at this time until we did manage to clean out a small store room and convert this into a staff room. Later I remember this little room became the School Library! ... The young children in those days were from Bovington mostly, but the older ones were brought in from as far as Bere Regis and beyond in the North, to Lulworth in the south, West Stafford in the West and East Stoke in the East. Bus loads were disgorged each morning on the Garrison car park.

"Inspite of the poor buildings and lack of facilities it was a good school and many ex-pupils and staff hold some affectionate and grateful memories of it... One problem for the school in those early post-war years was the difficulty in attracting the staff – not because of the school, but because of the shortage of houses. To help relieve this situation, the council built three pairs of houses at the corner end of Cologne Road. These were to house six teachers and their families and did so long before the later development of Cologne Road and Duncan Crescent."

Bovington Hospital

IN 1947, the hospital was still of considerable importance and grew even more valuable when the military hospital at Shaftesbury closed down. Bovington had a very good maternity ward which, under the National Health Act, could be used by civilians. Under the town planning scheme it was scheduled for rebuilding (this did not actually happen until Phase II of the major rebuild which began in 1960). Gen Duncan noted in his handover notes in 1949 that the OC hospital (Major Jacobs RAMC) had three Medical Officers working under him and was supposed to have had a Matron and 12 nursing sisters, however: "... the supply of these women is as short as that of nurses elsewhere in the country. I have always regarded the efficient running of the hospital as a fact of prime importance in the camp."

Welfare

A VOLUNTARY Infant Welfare Centre was run by the ladies of the camp with the SSAFA District Nurse (later replaced by a Health Visitor appointed under the NHI Scheme) always in attendance. A Married Quarter was later allocated to the Health Visitor and the first one (Miss Badhurst) came into residence in July 1949. In addition Duncan rightly pointed out: "What people do not realise is that this camp differs entirely from the ordinary village life, in that there are no older women, grandmothers and mothers etc, to whom the younger women can turn for advice. It is therefore essential that they should have a really sympathetic and understanding woman to whom they can turn for assistance and I have every hope that Miss Badhurst will fit the bill."

NAAFI Shops

MR F J THARME of Duncan Crescent was employed as manager of the NAAFI shop at Lulworth Camp for eight years from 1947. He writes: "Of course the NAAFI in 1947 was different to the shop today. The only people permitted to use the shop were Service personnel, their families, and civilian employees. Each month the Orderly Room presented us with a list of civilians entitled to buy at the shop ... Each month also the NAAFI was inspected by the Colonel, accompanied by the Adjutant and RSM, but I never found out for what particular reason. Another strange custom, we were allowed to change cheques for Army Officers – up to £15.00 from the rank of Major and above. Full name and rank had to be printed on the reverse, that was quite a laugh if they had quite a few christian names! Every month there was a PRI meeting which I had to attend with army personnel from the camp plus an Army wife to put forward any complaints about the shop. There were some interesting meetings and some of the complaints put forward were quite unbelievable."

The Bovington Piggery

A FAMOUS Bovington character was honoured in 1946, after spending twenty three years managing the Royal Tank Regiment Piggery at Bovington. His name was Mr H J Christopher and the following extract is from a piece that appeared both in the local papers and in The Tank:

"A well known member of a well known Dorset farming family, Mr Christopher has been prominent in Dorset farming circles or the past fifty years. He retired from active farming at Broadmayne in 1923, and since then he has been managing the Piggery, judging at the Royal Counties (Reigate, Bournemouth and Reading) and other shows and he has been chairman of the County Agricultural Society.

"During the war years, the Piggery consisted of three hundred pigs, which had an output of over six thousand individual rations each week (ten bacon pigs per week). Large grants have also been made from the account between 1941 and 1945.

"Mr Christopher, who is now seventy-three, retains all his old vigour, and looks many years younger. He still takes a great interest in Regiment and will be seen watching with the greatest enthusiasm any event at Bovington in which we are represented. He has kindly agreed to continue to run the Piggery.

"Recently, at the Officers' Club at Bovington, in the presence of a small gathering of Officers of the Regiment, Lieut-General Sir Charles Broad presented to Mr Christopher a silver cigarette box as a token of the appreciation which is felt in the Regiment at the great success he has had, and is having, in managing the Piggery. Sir Charles thanked him for his many years of loyal and untiring service to the Regiment." A Commander, RAC Centre was later to write in his handover notes when commenting upon the excellent work of the Piggery: "you will find this an invaluable source of revenue and without it operations the Centre would be very seriously hampered. The administration of the funds is done by the Staff Captain, distribution of the money being made by me personally."

Bovington Camp: queue outside the new Globe Cinema – film going reached its peak in the 1950s.

A new cinema

IN 1946 – 47 a new cinema was built opposite the Garrison Theatre on the other side of King George V Road. It was constructed by Italian POW for the Army Cinema Corporation (AKC) and later called The Globe Cinema.

RAC War Memorial Benevolent Fund

AFTER THE war it was decided to raise the RAC War Memorial Benevolent Fund and an appeal to the Nation was made by the three Patrons of the Fund, Winston Churchill, Field Marshal Montgomery and Lt Gen Sir Bertie Fisher. The text of their appeal read as follows:

"Although nearly 18 months have passed since the end of the war, we feel that the gallant exploits and the magnificent contribution to final victory of the officers and men who fought with the armoured cars, tanks, and special weapons of the Royal Armoured Corps will still be fresh in everyone's memory.

"For this reason we now bring to your notice the formation of a Royal Armoured Corps War Memorial Benevolent Fund and seek, as its patrons, to enlist the support of your readers on its behalf.

"Before the war ended, it was apparent that the personnel themselves of the Royal Armoured Corps were anxious to create a fitting memorial to their fallen comrades: to that end they began to subscribe to a fund which has now reached the total of £19,200.

"The purpose to which this money should be devoted has been carefully considered. The outcome is the Royal Armoured Corps War Memorial Benevolent Fund, designed, at the express wish of the Royal Armoured Corps itself, firstly to foster benevolent work among all ranks past, present and future of the Corps, and their dependants, and secondly to provide, in due course, for some small and comparatively inexpensive visible memorial where the names of all the fallen of the Corps shall be recorded.

"The Fund's Charter has been drawn as widely as possible to cover all forms of benevolence. A strong Committee of Management, representative of all components of the Corps, has been formed, and the existing Royal Armoured Corps Assistance Fund, which stands at £40,000, had been amalgamated with the new venture and supplies tried and proved facilities for its administration.

"It is intended that the Fund shall operate through the normal agencies for the investigation of of necessitous cases. It will co-operate with, and strengthen, the existing Cavalry, Yeomanry, Royal Tank Regiment, Reconnaissance Corps and other Regimental and Old Comrades' Associations by enabling them to give more valuable help than they can do individually and unaided. The welfare of those units of the Royal Armoured Corps that have no such parent bodies will be a direct charge upon the Fund. The ultimate intention is that no officer or man who at any time serves in the Royal Armoured Corps, or his dependants, shall go without help if in need.

"We feel that there must be many who wish either to commemorate a husband, a son, a brother or a friend who died fighting in the Royal Armoured Corps or to give thanks for one who has safely returned. We suggest that there could be no better way of doing so than by sharing in the effort, begun by the serving members of the Royal Armoured Corps, to build up a strong and permanent fund which will care not only for those who have suffered as the result of the war – a primary consideration – but for those who, today and in the future, carry on the proud traditions of service of the men who have not come back.

"No donation can be too big and no donation will be too small to be welcomed and acknowledged. There may be, however, some who would prefer to send an annual subscription on their own particular day of remembrance, and, big or small, such subscriptions will be received with special gratitude.

"Cheques and postal orders should be crossed and made payable to the 'R.A.C. War Memorial Benevolent Fund' and should be sent to the Secretary, R.A.C. War Memorial Benevolent Fund, Bovington Camp, Dorset.

We are, Sir

Yours faithfully,

WINSTON S. CHURCHILL
Colonel, 4th Queen's Own Hussars.

MONTGOMERY OF ALAMEIN
Colonel Commandant, Royal Tank Regiment

BERTIE D. FISHER
Colonel 17th/21st Lancers   December 17, 1946."

When the Fund was raised a sum of money was put aside for a visible memorial to those members of the RAC who gave their lives during the Second World War. The original concept was for some form of memorial in the Hyde Park Corner area of London, but as we shall see, after over twenty years of hard work and frustration, the Committee decided to abandon this idea and to build a memorial at Bovington Camp which would be of practical value to the present serving members of the Corps. The Central committee agreed that a Memorial Hall to replace the existing Garrison Hall would best meet the need and in 1968 the foundation stone was laid. The Fund is used for many other purposes, such as: giving assistance with school fees, clothing (including school clothes), meeting debts or HP arrears, rent or mortgage arrears, convalescent holidays, house repairs, removals, funeral expenses, Christmas grants etc. This side of the Benevolent Fund work can best be summed up in the words of one of its past Chairmen when he said: "The work in connection with the main aim of the Fund continues and I am confident that we will be in a position to offer a helping hand to those ex-members of the Wartime Regiments of the Royal Armoured Corps and their families who may be suffering hardship, through no fault of their own, for as long as that helping hand is required".

RTR Association and Benevolent Fund

THE RTR had maintained an office at Bovington pre-war (since 1924) and through WW2, for the administration of their Regimental Association and Benevolent Fund. In 1944, it had been expanded to include an office for the Representative Colonel Commandant RTR (Lt Gen Sir Charles Broad). The Association and Benevolent Fund are still run from Bovington, but the Colonels Commandant now operate via RHQ RTR in London. The Benevolent Fund's aim is to assist the less fortunate members of the Tank Corps, Royal Tank Corps and Royal Tank Regiment and their families who are in difficulties through no fault of their own. The Representative Colonel Commandant RTR is the President, while the senior serving RTR officer at Bovington or Lulworth acts as Chairman of the Committee. The RTR Association has the aim of promoting by any means considered necessary, including financial aid, the efficiency and esprit-de-corps of the Royal Tank Regiment. The Regimental Secretary, RTR, looks after the day-to-day business of both and in addition, is Secretary of the RAC War Memorial Benevolent Fund.

This sporting life

ONE SIGN that Bovington was returning to peacetime soldiering was the large increase in a wide variety of sporting activities, which catered for all tastes, from cricket, athletics and other team games, to the more individual pursuits such as golf, sailing, motorcycling and shooting. RAC teams normally took on the title of the Ironsides, while Wings and Schools ran their own more modest affairs. "The first postwar Ironsides cricket match was played at Bovington on July 15th and 16th 1946, and resulted in a win for the Ironsides by 5 wickets, after a most exciting finish", so read an account of the first post-war match against the Dorset Rangers, the winning hit being made with just ten minutes to spare. At Wing level these notes from Lulworth Camp give some idea of the pleasure which time for sporting relaxation brought:

"The Gunnery Wing cricket team have fully realised expectations in their ability to play entertaining cricket and addition, win! ... The Sportsground is a hive of activity these days; a new spirit is abroad, running, jumping and various field events are being practised very assiduously. I did hear that our old rivals the D & M Wing, are to be shown the way home in the Garrison Sports. Well, here's hoping!" As well as their opponents, all the teams had to compete against the usual vagaries of the English summer weather, but sometimes they were in luck: "In the midst of the week of rain and storms came one fine Wednesday afternoon – August 14 (1946) – the day selected for the D & M Wing sports. The fates were indeed good to all those planned this highly successful meeting ... It was well worthy of being remembered as the first peacetime Sports Day."

In addition to the serious sporting events there were comic races, sideshows, tea tents and even "Smoky the clown plus his donkey"! After the prize giving, the D & M Wing and Wireless Wing threw open their doors and the families were allowed in: "In the Wireless Wing the voice recorder held sway. In the Mechanical School, apart from the comic strips in the Cinema, small boys watched open mouthed as the wheels went round – without putting a penny in too. And to give a finishing touch to the day an All Ranks Dance was held in the Garrison Hall. Midnight saw many tired but happy folk wandering their way bedwards, yes, it was a good day and especially many thanks to the Clerk of the Weather, who must have turned off the taps and taken a day off".

Sailing too had its ups and downs thanks to the weather: "The Ironsides Yacht Club having acquitted itself fairly well last season, hoped to enter the area this year with more boats and increased membership. The last race of 1946 found both the dinghys reefed down with the crews bailing madly to try to help keep pace with the incoming flood. With Poole Harbour getting the upper hand very gradually, but surely, both boats had to make for the shore ... Having had our bad weather for this in full measure, we are looking forward to a sunny summer. Poole Harbour offers wonderful opportunities for interesting sailing. A sail round Brownsea Island, or up to Arne for a bathe on the Sandy Beach is one good way of spending your afternoons off."

Bovington (Services) Motor Cycle Club

THE CLUB was formed on 5th March 1946, to cater for the many motorcycling enthusiasts in Bovington Garrison – and there were plenty! The initial membership, quickly numbered over 50 all ranks coming mainly from the OCTU, D & M and Gunnery Wings and the REME Workshops. A club room was organised in a Nissen hut (courtesy of the CO Wireless Wing) and this was gradually made: "more like a club room and less like a Nissen as time permits!"

Trials were held on a tricky course laid out on the Driver Training Area and all those who took part enjoyed themselves immensely, as did the spectators who appeared to like the hill climbs and descents best as these: "Involved a steep climb, with some loose going a third of the way, weaving between trees to a letter S bend at the top, the last curl of the S being a very tight turn. This caused a lot of trouble and, as on the other sections, as more riders cross over to a second and parallel gully in that sandy soil peculiar to this part of Dorset". The club soon had a highly successful and competent display team which toured in many parts of the country giving displays of "Motorcycle Trick and Precision Riding".

Capt Iremonger Watts and Capt Fred Cornish, MM, led the team in those early days, Fred Cornish later taking them to the White City to perform at the SSAFA Tattoo where he was presented to the Princess Royal. The whole programme took about 25 minutes, every minute being filled with: "action of real interest, entertainment, and examples of excellent riding". Normal displays were carried out on standard 500cc BSA machines as issued to the Army, but the 'Flaming Hoop' and 'Wall Jump', a standard 350cc Matchless was used, Beryl Cornish, Fred's widow, told me how he went to the BSA Works and after begging and borrowing: "they eventually gave him many motorcycles for the team, including one very small folding model".

Piscatorial escapades at Bovington

"PROBABLY ONE of the least known pastimes of Bovington is fishing, and we think it is time that this subject be introduced for those who follow the gentle art and who may come to the RAC Centre one day. A brief summary of available coarse fishing follows. The River Frome, to the south side of the camp, flows gently through the meadows in the direction of Wool Bridge Manor, the picturesque home of 'Tess of the D'Urbervilles.' Fishing is allowed for about half a mile immediately to the south of the camp, and the boundaries are marked by W.D. Boards. The west boundary is a small stream which enters the main river from a wood, and the east boundary terminates opposite a fishing hut on the south bank.

"A good variety of coarse fish can be found in this stretch of the river, the main species being pike, roach, dace, gudgeon, grayling and an occasional perch. Eel abound and give the angler plenty of practice in unravelling knots. The fish are of an average size, and although no specimen pike have been caught, they are reputed to have been seen by the local enthusiasts. who tell the tale of large, dark shadows darting into the depth of the pools.

"Most of the fishing is done in the evenings or at weekends, and it is no uncommon sight to see the enthusiasts scurrying across the fields to catch the last of the daylight hours, and absolutely oblivious of the farmer's pet bull. No one, of course sees his return, but the catch is a favourite topic for many days, and great tales are told of monster fish which escaped. This can be appreciated by the arm stretching one sees in the Mess and the stories that the river dropped its level by 6 ins. when the monster was landed."[28]

Military activities 1945-50

NOT ALL was fun and games of course, the serious side of training still had to continue, although some of this clearly had an element of fun involved. One such event was undoubtedly the monthly tank race and obstacle crossing demonstration. It was started in 1943 by the D & M Wing when it was found that many students had little idea of the maximum abilities of their own units' vehicles and no conception at all of the performance of the other types of AFVs in other RAC Units.

So it was decided to demonstrate to each course the maximum cross-country speeds of each type of vehicle and to construct a number of obstacles of different types, which could be used to demonstrate the maximum obstacle crossing performance of each type and the method to be employed in driving over the bumps. "The value of these demonstrations to students of other Wings of the RAC School was soon appreciated and their popularity as a spectacle spread to other Instructional Establishments. Recent demonstrations have included no secret equipment and have therefore been open to spectators from all arms of the Services."

The demonstration consisted, in 1946, of three distinct phases – a handicap race, an obstacle crossing demonstration and a tank flame throwing demonstration. Vehicles taking part in the race were handicapped at the start, the handicap being based on previous experience with the aim of staging as close a finish as possible, depending upon the skill of drivers and the selection of ground by commanders. "The race is run in an atmosphere of excitement reminiscent of the race course."

The course was 1½ miles long over many types of going and all was visible from the stand adjacent to the finishing post. In addition to one of each of every type in service obsolete 'runners' were also borrowed from the RAC School Museum for the occasion. It was said that the fastest vehicle covered the 1½ mile course in about 3½ minutes, an average of 25.71 mph! **Comet, Churchill** and **Sherman** only took part in the second part and comment on the Comet was: "At 28 mph a **Comet** flew over an 18 foot trench but it was essential to keep the tracks turning in the air or the tank will attempt to stand on its nose on landing!"

Demonstrating Panthers and Jagd-Panthers

ONE EXTREMELY interesting group of AFVs to arrive at the D & M Wing in 1946 were three **Panthers** and seven **Jagd-Panthers,** for "investigation and demonstration purposes". The vehicles had been captured in course of production and had been completed under REME workshops supervision. They were in full battle trim, complete with the characteristic German camouflage colours, except for ammunition. They must have made quite a sight. Forty years on, just one example of each remains at the Tank Museum; the remainder must sadly have been used up as hard targets on the ranges.

The RAC OCTU arrives

A VERY special RAC Training Unit arrived in Bovington in November 1945, namely the 100 RAC OCTU. It came from Sandhurst, where its erstwhile accomodation was being prepared for opening, on 3rd January 1947, as the new Royal Military Academy Sandhurst. 100 OCTU did not remain in Bovington for long, moving to join the Infantry OCTU at Mons Barracks, Aldershot in July 1948. Thereafter RMA Sandhurst produced all the Army's Regular Officers, while Mons provided Emergency then Short Service Commissions, until it closed and all officer training was concentrated at Sandhurst. Lt Col (Retd) Dick Everard, MBE, attended the 100 RAC OCTU at Bovington. At that time training for the Emergency Commission in the RAC comprised a minimum of:

> 6 weeks basic recruit training at a Primary Training Centre.
> 12 weeks RAC basic Trade Training at an RAC Training Regiment
>   and attendance at War Office Selection Board.
> 12 weeks Pre OCTU course at Mons.
> 6 months RAC OCTU at Bovington.

Thus, the average RAC Officer Cadet had at least seven months service when he arrived at OCTU. Dick, who was commissioned into 2 RTR and went on to gain a Regular Commission, told me that remembers his time at Bovington as a: "marvellous summer holiday, after the disagreeable rigours of Mons throughout the dreadful winter of 1946/47 and the final crisis". He was a member of the OCTU Gymnastic team which used to perform at all the local summer festivals around Dorset that were: "… much more fun than cricket or athletics;" Another ex-cadet from 100 OCTU was Lt Dick, Rundle, who also was commissioned into 2 RTR.

His most vivid memory of Bovington concerned the pass-off parade: "The big 'thing' at the time was to perpetuate some nonsense at the friday night pre-passing-party that couldn't be cleared up before the parade started at noon the next day. We managed an old car tyre, a 'meeting in progress' board and a bike on the arms of the weather vane of the Sandhurst block and a fire bucket on the spike. Not much progress was made in getting them down by 1110 hrs but the fire brigade managed to dislodge the fire bucket at about 1157 hrs. The blood still runs a bit cold to think about the whole thing, but it seemed a good idea at the time!"

He recalled that his six months OCTU training was divided into: 4 weeks D & M, 4 weeks Gunnery, 6 weeks Wireless and 12 weeks Collective training to end. Coloured lanyards differentiated between the different periods – yellow for D & M, green for Gunnery, white for Wireless and red for Collective. Two troops entered the OCTU each month, even numbers going to 'A' Squadron, odd to 'B'. Healthy rivalry was maintained throughout, A Sqn wore a red bar on their white shoulder boards and B had green. Extra bars were awarded for sports colours – rugby, soccer, cricket and cross country.

Dick Rundle continues: "The rush of old motorbikes and cars into Bournemouth after Saturday midday Adjutant's parade had to be seen to be believed. 7s/6d a night bed and brekker somewhere behind the Central Station – Halcyon days!"

The Royal Armoured Corps Centre

"I CHANGED the title of this place from Central Schools, Bovington Garrison to HQ RAC Centre eighteen months ago." So wrote Gen Duncan in his handover notes, of Aug 1949, which continued: " I did this quite deliberately to foster a sense of unity among the people who live here and I think it has had a certain affect. I have continual trouble with outsiders who do not understand that the RAC Centre comprises the Schools, the Depot, Workshop, Hospital etc and persist in using the title as if it applied to the Schools only."

Course reminiscences

MR H WILTON-JONES of Doncaster was a Corporal Instructor at the Wireless Wing in 1947-48, he recalled that at the time pupils and permanent staff below the rank of sergeant lived in H-blocks overlooking the sportsfield and the road to camp (ie: in Allenby Barracks) with about six or eight in a room, while Sergeants on the permanent staff lived in bunks individually on the other side of the road with quite a walk to the Sergeant's Mess, also overlooking the playing fields. In the bunks, so many had electric fires, kettles and other illicit devices, that the fuses had been replaced with six inch nails, which were known to glow red hot and were hastily removed before Royal Engineers inspections. Surprisingly the wooden huts never burned down. Sgt's Mess fees were 2d (less than 1p) per day. He writes:

"The Centre worked a five day week, and special buses were run every Friday after duty to London, returning from the Union Jack Club at midnight on Sunday. In those days there was the RAC Club to stay in, located in one of the stately houses, in Grosvenor Square near the US Embassy, as well as the Union Jack and Chevrons Club. Usually the Centre went on block leave and one such occasion it was felt that the pay parade would be expedited if £5 notes were issued (a Sgt's pay in those days was 10s/6d (52½p per day), with the result that the commercial life of the Camp came to a halt that night because although everyone had plenty of money, there was no change left in any of the messes or canteens!"

As far as the Wireless Wing was concerned he recalled: "After the first 3 weeks, pupils spent 2 days a week on wireless schemes, namely with two pupils in a wireless truck, the operator in the back under the canvas tilt with the 19 set, and driven by an ATS driver. All schemes involved the use of R/T … and there was always a 'Tiger' scheme when pupils endeavoured to catch the instructors vehicles in between two of theirs. Instructors had to transmit to assist the pupils and much fun was had by all and surprisingly no road accidents resulted, partly no doubt because the civilian traffic density was very low".

Bovington Camp: 'Eyes right' as 100 OCTU march pass the inspecting officer on the main parade ground.

Bovington Camp: Monty back at Bovy as a father-figure – Field Marshal Bernard Montgomery proudly buckles the Sam Browne belt he has just presented to the best cadet at the 100 OCTU passing out parade in December 1947. The recipient happens to be his son, David Montgomery. Second from left is Brigadier Nigel Duncan, the Commandant of the RAC Centre.

Another new arrival in 1949 was the ubiquitous Chris Gray who came back to Bovington as an author on the D & M side of Publications Wing, that was by the housed in the hut in Elles Road which had been the Head quarters of the AFV School in 1940. He remembers that in 1949 HQ RAC Centre had moved down into part of Stanley Barracks but moved up to the huts near the Camp AKC Cinema when the Boys Squadron was formed in later years.

'The Camp had by now a brand new entrance from the Southern end where the new King George V Road had been built by Italian POW in 1947. A pathetic reminder that these prisoners were still in captivity two years after the end of the war and is supposed to have been painted on the pavement in the married quarters area in large yellow letters: 'SEND US HOME'.

The Italians came from Piddlehinton Camp. Park Camp at Lulworth was occupied by German POW from 1945 to early 1947 while they were building eight Other Ranks married quarters in the Oval at Lulworth Camp. The POW Camp was run by a Maj J Hopwood of the Pioneer Corps and Glyn Evans told me that he was "a great chap who did the Mess a lot of favours, like letting us have two POW as cleaners – excellent workers, while his personal batman, Fritz, who spoke faultless English, told me that he had been a student at Berlin University before he was drafted." Glyn also told me about a band concert he went to at Park Camp: "Fantastic setup, a 30-piece band perfectly dressed in black blouses with red ties made out of red bunting from the "Firing in Progress" range flags!

The RAC Depot returns to Bovington

THE RAC DEPOT came back into existence in January 1947, but its location then was Westwick Camp, Barnard Castle, County Durham. In those days it had a total strength of 53 Officers, 175 Warrant Officers and Sergeants and 1,200 Rank and file, which included a permanent staff of 275 all ranks, with a Colonel as Commandant.

Due to the reduction in strength of the Army in 1948 it was decided that the committment of receiving trainees en route from the Training Regiments to field and other units would stop. It was further decided that the future committment would be to hold and administer a total strength of about 25 officers, 80 WOs and Sgts and 300 Rank and file, which included about 120 all ranks as permanent staff with a Lt Col in Commandant. In July 1948, the RAC Depot returned to Bovington where it was to remain for another twenty years.

Retention of East Holme Ranges

AFTER A Public Inquiry in 1949, and over the next few years, the freehold interest was acquired by the Army on about 6313 acres of land, some 4057 acres of which being owned by one branch or another of the Bond Family. This included Tyneham village and Tyneham House, Gadcliff, Tyneham Cap and the coast to Kimmeridge Bay.

3 RTR comes to Bovington

IN SEPTEMBER/OCTOBER 1948 the 3rd Royal Tank Regiment moved to Bovington Camp, after six months in Gosport and the Portsmouth area. They were not there to provide soldiers to run the RAC Centre as was the case twenty years later, but rather just to use the barracks while they prepared for overseas service. They would remain at Bovington for about a year before moving to the Far East, with one Squadron (C Sqn) at Warminster, providing tanks and crews for the School of Infantry. B Sqn was the first sub-unit to leave UK on 31 May 49 when they began the first lap of their 9,600 mile journey to Hong Kong of the troopship *Dilwara*. They were followed shortly afterwards by the remainder of the Regiment who left Liverpool on 4th July on board the *Ordouna*.

7 RTR comes to Bovington

THE NEXT Regiment to arrive at Bovington was 7th Royal Tank Regiment, who moved there from Mooltan Barracks, Tidworth, in March 1950. Their stay would be longer than that of the 3rd, indeed it was the 7th who were to follow the 3rd in Hong Kong in 1952. However, they were certainly not to be left in peace, but at least they found the barracks clean as this extract from their "Tank Notes" showed:

"The main item of interest is the move of the Regiment from Tidworth to Bovington. The final

Bovington Camp: goodbye to 3 RTR, as B Squadron, 3rd Royal Tank Regiment march past Mark I at the saluting base outside the Tank Museum, en route for the troopship 'Dilwara' bound for Hong Kong.

decision was not made until late in February and now preparations are going ahead for the move at the end of March. Already an advance party is at Bovington armed with 'brushes and scrapers and machine, to make our barracks very clean', but thanks to the efforts of the 3rd Dragoon Guards, who thought they were moving into Bovington, the amount of work for us to do will not be so great. We shall occupy the Barracks vacated by the 3rd RTR, and its interesting to note that after a careful survey of the barracks and plans for the allocation of accomodation had been completed, a sketch plan was found in a disused hut, which showed the 3rd RTR layout when they were in occupation. Great minds think alike, as there was little difference between the two plans."

On 25th June 1950 the North Koreans crossed the 38th Parallel and invaded South Korea. American Forces in Japan, representing the United Nations, immediately went to their aid. On 29th July, 7 RTR was ordered to mobilise an armoured Squadron to be equipped with **Crocodiles (Churchill Mk VIII** tanks with flame throwers), as part of a British brigade (29 Independent Infantry Brigade) to be sent to Korea from the UK and support 27 Infantry Brigade which was leaving from Hong Kong. In addition to the Crocodile squadron there would be a complete armoured regiment (8th King's Royal Irish Hussars), equipped with **Centurion** tanks.

At that time 3 RTR was split up all over the place with squadrons in three locations – RHQ, HQ and A Sqn were in Bovington Camp, C Sqn was guarding an air base in Norfolk and D Sqn was at Gosport. The Regiment was under strength and contained many National Servicemen who were ruled too young to go to war (this rule was later changed).It was decided that C Sqn would be re-formed, all available regular soldiers being transferred in from the other squadrons. However, it was soon clear that many gaps would still have to be filled from another source, so it was decided to recall Regular Army reservists. In addition, the BBC broadcast an appeal for volunteers to join up for 18 months service in Korea. Those who responded were known as 'K' Type Volunteers.

The first batch of **Crocodiles** arrived at Bovington on 8th August, followed four days later by the first party of reservists and then by a steady stream of men and vehicles. This of course entailed much hard work both on the administrative and technical sides. The following is an extract from a 7 RTR account of the buildup entitled *C Squadron in Korea 1950-51*:

"What of the crews who, were to man the tanks and trucks? The regulars were an easier problem as they were already a part of the Regiment and their standard of training was known, neither had they been suddenly uprooted from their homes with the resulting hardships which others had to endure. There is no doubt that the reservists had the hardest time, for they had to leave their jobs and homes, without any warning, and, for the second time, take up a way of life

Bovington Camp: Churchill bridgelayer performing for a line of military attaches, 18 June 1950.

that was far from their choice. Contrary to expectations, they were far from down-hearted and, in most cases, already knew their jobs and were willing to get down to it. Without men such as these, the task would have been infinitely more difficult.

"The tanks were a different problem. Half of them had to be brought over from Germany, where they had been standing in vehicle parks for five years. Not only had they to be completely checked by the Squadron fitters and tank crews, but training had to be undertaken on them. Many a sleepless night was spent by the tank crews and Matador drivers.

"5 Troop was the first to be ready and, on August 26th, moved out of camp for 10 days training on Bovington Heath.

"Time was now getting short as the first tanks were due to move to Southampton for loading on September 16th, and thoughts were turning hopefully towards embarkation leave. How everything was finally fitted in, will forever remain a mystery.

"On October 12th, the Squadron embarked on H.M.T. *Empire Fowey* at Southampton and was seen off by many relatives and members of the Regiment, also the RTR Cambrai Band which competed so well with that of the 8th KRI Hussars."

The Armoured Reinforcement Group is formed

IN ADDITION to 8th Hussars and C Sqn 7 RTR, an armoured reinforcement group was established to operate partly in Korea and partly at the Commonwealth Base in Kure, Japan, to supply reinforcement crews and AFVs. I remember its formation as I was one of the young officers from other regiments (I came from 2 RTR) who had flocked to Bovington to go to Korea.

"I didn't make it on that occasion as the reinforcement rate was drastically reduced in late 1950/early 51 and I had to wait another year before getting into action with 1 RTR who served in Korea 1952-53. Nevertheless, we did a short familiarisation course on the **Crocodile** at Bovington and I helped with the formation of the ARG. My most vivid memory of that unit was its winter kit – sadly spartan by comparison with the really excellent items we were given in Korea during the bitter winter of 1952/53. The only major item of warm clothing was an enormous kapock – lined coat, which would stand up all by itself and I could crouch inside rather like a Red Indian in a tepee. It was gigantic, yet surprisingly enough it fitted the OC of the ARG, an exceptionally tall and robust officer, like a glove – I never did discover, however, if it actually kept him warm!"

The Fifties

AS WELL as the Korean War, the Army had three major continuing campaigns to fight in the Fifties, namely in Malaya, Kenya and Cyprus, however, the RAC was only really concerned with the Malayan emergency and then just in armoured car operations. Most of the RAC Regiments were in Europe, infact there were more British armoured units there in 1954 than at any time since 1945. There was also the debacle of the Suez operations in 1956, but this concerned only one armoured regiment (6 RTR), while operations in Cyprus against EOKA (1955-59) and in Kenya against the Mau Mau (1954-69) were mainly infantry-based. With all this operational activity it is still surprising that the Fifties also saw the start of a major reduction in the RAC, the Cavalry losing four regiments by amalgamation and the RTR three by the same process viz:

3rd and 7th Hussars	amalgamated to form	QOH in 1958
4th and 8th Hussars	amalgamated to form	QRIH in 1958
Bays and KDG	amalgamated to form	QDG in 1959
9th and 12th Lancers	amalgamated to form	9th/12th Lancers in 1960
3rd and 6th RTR	amalgamated to form	3rd RTR in 1959
4th and 7th RTR	amalgamated to form	4th RTR in 1959
5th and 8th RTR	amalgamated to form	5th RTR in 1960

Boys Squadron, RAC

ON THE credit side, January 1952 saw the formation at Bovington of the Boys Squadron, RAC, which in later years was to become the Junior Leaders Regiment. We have made this important and fascinating unit the subject of a separate study. (see page 129)

The School of Tank Technology

ANOTHER NEW unit to arrive in Bovington in the Fifties was the School of Tank Technology (STT), which moved from Chobham in November 1951. Its primary purpose was to give technical education to regimental officers on such matters as armoured vehicle design, including the problems involved in development and production. Three courses were run, Mechanical, Gunnery and later, Guided Weapons. Its secondary task was to provide a source of technical advice to the Director Royal Armoured Corps. It was redesignated as the Armour School in 1966.

Bovington Camp: the cinema in the foreground was built after the Second World War by Italian prisoners – this view, eastwards across the camp, is from the top of the power station.

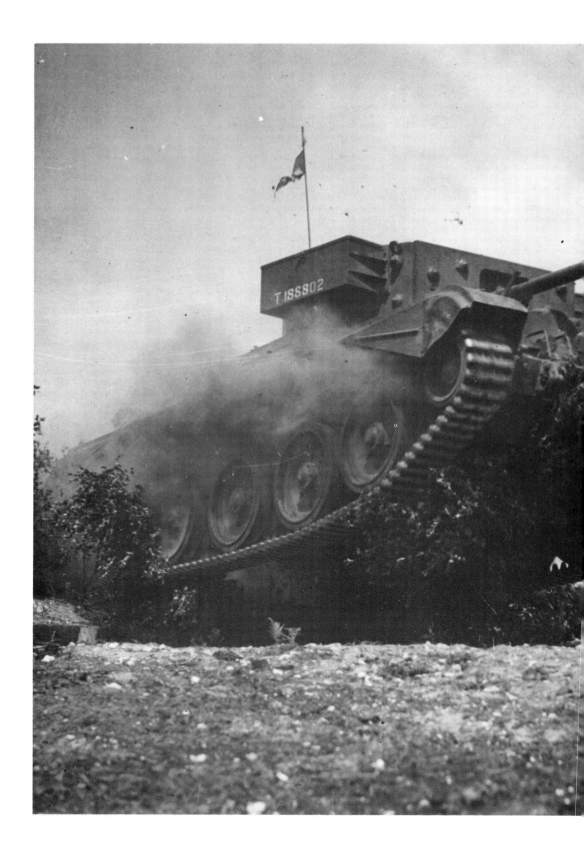

Bovington Camp: a Cromwell taking a 'jump' at 32 mph during the monthly tank race – it landed 31 feet away and stopped within a few yards.

Bovington Camp: first post-war reunion of Royal Tank Regiment old comrades, at the Cambrai dinner on 16 November 1951.

RTR Old Comrades celebrate Cambrai Day

THE ROYAL Tank Regiment has for many years celebrated the anniversary of the Battle of Cambrai (20th November 1917) as one of its most important battle honours. 1951 saw this anniversary celebrated in a very special way at Bovington when, on November 16th, the very first reunion ever of the Tank Corps Old Comrades was held. "F Lines dining hall was selected as the most suitable place for the celebration. The old dining hall which is so well-known to thousands of members of the RTR, past and present, was beautifully decorated and the dinner served would have pleased the shades of any ex-cook sergeant who may still be lurking in the building. Before gathering for the dinner a short service was held at the Garrison Field of Remembrance. A wreath was laid by the President, and poppies were planted by many members. ...Before the dinner the Old Comrades "got together" over a glass of "rum punch" The phrase "do you remember" was heard above the chatter more than once!

"During dinner the band played selections and afterwards the gathering were told how a telegram had been sent to H.M. The King, sending humble duty and loyal greetings to their Colonel-in-Chief and expressing the wish that His Majesty's recovery to health would be speedy and complete. Amid loud applause Col. MacLeod announced that a telegram had been received from the Colonel-in-Chief sincerely thanking the members of the Branch for their Loyal greetings and good wishes...

"Proposing the toast to 'The Regiment' Col MacLeod mentioned how, soon after he joined the regiment, he read the Order of Battle of Sir H. Elles, and he was struck by Order No. 4 – 'In the light of past experience I leave the good name of the Corps in your hands.' That sentence was an inspiration to all of them – to keep in front always the good name of the Corps.

"Responding to the toast, Brigadier 'Tommy' Price mentioned that he was one of the oldest member of the regiment – it was nearly 35 years since he stepped into his first tank...

"At the conclusion of the dinner the diners adjourned to the bar where an enjoyable evening (or shall we say night) was spent by all.

"An innovation at the dinner was the wearing of discs on the coat lapel. These were painted in battalion or company colours and helped in making introductions.

"Many old Tankies were with us and it was indeed pleasant to see such a gathering of the Regiment on such an occasion in Bovington, our hereditary home.

"It will be of interest to many to know that membership of the Bovington Branch is now 212."[29]

The Seventh departs

"BY THE time these notes appear in print we shall be, in the words of a famous poem, "Far away on the billow." Whilst our advance party will have been firmly established in Hong Kong and in the process of taking over from the 3rd Tanks". So read 7 RTR's Tank notes in March 1952. They had sailed from Liverpool in February 17th in *The Empress of Australia,* having left Bovington at an "unearthly hour" in order to catch the 0145 hrs train at Wool Station, no Regiment took their place at Bovington, nor would one do so until the late Sixties. Those left behind, however, saw to it that the camp was not neglected, as this short extract from D & M School Tank notes for the following July shows: "The Bovington Camp Garden Produce Association is busily preparing for its Annual Show to be held on July 21. The Unit lines are looking very trim, with an eye on the Unit Lines Cup. We very much regret that the competition did not take place earlier, when we had a wonderful display of tulips round the Orderly Room area, all specially cultivated in the RAC colours – red flowers with each petal trimmed with yellow!"

More houses for Camp workers

THE FIFTIES saw more houses built in Cologne Road, a few were private bungalows, but mostly (40 huses) built by the Council, deliberately designed to cope with an extra 64 plus, civilian staff who were to be employed in Bovington Camp from 1959/60 onwards. Attempts were also made to redevelop parts of Tin Town to: "tidy up an area which had long been a cause of concern", was the way it was put in one planning application.

Married quarters at Lulworth Camp

1952 ALSO saw the first major postwar building of married quarters at Lulworth Camp – 18 soldiers houses in Vale Road and 13 for officers in Bindon Close. Both these new roads were located just south of the camp, overlooking West Lulworth and the Cove. As residents of No 10 Bindon Close on two separate occasions, we have fond memories of our seaside quarter, with its breathtaking views over to Portland. Mupe Bay was just over the other side of Bindon Hill and we spent many happy hours there swimming and splashing about in the rockpools.

Bovington Camp: old Bovy burnt in the early hours of Sunday 9 August 1953 – two of the six huts that housed the Boys' Squadron were gutted.

Bovington Camp: the 1953-built Bovington Secondary Modern School, at the corner of Cologne Road.

And a new School!

THE FIRST plans of the Dorset County Council for the building a new Secondary Modern School for 450 pupils, were broached in January 1949, with the intention of starting building 1949/50. It would take some three years to complete this splendid new school at the bottom of Cologne Road, as Mr Morley recalls: "In 1953 a most luxurious school building was opened, about a mile from the centre of the camp at the corner of Cologne Road... it was and probably still is, the finest school in the County, with a very large Assembly Hall and spacious Crush Hall, good sound classrooms, a well equipped PE Hall with separate showers for boys and girls, a five acre playing field as well as an open air swimming pool. Children from about a 6 mile radius came to the school and a number of buses gave us transport. The number of pupils was 500 plus. There was also a two acre plot of ground at the back of the school used as a garden/farm for rural studies, incorporating horticulture, garden and farm crops, animals, chickens, rabbits, pigs, bees and even sheep."

The Garrison Church rededicated

SEPTEMBER 1953 saw the rededication of the Garrison Church of St Christopher. The old church had been lengthened and many improvements carried out, however, "even with the increased seating space, the congregation for Harvest Festival on October 4th overflowed into vestibule". The Colonel of the Duke of Wellington's Regiment presented a bell to the church. It had been captured in North Africa by 145 Regiment RAC (8th DWR) between Medjez-el-Bab and the Cap Bon peninsular during May 1943. A tank named "Diana" had engaged an enemy OP in a mosque and the bell was shot down during the engagement. It was found to have the name "Diana" engraved on it.

Alterations at Lulworth

MEANWHILE, OVER at Lulworth building work was in progress as this extract from the Tank in February 1954 explains: "Any old Lulworthian entering the sacred precincts of the camp at the present moment might well feel himself completely at a loss. Due to the fact that a new – and we

118

hope, magnificent — cookhouse and dining room are to be built, most of the area around the guard-room is being demolished. In order to get to the Orderly Room it is advisable to use a large scale map and follow the instructions erected on the roadside most carefully, or risk ending up on the top of Bindon.

"Most of the old wooden huts, so familiar to Tankmen throughout past years, have been razed to the ground. The future entrance to the camp will be situated midway between the old west and north gates, whilst even the M.I. Room has been moved to the east end of what was the Officers' Mess in days of yore. A host of workmen are kept busy tearing up roads and laying down main with but one object in view — to further the ACC in the pursuit of the culinary art and to improve the amenities of the modern soldier. May he be worthy of it!"

The Camp itself was not the only place where work was to take place: "Work is proceeding on a new "Mover" on Heath Range. This has become necessary because the Atomic Energy Authority want to lay the "drain" from Winfrith in Worbarrow Bay, and Bindon Range will be out of use for some months as a result." (Tank notes, January 1959).

"Old Soldiers Never Die!"

THE RAC DEPOT staff possessed some remarkable old soldiers over the years, none more extraordinary than Tooper Henry Charles Fenn who retired from Bovington in 1960, at the age of 65, after 45 years service (39 years with the RTR), the last fifteen of which were spent at Bovington! One reason for his long service might well have been the "New Look" catering then being enjoyed at the Depot:

"We think it time that the soldier claiming gastronomical idiosyncrasies in the Unit gave praise and credit to our cooks, ably led by Sgt. Graham, ACC. We quote a typical menu for lunch and this is not specially selected:-

Curry	Milk Pudding
Braised Steaks	Trifle
Roast Beef	Rhubarb Pie
Cold Meats	Custard and Jelly

We find the cafeteria system working well and strange as it sometimes appears there is not a rush for the braised steak; food seems to be completely an individual choice and our variety caters for that taste. The only complaint has been for more "Lelikogs" sugar frosted flakes".[30]

Bovington Camp: the re-dedication of St. Christopher's — the Garrison church.

Bovington Camp: memories of 'Diana' – seen when she was at the corner of Somme Road and Swinton Avenue – whose inscrutable Chinese Eyes, painted on her sides, were the personalised make-up for this 'Male' tank.

Do you remember Diana?

TO CLOSE this brief roundup of the Fifties is a short piece written by Sgt Ken Chadwick at the end of 1959, when he was serving at Bovington which he entitled "Do you remember Diana?", particularly appropriate in view of the inscription on the church bell.

"Recently I read a book entitled *Tinned Soldier* by Corporal Alec Dixon; it was description of life in Bovington Camp during 1919 and the early twenties. It seems to me that the home of the Tank Corps has not really changed. The wooden huts are the same, many of them still have the original fittings; the hospital and many of the quarters are still in existence. The soldiers seem different, of course. And new techniques have been evolved in dealing with the mixture of short and long term Regulars and the many types of National Servicemen, but essentially the soldiers are the same as their forefathers of 40 years ago.

"Life goes on much the same, but perhaps the most striking difference is that the cinema has been moved to the other side of King George V Road. The ground upon which the old picture palace used to stand has been cleared, and the derelict tank, which often served as a general waiting room, has disappeared!

"Do you remember Diana? Her name and the "Chinese Eye" painted upon her sides proclaimed that she was one of the 4th Battalion's tank. Now she is in honourable retirement in the RAC Tank Museum and the corner of Swinton Avenue boasts only waste ground and a telephone kiosk.

To my mind, one of the intangible things which had altered is that the present day soldiers have less fun than their predecessors; there is more amusement provided but less fun is got our of life. Take Diana for instance, the early crewmen derived considerable amusement from naming their tanks and designing Section recognition signs.

"The earliest tanks were painted under the direction of Mr. Solomon J. Soloman, an eminent artist, who was serving in the Royal Engineers. As the tanks were placed on the railway flats for transportation to the four companies, the legend 'With care to Petrograd' was stencilled upon the hulls and protective coverings. Before the tanks went into action a name, prefixed by

H.M.L.S., was painted across the front plate, between the tracks. The first names were adopted purely at the whim of the crews but soon a Regimental system was adopted in which all names had to conform to the Battalion's initial.

"Later, to enable aeroplanes to determine the nationality of the tanks in action, red and white stripes were painted on the front horns of the tanks. For the crews to recognise the other tanks and to be of assistance to the Infantry, Section recognition signs were adopted. The signs often commemorate events in the early battles, such as the sign of the Broken Bridges, which was a common occurence in the days before weight plates were devised. Or the occasion when all the crew commanders dipped their hands in a tin of red paint and made the mark of the Bloodstained Hand on the nose of the tanks.

"All that was fun born of expediency. These days, apart from a few progressive soldiers, the main concern is the lack of selection available on the C of E juke box. Would that the long lasting pop record "Diana" could be smashed for ever, and that "Diana" the **Mark V** could once again be the centre of the RAC!"

The Early Sixties

THE NUMBER of operational tasks undertaken by the Army did not diminish in the early Sixties as Great Britain continued to divest itself of its Empire. Problems in Aden continued all through the Sixties, including the Radfan operations against dissidents from the Yemen in 1964, and the inevitable Internal Security problems during the eventual extrication from Aden in 1967. Tanks and armoured cars were used throughout, with detached squadrons operating in the Persian Gulf. In the Far East, the end of the Malayan Emergency in 1960 was followed in 1964 by confrontation against Indonesia involving mainly armoured cars and infantry. The shortage of infantry was highlighted towards the end of the 1960s when events in Northern Ireland occupied more and more manpower, while United Nations involvement in Cyprus, keeping Greek and Turk from each others throats, required still more troops. As in the Fifties, the bulk of the RAC was still in BAOR supporting NATO, but increasingly regiments in Europe (including those in UK) found themselves with detached squadrons elsewhere in the world. The cuts also

Bovington Camp: Vehicle Squadron petrol point around 1960, with a galaxy of AFVs – there are a Conqueror and Centurion behind the pumps, and a M44 SP Howitzer, Ferret, and Saladin on the near-side.

continued, 5 RTR being disbanded in 1969, while 10H and 11H amalgamated to form the Royal Hussars (PWO), the Royal Horse Guards and the Royals to form the Blues and Royals, and 3DG and the Greys to form the Royal Scots Dragoon Guards, all between 1969 and 1971. In addition, the remaining RAC Regiments of the Territorial Army were amalgamated to form just one single RAC TA unit, the Royal Yeomanry Regiment, in 1967.

The cuts would have been even more severe had it not been found possible to 'save' regiments by employing them in roles previously performed by ERE (Extra Regimentally Employed) personnel, so the task of providing the 'labour' at the RAC BTU at Catterick and the RAC Centre Regiment in 1968 and, as we shall see, this system was to last for two decades, with numerous RAC Regiments taking a one or two year tour in Bovington and Lulworth, their soldiers providing the administrative backing to keep the RAC Centre running smoothly.

The end to National Service

THE SIXTIES also saw the end of National Service, which had, since the first conscription in 1939, seen nearly 4 million men called up for the Army alone. Although the last National Servicemen would not leave until the early summer of 1963, the 'old order' changed rapidly in the Sixties with the new, much smaller, all regular force taking over. Thus, the overall training requirement was drastically reduced and so the transient population of Bovington and Lulworth shrank accordingly.

The composition of the Garrison in the Early Sixties

IT IS relevant to look briefly at the composition of the RAC Centre and to list the units which made up the two garrisons viz:

RAC Centre comprised:
Headquarters
Driving and Maintenance School (including the Royal Artillery and Royal Engineers Wings)
Signal School
Gunnery School
Tactical School (including a Combat Development Cell)
School of Tank Technology (including the Tank Museum)
Equipment Trials Wing
Publications Wing
Junior Leaders Regiment, RAC
RAC Depot
RAC Team, Army Works Study Group

In addition, the following units were also situated Bovington and Lulworth:
Medical Reception Station, Bovington
18 Command Workshop, REME
16 Army Education Centre
Civilian Establishment Pay Office
15 Independent Company, WRAC
Married Quarters Administrative staff
Area and Garrison Works Offices

In general terms, the responsibilities of the RAC Centre were as follows:

a.   Corps training, in particular the training of unit instructors for all RAC units.
b.   Initiation of technical training doctrine for the RAC and giving advice on technical training policy.
c.   Corps training of young officers in first commissioning
d.   Instructing officers and the RAC and other arms in the basic and applied technology of AFVs and weapons.
e.   Training of Commonwealth and foreign students as ordered by the War office.

f. Training Junior Leaders and Junior Bandsmen in the JLR, RAC

g. Advice on technical and tactical training publications, on the working of RAC ranges and details of range practices.

h. Provision of RAC travelling instruction teams to units at home and abroad.

j. Acceptance of visits and organisation of demonstrations as asked by the War Office.

k. Liaison with other arms training establishments in UK, and with RAC training establishments in the Commonwealth and Allied countries.

l. Investigation and trials of equipment in service or prototype.

m. Assistance to RAC Regiments in their conversion from one role to another.[31]

n. Combat Development and Works Study projects as directed by DRAC.

It is useful to compare this list of responsibilities with those undertaken during WW2 and to see how they have gradually evolved. Compare again with the present tasks of RAC Centre (see later) and it is very apparent that the Centre is constantly changing its detailed structure in order to best deal with the responsibilities it is given to perform.

The RAC Depot

IN GENERAL terms the Depot was responsible for the holding and drafting of Officers and Other Ranks of all RAC Regiments and for the provision of help to regiments, especially those abroad, who did not have ready access to the facilities and organisations at home. To understand exactly what it is entailed I asked Maj (Retd) John Rix, late RTR, to explain. He served as the Other Ranks postings and release officer in the Depot from May 1965 to May 1967. He writes: "The Job: Every year about one thousand soldiers were posted and passed through the Depot Squadron as 'Holdees' (ie: on held strength of RAC Depot).

"About half were for onward postings to ERE appointments, some in such faraway places as Singapore, Hong Kong, Washington and the Caribbean. Others went to more humdrum jobs in the UK. Our job was to process them for medical, kit, banking facilities etc, and to arrange briefings so they had some idea of what to expect when they reached their destinations. The other half of the Holdees were: compassionate cases, Medical cases with Pulheems of HO[32] (about 80 at any one time), also the returned absentees and deserters.

"On the release side, most men were quickly processed, sent on pre-release courses (to learn the rudiments of a civilian trade) and descharged, although a few were held for as long as six months for special reasons.

"Everyone who came, whether on posting or release was interviewed by me. I had a staff of NCOs and civilians (mostly retired WOs) to process, control and employ the Holdees. Initially all seemed either to be sent on leave or employed in one of the messes or stables – I changed all that!

"The Staff: The Depot was a strange mix of people and departments all very much aware of their independence. There was an RHQ, commanded by a Lt Col, with an adjutant, Chief Clerk and Orderly Room. They did all the Pt II orders, courses material and mobilisation plans, and held up the mail for at least two days. HQ Squadron, was responsible for all accomodation and the normal functions of a regimental HQ Squadron (ie: administration). WRAC was commanded by a captain who was also responsible for the WRAC in Lulworth as well. They provided an excellent service as drivers, cooks, clerks and storewomen.

"In Tank Park Squadron changes came after a year. There was a lot of talk about QRIH coming to Bovington as the RAC Centre Regiment and that they would then provide all the staff and manpower in Bovington and Lulworth. To make the transition easier a number of organisational changes were made which included RHQ taking direct control of the Tank Park Squadron and the WRAC. This RHQ gained a second in command (ex OC Tank Park Sqn) and Asst Adjt (late OC WRAC). In addition a shadow 'Bovington Centre Commander' was "imposed" and an RHQ, leading not unnaturally, to friction at times between him and the Depot CO. This situation was ameliorated about 6 months later when he was moved into HQ RAC Centre."

John became quite a legal expert during his tour at the Depot, taking part in no fewer than 33 District Courts Martial, mainly as defending officer, but also prosecuting three or four times, or as a member of the Board. He prepared about ten DCMs for trial and even a General Court Martial (of an RTR Officer). He attended many magistrates courts in the South of England, even as far afield as Ascot, in order to give evidence on behalf of various RAC soldiers. He told me of one unusual case, where an NCO was employed for a few months as Assistant Provost Sergeant in the Garrison Guardroom, while he waited to be released. Two days after his discharge they discovered he had perpetrated a series of frauds locally. John had him arrested by the Civilian Police and brought back to Bovington. He was placed in a cell in the Garrison Guardroom to await trial.

One night he persuaded the Guard Commander, who was a student attending a course at one of the schools, to allow him to lock up the other prisoners for the night, ie: to have the care of the keys. The student was only too grateful, as he had a TP (teaching practice) to prepare for the next day. The NCO crept out of the Fire Exit door late that night and John got a letter from him posted in Australia!

Bovington Camp: Royal Armoured Corps Centre, Regimental Headquarters Block.

Headquarters, Director Royal Armoured Corps comes to Dorset

"CENTRALISATION and rationalisation of this grand scale was all the rage in defence matters in the Sixties," commented Kenneth Macksey in his *History of the RAC (1945-1975)*. Many of the administrative functions of the three Services were rationalised, including some of the Whitehall defence departments in the move towards creating a single Ministry of Defence. One of the effects of this was to "streamline" the old War Office, by moving out of London various departments, such as the Arms Directors.

Thus, HQ DRAC left Whitehall in 1965 and moved down to occupy an old wooden bungalow-style married quarter close to the Officers Mess and the Bindon Firing Point, in Lulworth Camp. Maj Gen Jock Holden was DRAC and Brig (later Maj Gen) Geoffrey Armitage was the Commandant RAC Centre. Gen Geoffrey told me: "Arms Directors were turned out of the War Office in 1965, and we had to find quarters and an office for DRAC at the Centre, Gen Jock at one time threatened to oust us from Cambrai House,[33] but a suitable residence was discovered at Charborough, while his office was established at Lulworth. As he started to sign an important letter a tank let off a round outside and the General's pen went through the paper. He was on the telephone to me at once: 'Get me an office at Bovington and quick!'

"Hulldown House, so called, was the choice and I myself in due course enjoyed my turn as DRAC there." Hulldown House was the name (chosen by Gen Jock Holden) for the pre-war brickbuilt nurses home which HQ DRAC then occupied. His staff were later to explain the choice of name as being somewhere that DRAC could observe the doings of Bovington and Lulworth, yet maintain a low profile, so that Commandant RAC Centre could get on with his job without too much interference – one might also add that a hull-down position enables the occupier to bring his guns to bear whenever and wherever he wishes, yet remain completely protected!

Gen Geoffrey Armitage had many amusing memories of his days at Bovington as the following extract shows: "There were plenty of visitors, and I recall some amusing moments. James Ramsden, Secretary of State for War, stayed with us on one occasion. Driving back after dining in the Mess just before Midnight, I remarked that the **Chieftain** test crew would be about to set off from the hangar to a night run. 'Let's see them,' said the Minister, and a few minutes later he was clambering onto the tank in white tie and tails.

"For one DRAC's conference Cambrai House was full of top brass, including the CIGS and the Military Secretary. I took the CIGS up to his room, on returning from the Lulworth Mess and then went to let my three spaniels out for a run. As they were stretching their legs, another staff car drove in. The MS, no less. No time to put the dogs back in their quarters, so we ascended the stairs midst a flurry of canine attention. I bid the General goodnight, and set off for the front door. To my horror, two dogs were carrying socks with suspenders attached, and the third proudly presented me with a bedroom slipper. Back to the great man's room to return his property. My explanation was received in silence, and I imagine my dossier in the War Office being inscribed 'odd'.

"Plenty of foreigners came too, I enjoyed visits to America, Canada and France to stay at comparable establishments.

"I started gundog training classes for the officers, whose retrievers were notoriously ill-behaved in the shooting field. Great fun, and we were joined by a number of civilians and their gundogs."

A building boom

THE SIXTIES was undoubtedly the decade when more rebuilding was started at Bovington and Lulworth than at any time since the beginning of World War II. This boom covered living accommodation (eg new married quarters, new bachelor accommodation at messes and new civilian housing), new shops and the amenities such as clubs, and new general military accommodation including instructional facilities: To list the major work in the Sixties under these headings:

a.   Living accommodation

1961	–	30 soldiers married quarters at Cranesmoor Close, Residential Caravan Sites' at Bovington (off Cologne Rd) and Lulworth (off Vale Rd).
1963/64	–	14 semi-detached civilian bungalows on the Alamein Estate (off Cologne Rd), 53 Officers and 61 Soldiers married quarters (officers – Robertson Road, Heath Close, and Sewell Rd, soldiers Purbeck View, St Julien Rd, Higher Wood Swinton Ave and New Road)
1964/65	–	10 soldiers married quarters at the Oval, Lulworth Camp & The White House (Commandant's house) also at Lulworth Camp.
1965	–	8 semi-detached civilian bungalows on the Alamein Estate
1967/68	–	43 soldiers married quarters (Lawrence Close and Thomas Hardy). Seven Storey Officers mess at Bovington to house III single officers.

b. Amenities

1960/61	–	Civilian canteen at Bovington near 18 Comd Wksp (it cost some £13,500 and was fitted with the most modern kitchen equipment, had a bar and catering accommodation for 200) Extension to British Legion Club House (Cologne Rd)
1961	–	NAAFI Family Shop Bovington

1961	–	Betting shop in Fish St (now Windsor Close) 1000 gal petrol tank at Redlands Garage (now Alamein Garage)
1962	–	Alterations and extensions to the Garrison Garage. NAAFI Junior Ranks Club
1964	–	New County Primary School (off King George IV Rd)
1965	–	Beehive Cafe (in site of demolished cafe at end of Fish St, with two flats above).
1967	–	Further extension to British Legion Club
1968	–	RAC Memorial and Recreation Hall
		An Army Education Centre (Anderson House), which includes a library; a squash court and new Sports Pavilion.
1969	–	Redevelopment of Smiths Handy Stores into a Shopping Centre (containing 7 shops with stores, plus car parking space).

c. Military Buildings

1961	–	Five brick built barrack blocks in JLR Camp (Stanley Bks)
By 1965	–	Stanley Barracks completely rebuilt
By 1968	–	Phase 1 of rebuild completed including:- D & M School – offices, stores, classrooms, Exhibition Hall, Vehicle Instruction Sheds and Vehicle Hangars.
		A Vehicle Wash and POL point.
		An LAD – since changed to the Light Repair Section of 18 Command Workshop REME
		A Central Servicing Station with built-in Tecalamit servicing equipment
		The Technical Stores and Vehicle Squadron Offices
		Two buildings to accommodate the RAC Centre Regiment's Offices, stores and tradesmens shops.
		A Central oil fired Boiler House

A point of interest is that the main D & M School block, the RAC Centre Regiment's RHQ Block and the Army Education Centre were all built in a form of construction known as CLASP. This stands for "Construction of Local Authorities Special Project" and was a form of pre-fabricated construction which was the brain child of Sir Donald Gibson, the Director General of the short-lived Army Civilian Works Organisation. But the rebuilding of Bovington was not without its funny side, as one wag wrote in the TANK: "It is rumoured that when the cookhouse near the Globe Cinema was demolished, a packet of haversack sandwiches was found wrapped in a 1923 newspaper – the sandwiches were as fresh as the day they were cut! Nearer home (RAC Depot) our cookhouse is now due for a facelift preparatory to the D & M School messing with us whilst their cookhouse also had a do. It is quite amazing the moans that went up when the troops knew they were leaving our cookhouse which must be well on the way to becoming an historical monument!"

1969 Phase II began – full details given in the next decade report.

Lulworth was almost completely ignored in this orgy of building and it would be some years before modern buildings replaced the old. Not that such things worried the inmates of that delightful camp – instead of new buildings they merely rearranged the old ones, as this quotation from a February 1960 copy of the Tank magazine describes: "The Tin Tabernacle outside the Instructional Wing has now been dismantled and is to be used elsewhere for housing vehicles. This was one of the Lakeman 'temples', of which there are a number still standing in various camps, and in which were carried out so much developement of mountings and brackets and things during the war. But this is not really a sign that Lulworth is being rebuilt at long last. Infact, members of the Orderly Room are getting so restive that covetous glances are being aimed as parts of the Instructional Wing buildings. It will indeed be a sad day if your scribe gets ousted out of his sunny office after all these years!"

The first RAC Centre Regiment

ON 15 AUGUST 1968, the Queen's Royal Irish Hussars moved to Bovington and on 4th September assumed administrative responsibility for the RAC Centre. They were the very first RAC Regiment to do the job, and as they reported in their Regimental Journal they had mixed feelings about the task they were taking on:

"Our new role is hardly exciting and is often frustrating, but we have been given a job to do and we intend to do it well. A glance at the Squadron nominal rolls at the end of this journal will show how the regiment has changed shape to fit the establishment.

"RHQ and Headquarters Squadron retain their basic composition and role, except that the HQ Squadron has lost MT to 'C' Squadron.

"'C' (D of E) Squadron has expanded to a strength of 156 and is responsible for 186 vehicles of all types. These include Chieftain, Centurion, Saracen, Saladin, Ferret. B vehicles ranging from 10 Tonner to Mini-van – and one Corporation – Type road sweeper! Many of the B vehicles are driven by civilians and some of the lighter vehicles by WRAC girls. The Squadron's main tasks are to provide vehicles for the Schools to instruct on and to lay on demonstrations, both static and mobile, for a seemingly endless stream of visitors. The number of official visits to the RAC Centre amounts to some 150 per year, a visit comprising anything from the crowned head of a middle eastern kingdom and his entourage to a party of schoolboys, but one thing seems to be common to all visitors – the wish to ride in an armoured vehicle.

"'B' Squadron, with a regimental strength of 3 officers and 40 other ranks, is but a poor shadow of its former self. They have taken on the duties of the old RAC Depot, that is to say the documentation and employment of men returning from overseas for release, discharge from hospital etcetera. In addition they have on their books, senior officers batmen, Sandhurst grooms and anyone in the RAC who is for the time being homeless.

"'A' Squadron is at the Gunnery School, Lulworth, where they administer the School, own and maintain all the vehicles, and provide the labour force for the running of the ranges.

"The regiment is also responsible for providing a troop leader and crewmen for the RAC Equipment Trials Wing at Bovington and an independent troop for 6 Infantry Brigade in Catterick.

"The fact that we do not have our own Officers' or Sergeants' Mess or Squadron Rest Rooms is a bitter pill but, as with so many other things, we must adapt ourselves and make the most of what we have.

"Morale remains high, and we have the satisfaction of knowing that though we as a regiment will derive little benefit from this tour, the RAC Centre has received a much needed shot in the arm from our presence, a fact that has been remarked on by numerous visitors."

Perhaps the most important visitor the Regiment had during its tour was their Colonel in Chief, HRH Duke of Edinburgh, who came to Bovington on 20th March 1969: "The major event of the year was the visit to the Regiment in March by the Colonel in Chief. This was the greatest success in spite of unpredictable weather. Prince Philip arrived in the Royal train at Wool station, which in true local form remained quite unchanged and therefore presented the rather unprepossessing station scene that all of us have known for almost two or three generations. He moved on to inspect a Guard of Honour outside the Officers Mess, saw 'C' Squadron put their vehicles through their paces on the demonstration area and drove a **Chieftain** himself – this he appeared to enjoy; however, like most of us over 4ft tall found that there was little or no leg room. His Royal Highness then visited the Corporals Mess, lunched and was photographed with the officers and spent the afternoon with 'A' Squadron at the Gunnery School, where he fired Chieftain. After tea with the Wives Club he returned to his train to change for Dinner in the Officers Mess, before which he had a drink with the Warrant Officers and Sergeants in their mess. This most happy and informal visit had a great boost effect to the Regimental morale and brought the Regiment very close together for this day."[34]

Royal Armoured Corps Memorial Hall

THE ROYAL Armoured Corps Memorial Hall, Bovington was opened on Saturday 12 April 1969, by Gen Sir Charles Keightley, President of the RAC Benevolent Fund, in the presence of a large representative gathering which included Sir John Colfox, High Sheriff of Dorset, Field Marshal Sir Richard Hull, Colonel Commandant Royal Armoured Corps, Colonels of Yeomanry and

Bovington Camp: Royal Armoured Corps Memorial Hall, opened 12 April 1969 – with a striking sculpture on the front.

Cavalry Regiments, the Colonels Commandant Royal Tank Regiment, and representatives of all existing and wartime Regiments of the Household Cavalry, Royal Armoured Corps and Reconnaissance Corps. The gathering also included a large number of widows and families of those who gave their lives serving in the Royal Armoured Corps 1939-45.

After the address and formal opening by the President, the hall was dedicated by the Rt Reverend Victor Joseph Pike, Bishop Suffragan of Sherborne, who as Canon Victor Pike was known to many past and present members of the Royal Armoured Corps, as Senior Chaplain, 11th Armoured Division, Assistant Chaplain General 8th Army and subsequently as Chaplain General to the Forces 1951-60.

The foundation stone had been laid, at a small informal ceremony on September 22 1968, by Brig Sir Henry Floyd, and Maj Gen R Briggs. The Tank magazine for 1969 reported:

"The building consists of a main hall with stage and changing rooms, a kitchen, bar and servery, and a Memorial Room, which will be available for meetings and as a reading and writing room. In this room will be found a portrait of His Majesty King George VI, who was Captain General, Royal Armoured Corps. It is a copy by Mr Robert Swan of the original portrait by Commander Denis Fildes, which belongs to the Staff College, Camberley. Below the portrait will be a Roll of Honour of all the units which together formed the Royal Armoured Corps, 1939-45. The motif of the Memorial Sculpture on the external east wall of the hall is both historical and military. The design is based on the idea of the Roman Eagle, from which our present standards and Guidons derive. The sculpture characterises the Corps by expressing its armour, mobility and vigilance, whilst reflecting the toughness of the tank and the scars of battle. It is framed by Churchill tank tracks. It was designed and made by Mr. Peter Barker-Mill and kindly presented by Messrs. J. Brandt and Partners, the architects of the hall."

The Junior Leaders Regiment, Royal Armoured Corps

THE FIRST boy soldiers to be posted to Bovington began training in January 1920. They were all under fifteen on enlistment and were considered to be of sufficiently high academic standard to be able to pass the Army Certificate of Education 2 during their first year of service. There were initially forty of them but their number soon grew to 200. They had been recruited in order to make up for the lack of qualified mechanics volunteering for the Tank Corps. Their training, therefore, concentrated on the technical aspects of their trade training. Nevertheless, a considerable portion of their time was devoted to elementary theoretical work, physical training, drill and organised games. This scheme came to an end in 1924 with the opening of Army Apprentices' Schools.

The next boy soldiers to arrive in Bovington did so when the Boys' Squadron RAC was formed in January 1952. Initially there were 44 Junior Soldiers but their number soon increased to 200. They were 15-16 year olds who were to be trained to take their place as crewmen in the Regiments of the Royal Armoured Corps and normally spent two years at Bovington. The Junior Leaders' Regiment RAC developed from the Boys' Squadron. This development took place gradually during 1956 with a steady increase of numbers and the formation of a second squadron. When the Regiment formally came into existence in January 1957 it was commanded by a major but during 1958 the appointment was upgraded to Lieutenant Colonel. During this year the strength of the Regiment rose to 400, (including 100 Junior Bandsmen) and a third squadron was formed.

The role of the Regiment then was "to produce and train the future warrant officers and sergeants of the Royal Armoured Corps". The emphasis on the educational side of training continued to be on "Education for Promotion" but the Education Wing was also responsible for providing evening activities for every boy. Hobbies ranged from meterorolgy to motor maintenance. Furthermore, many Junior Leaders attended Outward Bound courses. Indeed, the training aim of the Regiment, to quote the Regiment magazine of Summer 1958, became: "to mould and develop the character of the boy so that he leaves the Regiment a trained leader, qualified in a crewman trade, holding at least a second education certificate, and having been trained at the Army Outward Bound School".

This continued to be the purpose of the Junior Leaders' training for many years. There were, of course, occasional changes in the training organisation. In 1959, for instance, a separate Pass Off Troop was formed with the object of bridging the gap between the ordered pattern of life of a Junior Leader and the comparative freedom of a trained soldier. In 1963 the organisation was changed again. Each Intake was divided into two squadrons in one of which a new boy spent four terms doing General Military Studies and Education before joining a combined squadron to do gunnery, radio and driving. He then spent his final term preparing for Pass Off.

In 1963 it was also decided that in future the best ten Junior Leaders in Pass Off Troop should be selected for a parachute course and a further ten would be tested for suitability for pilot training. In 1969 the squadron organisation completed its full circle. It was decided to abolish Pass Off Squadrons. Henceforth there would be three parallel squadrons and a boy would remain with one squadron throughout his time at the Junior Leaders' Regiment.

"Tailor-made" Barracks

IN 1965, the Junior Leaders Regiment finally moved into the recently completed Stanley Barracks which had been "tailor-made" for a junior leaders unit, had cost £1¼ million to build and taken five years to complete. The new complex replaced the original hutted camp and occupied 29 acres excluding the playing fields. The boys now lived in excellent accommodation and surroundings. They slept eight to a room, junior NCOs having their own private rooms. The new spacious dining hall served high quality food, while the sports facilities included an olympic size swimming pool, gymnasium, squash courts and a fencing room. The Assembly Hall could seat 600, there was a NAAFI club with a shop, hairdressing salon and a restaurant cum-lounge to seat over 100. Adjoining the club was a library – reading room, billiards, games and TV rooms. Instructional facilities were just as spacious and well conceived, while the facilities for sports (rugby, hockey, soccer, cricket, athletics, tennis etc), indoor hobbies (woodwork, art and modelling for example) and outdoor pursuits (including mountaineering, sailing, karting, water-skiing and sub-aqua diving) were supported. These excellent facilities certainly produced the desired results – a press-handout at the opening of the new barracks explained that of the Junior Leaders then serving in the Regular Army (over 11,000 in all Corps), 41% had become sergeants by the age of 27.

'Freedom of Wareham'

IN 1970 the Regiment was granted the 'Freedom of the Borough of Wareham' in recognition of the close friendship which exists between the Regiment and the local community. In 1971, to commemorate fifty years of boys' training at Bovington, HRH The Princess Anne visited the Regiment as Inspecting Officer of the Spring Pass Off Parade. In the same year the system of Army Certificates of Education and their Junior Army equivalents came to an end. The Army Certificate of Education was replaced by the Education Promotion Certificate which was primarily for soldiers already within the promotion bracket and was therefore unsuitable for Junior Leaders. Consequently the aim of education in the Regiment had to be changed from Education for Promotion to Education in Support of Training and Service in the Army. Furthermore, the raising of the school leaving age in 1972 meant that henceforth the boys would not be able to enlist until they were at least 16 and consequently future courses would be of only four terms (15 months) duration. Nevertheless it was decided to continue to give all Junior Leaders a basic military training, coupled with education and character building training, and still to qualify them in one, and if possible two **Chieftain** tank turret trades as well as teaching them to drive.

The revised course started in January 1974 and it was during this year that Junior Leaders of the Army Air Corps and Royal Military Police joined the Regiment to undergo their basic training. After leaving Bovington they continue their training elsewhere. The AAC go to Middle Wallop in Hampshire and the RMP go to Chichester in Sussex.

In 1974 the aim of the Regiment was stated to be: "To give Junior Leaders of the Household Cavalry, the Royal Armoured Corps, the Army Air Corps and the Royal Military Police, the character and leadership training which combined with educational and military training will fit them in due course to reach the rank of sergeant or warrant officer." This was very similar to what it had always been. By 1977, however, the aim had changed radically. The emphasis was no longer on potential leadership but on operational efficiency as a crewmen – "to produce by employment training and education a soldier able to take his place in an operational regiment ... and in so doing to develop quick reaction, self reliance and alertness and to promote character and leadership early in his adult service". This was refined in 1983, so that the present aim of the Regiment is "to train a soldier to take his place in an operational troop with his leadership potential developed as far as possible".

In 1985 a further change took place. The tank gunnery course was transferred to Catterick and the course at Bovington was reduced to one year – three terms of 14 weeks each. The Junior Leader, RAC, now leaves Bovington to learn his armoured vehicle trades at Catterick, Yorkshire, or to take a clerical course at Worthy Down, Hampshire, before joining one of the nineteen Regiments of the Household Cavalry and Royal Armoured Corps. In 1985 too, the young Apprentices of the Royal Army Pay Corps joined the Regiment at the start of their Army careers. After completing their basic training and studying for one or more GCE 'O' levels, they go to Worthy Down to continue their studies. From its inception the Regiment had its own Band School and this trained young musicians for service in one of the bands of the Household Cavalry or Royal Armoured Corps. In 1986, however, the Regimental Band was disbanded and the Army Junior School of Music was established, the larger of the Army's two shcools catering for the young musician. In addition to the development of the young bandsman's musical ability, the two-year course teaches the basic skills required of the soldier. Although having a separate identity, the School also forms an integral part of the junior leaders' Regiment RAC, and, as such, makes full use of the facilities provided for general military training, sport and leisure activities. Apart from training Junior Bandsmen for the Infantry Regiments of the Scottish Division, the Queen's Division, the King's Division, The Prince of Wales' Division, the light Division and the Parachute Regiment.

In addition to Princess Anne visitors to the Regiment have included the Duke of Gloucester, the late Lord Louis Mountbatten and Field Marshal Montgomery, and General George S. Patton, son of the famous American commander.[35]

6   MODERN TIMES 1970-85

AFTER THE turmoil of amalgamations and disbandments of the Fifties and Sixties, the Seventies heralded a period of camparative stability. The main role of the Army and thus that of the RAC, was now firmly in Europe as an integral part of NATO, so the majority of armoured and armoured reconnaissance regiments were stationed in BAOR. However, the disturbing upsurgence of the troubles in Ulster which began in 1969, was to lead to a continuing RAC involvement in Northern Ireland, not just in their normal mounted role, but also acting as dismunted infantry. Tours in Ulster became the 'norm' for all units BAOR with RAC regiments taking their turn patrolling, assisting the Ulster Defence Force and the Police, to keep the peace, guard prison camps, etc.

This stretched manpower resources everywhere making it even more difficult to ensure that the AFVs left behind in BAOR were probably maintained by the small regimental rear parties, while the bulk of the unit's personnel went to Northern Ireland for short six months tours. Regiments were now well equipped with modern AFVs, such as the **Chieftain** main battle tank, the **Scorpion** Combat Vehicle Reconnaissance (Tracked) and **Fox** CVR (Wheeled). Naturally all this had a considerable effect upon the RAC Centre as they had to teach the new weapons, vehicles and equipment to potential regimental instructors. New techniques had to be taught and the entire RAC Centre had to become even more flexible.

Take for example one of the new weapon systems of the Fifties, the long range anti-tank guided missile. A Guided Weapons Wing was formed at Lulworth as an integral part of the Gunnery School. It taught heavy LRATGW, such as Malkara (held by the Parachute Squadron RAC) and Vigilant, a light ATGW, which was mounted on **Ferret** scout cars. Then in the Seventies it was decided to switch all LRATGW to the Royal School of Artillery and the GW Wing closed down. In 1984, however, for reasons which need not be explained here, LRATGW was again put under RAC control, so GW training is once more taking place in Lulworth, albeit on a much reduced scale.

Organisation of the RAC Centre

THE ORGANISATION of the RAC Centre of the Seventies and early Eighties showed only a few changes viz:

a.   The main schools lost their vehicle squadrons which became part of RAC Centre Regiment
b.   School of Tank Technology was renamed as the Armour School.
c.   Tactical School moved from Lulworth to Bovington and lost its Combat Development cell to HQ DRAC
d.   Equipment Trials Wing was renamed as the Armoured Trials and Development Unit and became an MOD controlled unit
e.   Publications Wing is now the Training Development and Publications Wing (TD & PW)
f.   Various minor or ancilliary units have come and gone.

Building continues

THE MODERNISATION of Bovington continued unabated in the Seventies and, during Phase II, the following buildings were completed:

A separate compound and buildings to house the Armoured Trials and Development Unit, to the NW of the Camp. In view of the classified nature of some of this unit's work, it had to be protected against unlawful intrusion to a much higher degree than the rest of the camp. It also required a new access road

Signal School Block

Armour School Block

A Guardroom, with attached weapons training theatre, armoury and small arms ammunition store

A Band practice room

A Simulator building to house AFV driving simulators (came under the aegis of the D & M School)

A Medical Reception Station which included a Dental Centre and Station Medical Centre

An Accommodation Exchange store

Works Offices for the Property Services Agency, DOE

Living quarters for the Manager of the NAAFI Families Shop.

New buildings were not the full extent of this phase, which also included the modernisation of certain existing buildings such as the Sandhurst Block (kitchen and dining hall), 30m range, the Armour School, machine shop, the Gymnasium and SKC Cinema, (later to be called the Services Sound and Vision Corporation (SSVC) Cinema), while Rhine Road was straightened.

On the civilian side, a branch of Lloyds Bank and an electrical shop were built on land leased by the MOD, just to the south of the NAAFI Families Shop. A few more civilian privately owned bungalows were added to Cologne Road, while married quarters accommodation was also not forgotten, 125 soldiers married quarters being built by 1975 (24 in Elles Road, 30 in Lawrence Close, 45 in Purbeck View and 26 in Thomas Hardy). In addition, 45 mobile homes were located in the Higher Wood area and 16 in Arras Crescent. These were always considered to be temporary accommodation only and were in fact all removed by 1984.

The Bovington Officers mess was extended towards the end of Phase II, a West Wing being added, containing 51 additional bedrooms, plus a small ante-room and dining room for use on special occasions. The officers themselves also funded a small swimming pool (open air) which was built between the side of the existing mess and the new West Wing. It has proved a great delight to all concerned, both on hot summer days when the officers families are perhaps the main users, and on certain Guest Nights throughout the year when the bathing has been perhaps slightly more unexpected for some of those entering the pool!

Phase II was followed by two further phases III and IV, which ran concurrently and encompassed the following:-

A new Headquarters Building (see later), to house HQ DRAC, HQ RAC Centre, Training Development and Publications Wing, The Tactical School, the RAC Army Works Study Group, CEPO (Civilian Pay Office), RAC and RTR Benevolent Fund offices, a Courts Martial Centre and a large, well equipped lecture theatre to seat 150. A fire station, to be manned by the Army Fire Service (sadly since closed due to cuts in the AFS and now used by the Cadet Training Team).

Accommodation for the RAC Mobile Display Team

A store for the Armour School

An extension to the WOs and Sergeants Mess to provide a further 24 bedrooms, plus more ante-room space.

Work of a general nature to enlarge the Accommodation Exchange Store and the D & M School (including 10 more vehicle instruction sheds) provide extra hangars for vehicles and to enlarge the simulator building.

Fire at the Garrison Garage

ONE UNEXPECTED alteration occured to Bovington at 10am on 9th October 1979, when a fitter doing some welding on a car in the Garrison Garage (the Red Garage had changed its name to Garrison Garage about 1960) caused and explosion leading to a fire which completely gutted the premises. The garage was rebuilt a few months later.

1979 saw a further 27 soldiers married quarters being built at Lower Cranesmoor, bringing the grand total of married quarters currently occupied in Bovington to 520 (84 officers and 436 soldiers).

Lulworth did not share in this building boom however, for the record, the total married quarters occupied there currently is 78 (16 officers and 62 soldiers).

Opening the new headquarters building

FIELD MARSHAL the Lord Carver of Shackleford, GCB, CBE, DSO, MC, opened the new headquarters building on 12 July 1978. It had taken two years and nine months to complete, the contractors, WE Chivers & Sons Ltd, having started work on 20 October 1975. The site of the new building was roughly where the RTC Depot Officers' Mess had been located. Originally

Bovington Camp: headquarters building, opened 12 July 1978, with the Carver lecture theatre attached to the rear – the larger building in the middle distance is the 1938 Sandhurst Block.

built in 1924 this wooden building became the RAC Centre Officers' Mess and was eventually demolished in 1969. The only changes in occupancy to the list given above were that the RAC Army Works Study Group no longer existed, while CEPO had been replaced by the more easy to understand title of Area Civilian Staff Manager (ACSM). The lecture theatre (appropriately named the Carver Hall) now has the most modern TV equipment as well as slide, cine projection, etc. It has its own full-time Manager and is much used forming extremely valuable addition to training facilities of the RAC Centre.

A new Garrison Church?

ALTHOUGH THE rebuild synopsis included a new interdenominational church in its final phase, the actual church building has remained just a gleam in the eye of every Garrison Commander. The church of St Christopher was inadequate to serve the needs of the JLR as well as the rest of the Garrison, despite the fact that it had been lengthened in the Fifties. Most Junior Leaders' services had to be held in their gymnasium or in a classroom.

In 1967, the Revd CJ Browne, who was then the Senior Chaplain in the Garrison, had the idea of using furnishings from a defunct church at Hilsea (near Portsmouth) to establish a new church for the Juniors in one of the empty huts of Allenby Barracks, quite close to the Tank Museum. Vehicles were sent to bring back pews and other furniture, while labour was obtained from the nearby athletics track – the JLR Chaplain, the Revd Jim Browne, would grab a squad doing fitness training and run one mile with them for each hour of labour they provided! Thanks to this enthusiasm, and to the carpenting skill of Clifford Browne, the church was built.

Later it was dedicated by the Revd C Stubbs-Bromley, QHC, MACF, who was then District Senior Chaplain. Later, we are told, in response to a particularly heretical sermon by an unknown garrison chaplain, the old Garrison church burnt down and the JLR Church became the Garrison Church.

This was about the middle of December 1979 and the Church of St Albans remains the Garrison Church to this day, although there are now moves afoot to build nearer the centre of the Camp. It has been proposed that the Band Practice Room and offices, near the main square to the south of the Sandhurst Block be converted into a church as the Band Block is no longer required, no more RAC Regimental Bands being stationed in Bovington, while the Army Junior School of Music has all the necessary practice facilities any visiting band may require. It is an attractive solution and would then release the Allenby Barracks hut – the last remaining WW2 'spider' in the camp – to be taken over by the Tank Museum and restored to its former glory as wartime barrack rooms with NAAFI canteen.

Bovington Camp: Workshop opening ceremony, 3 June 1985 – the principal participant in the drive-past being this new Challenger, set to become the British Army's main battle tank.

A new Workshop

PERHAPS THE most ambitious part of the rebuild of Bovington Camp – certainly the largest single building – has been the erection of a new Workshop on the site of the existing 18 Command Workshop, REME. The rebuild officially started on 21 May 1979, when the Paint Shop (building 51) the only building not scheduled to be demolished, was rebuilt. DOE/PSA DW (Army) Chessington managed the rebuild programme with Cementation Construction Ltd as the main contractor. Work was undertaken in three stages so as to allow the Workshop facilities to be transferred to other buildings within the RAC Centre in order to minimise disruption to the Workshop operation. Buildings 103 to 106 were constructed in the first phase, then Buildings 101, 102 and 107 as phase 2 then Buildings 108 and 109 and the Test Track facilities as the third stage. In February 1982, the workforce vacated their temporary accommodation and the Main Workshop (Bldg 101) was taken over. The final handover board (for the Test Track facilities) was convened on 25 November 1982 and the official opening ceremony held on Friday, 3 June 1983. The opening was performed by Maj Gen TB Palmer, then Director General of Electrical and Mechanical Engineering. On 1 April 1985, the Workshop was retitled as 18 Base Workshop REME and has become responsible for the base overhaul of the UK fleet of main battle tanks and their derivatives, in addition to the continued support it provides to RAC Centre and other units in South West District.

Bovington links with Lawrence of Arabia

WE HAVE mentioned the strong links which have existed between Bovington Camp and Col TE Lawrence, who served as TE Shaw in the ranks of the RTC and lived in a cottage at Clouds Hill. It was while returning to his cottage from Bovington Camp Post Office on 13 May 1935 on his motor cycle, that he swerved to avoid two boys on bicycles and sustained a fractured skull. He died in Bovington Camp Hospital without recovering consciousness, on 19 May 1935, and was buried in the cemetery of Moreton Church. On 20 March 1979, Gen Sir John Hackett, GCB, CBE, DSO, MC, MA B Litt, LLD, unveiled a commemorative plaque at the Medical Reception Station, Bovington Camp, which reads: "NEAR THIS SPOT LAWRENCE OF ARABIA DIED 19 MAY 1935. PRIVATE ROYAL TANK CORPS 1923-1935".

A few years later, on the 13th May 1983, Tom Beaumont, who had been Lawrence's armoured car driver in those heady days in the deserts of Arabia, planted a tree close to the spot where the tragic accident had occured 48 years earlier. The plaque at the base of the tree reads: "NEAR THIS SPOT LAWRENCE OF ARABIA CRASHED ON HIS MOTOR CYCLE AND WAS FATALLY INJURED 13 MAY 1935".

Reorganisation of children's education in the area

DURING THE mid-Seventies, a large comprehensive school – The Purbeck School – was opened at Wareham. It began taking pupils from a wide area, including Bovington and Lulworth, and quickly reached the 1,400 mark, making it one of the largest schools in the County. Bovington County Modern School became a 'Middle School', that is to say, one catering for 9 to 13 years old. Although the numbers of pupils have thus dropped, it remains an excellent, well-run school with splendid facilities. Bovington First School (5-9 years) was built in 1964, and its location in the middle of the camp makes it ideally suited for attendance by children from the Garrison. It is well used to handling the problems encountered by Army children who have to move from school to school as their parents are posted from camp to camp. It is complemented by two more First Schools in the local area, both open to Garrison children – St Mary's RC School in Wool and West Lulworth First School. Bovington and Lulworth Camps also both have thriving Nursery Schools.

A caring community

UNLIKE A normal small town or village, there are very few long-term residents in Bovington or Lulworth Camps as even the instructors generally stay only for 2-3 years, while course students are here for much shorter periods. This means that there is a continual turnover in the occupancy of the married quarters, so it essential for new arrivals to be able to turn to someone for help and advice. This important job is the prime responsibility of the Families Housing & Welfare Service (FHWS) whose offices are now in Hulldown House. The Families Housing Commandant's responsibilities include married quarter estate management and the welfare of both individual families and the Garrison community in general.

For its married quarters FHWS coordinates the work of the Accommodation Services Unit (ASU) who provide the furniture and the Property Services Agency (PSA) who are responsible for the upkeep, repair and redecoration of the houses. There are a number of FHWS Estate Wardens who examine each quarter before a new family moves in and place orders for any work required by PSA. The handover and takeover of married quarters can be a touchy subject, so it is useful to have these wardens available to sort out problems before they escalate. FHWS has an Army Welfare Assistant based at Hulldown House to assist with family problems, while they run an Information Room to help with the general day to day queries raised by Army families.

There is also a Community Organiser who coordinates the activities of all the Clubs and voluntary organisations in the Garrison. He is in addition the Manager of the Memorial Hall, where many social activities take place. FHWS are responsible for producing the *Bovington Garrison Guide,* an attractive booklet which is a mine of information for families. A copy is issued to every married quarter and is revised annually. It is well-produced and is packed with valuable information presented in a modern manner – even using the stripcartoon approach to getting certain messages across.

Lulworth Range Walks

ONE EMOTIVE issue that was settled to most people's satisfaction during the early Seventies, was that of public access on the tank gunnery ranges around Lulworth Camp. As we have seen, considerable areas of land had been taken over and then purchased during and after World War II, so that it could be used for training. Perhaps the area which epitomised the energetic crusades over the years to "Get the Army Out!" has been the Tyneham Valley. The work of the Tyneham Action Group reached a crescendo in the late Sixties and early Seventies, receiving an unexpected boost from the Nugent Commission, who, in their report of July 1973, advocated the total release by the Army of all land in the Lulworth area.

This recommendation took no proper account of the harmful effect such an action would have on the combat readiness and efficiency of the Royal Armoured Corps, nor the severe financial effect such a withdrawal would have on the local economy. As the welter of claims and counter claims grew, the local people decided at long last to make their own voices heard, in order to counter the vociferous and better orchestarted chorus of protesters, who mostly hailed from everywhere except the actual area concerned!

Fortunately the local people were able to organise themselves and at last get someone to take notice of the "Keep the Army in Lulworth" campaign. One of the founders of this movement, Mr John Wright of West Lulworth told us: "We did a house to house poll of East and West Lulworth, which showed that 85% wanted the Army to stay, 10% had no thoughts about the matter either way, and only 5% actually wanted them to leave. We then arranged a meeting in the village hall which was packed and included our MP, Mr Evelyn King, who admitted that he had come with some doubts about our efforts. He was very surprised and impressed by the strength of local feeling and as a result arranged for a meeting with the Under Secretary of State for Defence Mr (now Sir) Peter Blaker, to whom we were able to put our viewpoint and to which he listened very carefully. Southern Television sent a reporter and a photographer. The BBC favoured the other side. We also wrote a letter to Her Majesty the Queen which we delivered to Buckingham Palace and this was shown on television the next day. ...When the final decision had to be made, the then Secretary of State for Defence, Mr Roy Mason, to his eternal credit, decided that the Gunnery School should remain at Lulworth. One does not know how much influence our efforts had on the result. I always thought the Nugent Commission's recommendation was a nonsense, but certainly we left the "Powers That Be" in no doubt about the views of the people most affected, ie: the local residents."

Perhaps Mr Mason was also influenced by the feelings expressed by at least one of the few remaining old inhabitants of Tyneham who were rehoused when the Army took over. In commenting upon an article written in the Bournemouth Evening Echo in 1969 which read – "A raw damp December day, the villagers left – the squire, gardener, postmistress, school teacher..." – she commented: "No school teacher as the school had been closed for 10 years, pupils – no school age children there then. Shepherd – no sheep had been kept for two years in the valley. Fishermen – all too old 80 and 90 in years to row a boat. Rector – who was already in the Army and left two years and so on!"

This book is not the place to open old wounds, however, little has ever been written about the other side and it is to the Army's credit that, instead of merely putting up the barriers again, they embarked upon a scheme designed to allow more public access, and to achieve this in a sensible and above all, safe manner. Thus were born the Lulworth Range walks. These paths mainly run along the seven miles of cliffs bordering the foreshore, although there are circular walks taking in the Tyneham Valley and the Ridgeway to Whiteway Hill. They link up with the Dorset Coastal Path at both range boundaries. In order to ensure that the paths would be safe for the public we enlisted the aid of a strange, yet charming and efficient "private army", namely a group of Ukranians who currently help the Royal Engineers to clear up the unexploded shells and bombs on old wartime ranges and training areas in UK. They methodically examined every inch of the 15½ miles of proposed paths with their metal detectors: "When the high pitched whine is heard in the earphones of the detector operator it indicates a find, the digger steps forward and carefully uncovers it. If it looks as though it is a 'memento of war,' the trained British Army Bomb Disposal Experts are summoned to defuse and blow up the find."[36] Eventually the paths were all cleared, marked and ready for opening to the public. They now open on most weekends and for the whole of August and have proved very popular.

Lulworth Camp: looking north-east, from the sky, in the late 1970s – when the Tactical School was still occupying a group of First World War huts (centre right).

Lulworth Ranges: spectacular coastal scenery, this view being from Cockpit Head over the Arish Mell Gap to Flower's Barrow Hill, Worbarrow Bay and the Tyneham valley – a beauty which led to a strident campaign for its release.

Lulworth Camp: aspects ancient and modern, the World War One huts having survived more than sixty years before they finally met the bulldozer and became the site of the new A-vehicle complex. The 1980s look came with the completion of the maintenance hangars.

Opposite, top **Lulworth Ranges**: wire-guided LRATGW Swingfire missile, which came into service after Malkara and Vigilant, and is seen at its launch from an AFV 438.

Opposite, centre **Lulworth Ranges**: firepower demonstration, down the Bindon Range towards the Arish Mell Gap – a troop of Scorpion CVR (T) are engaging targets, with a Royal Ordnance Factory light gun in the foreground.

Opposite, bottom **Lulworth Ranges**: note the lower sign, 'Lulworth Range Walks' – which through regular weekend and August opening gave large-scale public access to the coast and defused emotive appeals for the abandonment of military use.

Range Wardens

AS SOME 70,000 armour-piercing, high explosive and phosphorous smoke tank shells are fired on the ranges every year, some are bound to land on the paths, especially if they fail to explode and ricochet off target. Thus, on every single occasion before the walks are opened to the public, they must be searched carefully for unexploded shells. Those using the walks are continually warned to keep to the path and not to stray off the well marked boundaries, also of course not to pick up any suspicious objects.

The work of looking after the walks, advising the public and generally maintaining the area, is the job of a specially trained team of Range Wardens who are based near Range Control in Lulworth Camp. They work closely with the military range staff to ensure that the ranges operate efficiently and that the public is safeguarded at all times. Range safety during periods of firing is paramount both on shore and within the sea danger area, so there is now a sophisticated radar station on top of Bindon Hill and a number of MOD range boats operating out of Weymouth who regularly patrol offshore. The Lulworth Ranges are an area of spectacular beauty and, as Rodney Legg says in his book *Lulworth and Tyneham Revisited*, "there is a greater concentration of wildlife inside the Lulworth East Holme Ranges than in any of Dorset's official nature reserves."

Bovington Training Area

TO MANY people the Bovington Training Area looks like a desolate area of wasteland used only for tank driver training. It is however, one of the few areas in Dorset where the flora and fauna which were once abundant of Dorset heathlands, can now exist. It is also a very important wildlife habitat. Fortunately, as at Lulworth, the Army is seeing that the area is properly managed, despite the very evident changes to the landscape which AFV driving over the years has produced. At least this is now contained in a relatively small area and even there, the Bovington Conservation Group ensures that proper regard is paid to such factors as deer conservancy[37] (there are probably more wild roe and sika deer living free in the Bovington and Lulworth Training Areas than anywhere else in the county,) flora and fauna, sites of ancient monuments or those of special scientific interest. Contrary to popular belief, the Army does not just drive about in a totally uncontrolled manner, laying the countryside waste and not caring a jot about the damage done. In fact they take the greatest care to protect the area in every possible way.

Rebuilding at Lulworth

WITH THE future of the Gunnery School once again assured at Lulworth, the planners could begin considering the modernisation of Lulworth Camp, which has always lagged woefully behind Bovington. Even today much of the original camp is unchanged, although various buildings have been used for other purposes. A brief study of the migrating habits of the camp Medical Inspection Room will perhaps explain to the reader this peculiar Lulworth phenomenon:

1920	–	Medical Centre occupied site No. 1 near old main gate.
1930s	–	moved to new site 2
1946	–	moved to new site 3 opposite present Officers Mess
1953	–	moved to new site 4 where old "Tin Shed" Officers Mess was located
1966	–	moved to present site 5, not very far away from its starting place in the 1920s

We are uncertain about its future but if it is to keep up its wanderings then clearly another move must be on the cards!

To be fair some new buildings have recently appeared at Lulworth. The line of old WWI huts which used to be occupied by the Tactical School have been bulldozed away and their place taken by a splendid new vehicle area of hangars, washdowns, offices etc. Having had two blissful tours at the Tactical School I remember the old huts with considerable affection. On a summer's day one could hear the rabbits who lived underneath, scampering about, while on occasions internal grasscutting was required as it pushed its way up through the floorboards (This also happened at Bovington Camp and I well remember the Commandant's PA telling me she used to have to cut the grass regularly in the Brigadier's office, otherwise it pushed his carpet up and looked untidy!) No doubt modern buildings will take the place of the old, but it is to be hoped that they preserve some reminders of the old days.

RAC Centre Regiment

DURING THE Seventies and Eighties, ten RAC Regiments carried out the duties of RAC Centre Regiment – see Annex to this chapter for details. Their basic tasks did not vary much over the years, so the summary already given in the last chapter of the role of QRIH will stand for the others as well. However, the other activities which they were called upon to perform, were many and varied as these extracts from the TANK notes of 2 RTR (Bovington 1970-1972) indicate:

"Film Stars"

ON ARRIVAL in Bovington a memo appeared, asking for a troop to be formed with express purpose of bringing up-to-date a training film – 'Infantry/Tank Co-operation'. Duly, the budding film stars gathered together at the beginning of October, made themselves look like fighting soldiers, made their tanks resemble Christmas trees and Bovington Heath look like a battle ground.

"It did not take long for the glamour to wear off: the soldiers found themselves closed down on set and only their tanks were filmed. The three commanders were more lucky; they were seen padding through woods, bristling with guns, respirators, compasses, binoculars, etc, etc. Lt Geisler managed to lower himself into wet grass and crawl around, just to become a film star.

"The Infantry were seen out of their APCs, covered in war paint and charging around or rushing some imaginary enemy dug-out. The Rarden turret mounted on an APC caused great controversy. Eventually, the platoon commander claimed it as his, and this ungainly vehicle became a film star too.

"The last week saw the three Chieftains moving to Lulworth for firing sequences and this proved more interesting, especially from the gunners' point of view. There was some good shooting, and many disputes as to ranges on long range HESH shoots. A certain commander was proved wrong with his "dot 2 add a bit" on an urgent target, and some of the fire orders were a little strange:

"Action"	–	Commander
"HESH dot 2 Ant"	–	Commander
"Loaded"	–	Loader
"Action"	–	Film director
"Running"	–	cameraman
"Go"	–	commander
"Firing now"	–	gunner
"You missed"	–	the film crew

"Certain guest appearances were made in the film, by Lt-Col G L D Duckworth as the battle group commander, and Major Ralph Bagnall-Wild as the combat team commander. Lt Fanta Geisler was presumed to be 'the star', though everyone has his doubts about this fact. The crews were made up of ex-Hohne 'Badger,' drawn from various troops in Bovington 'Badger'.

"The premiere of the film will be in mid-1971 – rumour has it that champagne will be provided. Capt Mike Goodwin, 3 RTR, was the military supervisor and chief mediator. It was based on a book by Major Rob Ockenden – complaints should be addressed to him."

A Troop Leaders' course exercise

"AN UGLY rumour circulated around our working areas. Yes! 'An exercise on Salisbury Plain'. This brought on a rush of little DMS in the direction of the Tech stores and the sound of all the tools being assembled and issued, wafted on the breeze. The transporters arrived and after last minute checks, and cups of tea, on went their loads amid cheers and certain other words.

"The crews departed by road in the usual form of Army VIP conveyance to meet up with the tanks which had departed much earlier; no doubt due to their slower rate of progress. At the training area the coach arrived bringing all our budding troop leaders to their steeds.

"Sgt Bill Watt and his trusty charioteer Cpl John Horton again featured in Niner (Three Star) Hotel and did an excellent service to the Starving Troops Association. Training proceeded with tanks rushing in all directions, amid cries of "Hello .... this is .... get down from the .... Skyline".

"Night fell, and whispers were heard of "Night Attack", 'Gas'? 'Someone's Rover is bogged and 'Where's the paper, Bill?' New Zealand Farm became the home for some of us for the duration of the exercise whilst the tanks found some comfortable bushes in Ablingdon Furze and underwent attack after attack which sent them scampering about the Plain.

"As usual the ARV and its crew were in the limelight visiting some of the 50 ton brigade whose automotive parts had decided that they had had enough for the time being.

"The last day came and huge quantities of ammunition (Brocks type) were issued and opposing sides were manoeuvred into position on their start lines. Someone in the middle,, waved a red flag, and they were off.

"Soon we heard "You're knocked out!" "Contact!" "Replen" and other well known battle lines, whilst over the 'A' set drifted "Go left Driver! Driver go left! Oh Damn ... Blast" Boom, Thud, etc. The results of the exercise were as follows:-

| Chieftain engines – 3 | ... | Young Officers Ankles – 2 |
| Diesel Rashes – 1 | ... | Food Poisoning – 0 |

"Away we go to meet the transporters again and the YOs depart, being now thoroughly conversant with both types of Shovel Drill.

"As the end of the month draws near and the ripples of the last month subside, we look back in awe and wonder how on earth we ever got through it."

Open Day – Gallows Hill Demonstration

"AFTER NUMEROUS rehearsals we were all relieved when the morning of Sunday, August 1st arrived. All vehicles and crews were in position by 09.30 and the long wait started. Several families had camped on the area to ensure getting a good seat and the crowds started arriving from 10 o'clock onwards. Sgt Litchfield was in charge of the Static Line, assisted by a handful of D & M Instructors. This kept the families busy until 11.30 when the battle started.

"The Armoured Car Troop under Sgt Shipley advanced over the river to reconnoitre forward. This went smoothly until, from the area of the fir wood to the west, a troop of **Chieftains,** commanded by Sgt. Watt, opened up. The Armoured Car Troop, taken completely by surprise, quickly decided to withdraw the **Saladins.** After a quick appreciation, the Armoured Car Troop called forward a recce helicopter – another 2 RTR 'star' actor in the form of Sgt Harrison. He carried out a quick recce and reported back on the advancing tanks. Because of the helicopter's frightening report of a troop of **Chieftains** advancing, supported by the remainder of a Squadron, the armoured cars started to withdraw quickly. One of the **Saladin's** wheels soared high into the sky (thanks to Sappers' plastic explosives) and Cpl Aherne appeared with another **Saladin,** front wheel missing and wheel hub blazing. Sgt Shipley's **Saladin** was next to go, amidst explosions and clouds of smoke. The last remaining Ferret just managed to escape over the bridge before it was blown. The **Chieftain** Troop was cut off from advancing over the river and so they called up a bridgelayer. A successful launch and the **Chieftains** screamed over to follow up the fleeing Armoured Car Troops.

"We left the battle there and started demonstrating the automotive capabilities of RAC, RA and RE vehicles used at Bovington. This started off with a bang – the first **Ferret (Mk 1)** driven by Tpr. Farr, tried to jump the second of the double bumps! A very nasty sight, but luckily he landed the right way up and managed to continue. Apart from this all went well, and thousands enjoyed the static line during the lunch hour before moving to the arena for the afternoon."

Open Day arena display

"WHEREAS THE Gallows Hill Display was designed to show the public, held in the afternoon, provided more traditional "Tattoo-type" entertainment. The proceedings opened with a fanfare by the State Trumpeters of the Household Cavalry, with Cicero the Drumhorse. This was followed by the Massed Bands, consisting of the Cambrai Staff Band and a very large Junior

Leaders' Regiment RAC Band.

"The D & M School produced their idea of the Main Battle tank of the 1980s, with its revolutionary form of protection (make the armour of cardboard and all shots will pass harmlessly through). If nothing else, it succeeded in covering the crowd with a healthy mixture of coloured smoke and had to be escorted from the Arena by the Army Fire Brigade.

"A tentpegging display by the Blues and Royals followed; and then a display by the Junior Leaders, consisting of a drill demonstration, which included a feu de joie, and a very spectacular PT display.

"The Gunnery School reconstructed the first tank V. tank action of April 23 1918, which involved Lt Mitchell and an A Battalion Tank. The mock-ups of the **Mark V** and German Tank were excellent, and the crowning moment came at the end when the 'D' Battalion **Mark V** tank from the Tank Museum, still fighting fit after more than fifty years' service, traversed the arena at a leisurely 2½ m.p.h. The last time we had seen her perform was at the 50th Anniversary Parade four years ago in Germany. The Dorset Branch of the Royal British Legion paraded their standards and then we moved onto the climax (we thought) of the show.

"The KAPE team, back fresh from their annual tour of our recruiting area, provided an excellent procession driving display in their Ferrets, which held the large crowd spellbound.

Certainly Major Golding and Sgt. Scott could afterwards breath a large sigh of relief in that KAPE 1971 had taken place without any 'prangs'.

"The Parachute Squadron RAC produced a hair-raising freefall demonstration. Of the stick of four, two did perfect landings in the arena. The other two, unfortunately got caught by a wayward gust of wind when still 300 feet up and were last seen heading fast in the Salisbury direction. However, they did finally manage to make contact with Mother Earth without sustaining any injuries. All participants paraded for the Grand Finale – the Evening Hymn and National Anthem. During this, each Regimental Flag was lowered by a Junior Leader about to join that Regiment.

"Elsewhere around the arena the 30,000 spectators who attended could amuse themselves at a wide range of sideshows and static displays. These varied from displays of equipment put on by all the Schools and Wings, to Bingo and a Funfair."

Personal memories of the Eighties

MAJ GEN Simon Cooper has spent six of the last seven years in Bovington first as Commander RAC Centre (1981-83) then as DRAC (1984-87). His reminiscences of these six years begin: "My two tours were separated by a year only so it is hard to separate any reminiscences into the correct period. My abiding memories will be, I'm sure, the fun and enjoyment I have had serving in this part of the country which is, for me, so closed to home, the relaxed atmosphere and friendliness of everyone who lives and works or is associated with the two stations of Bovington and Lulworth, the seemingly endless stream of visitors that pass through the Centre and, despite the inevitable changes that have taken place during my six years association, the timeless face of the Garrison and this corner of Dorset.

"The most noticeable changes have been the removal of the original Bovington Workshop building to be replaced by the enormous new Base Workshop establishment, the final demise of the First War wooden huts at Lulworth including the four outside which King George V was photographed, and of course the Museum which is perhaps best described as a change from a collection of dead and dusty AFVs housed in extremely cramped and uninviting conditions to a living, comprehensive and unique historical record of the Tank, its antecedents and its people, in surroundings which attract visitors of all ages from the armoured vehicle buff to the harassed mother trying to amuse her children on a wet summer's afternoon.

"Of the hosts of visitors I have seen through Bovington, three stand out as particularly memorable. First was a Chinese delegation of 18 under Mr Yang De Zhi, Chief of the General Staff of the Peoples Liberation Army, which included a woman interpreter. They arrived in a bus at the demonstration area on Gallows Hill. On disembarking, or perhaps disgorging is a better word, from the bus they completely swamped their escort officers and all rushed forward to shake hands. Each was of identical height, each was intent on introducing himself in Chinese. It was impossible to identify Mr Yang or, worse, for some time to discover which was the woman interpreter. They were a delightful party and Mr Yang De Zhi, a veteran of the Long March and as ageless in looks as so many of his race, was fascinating to talk to and drank brandy after lunch with an aplomb that surprised me.

"In contrast the visit of the Crown Prince of Thailand had a nightmarish quality about it, which I know was not intended but left us all quivering. He arrived half an hour early to stay the night at Swinton House. His party of 14 which included his political mentor, his doctor, his personal servant and two Thai ADCs each armed with walkie talkie sets and, I suspect, pistols. His servant having removed his shoes on entering the house (he didn't put them on again until he left) inspected the Prince's room and pronounced it, after some discussion, suitable. It was then explained that we had rooms and beds to cope with his mentor, doctor and British ADC, but that the rest would be accommodated in the Mess. This was not well received but was, we thought, eventually accepted. After tea, during which at one moment the Crown Prince was stoking the fire himself, at the next being given his teacup by his servant on his knees (no Thai junior to the Crown Prince is supposed to talk to him with his head above the Prince's) a long discussion ensued about the protocol for dinner. The two senior Thais invited to our private party for the Crown Prince said that they could not attend as they were forbidden to sit at the same table.

"Eventually this problem was solved (there was no room for a separate table, the kitchen was hardly suitable and they refused the Mess) by them agreeing to sit on the same side of the table as the Prince and not looking at him. During and after dinner it was clear that the rest of the entourage ate in the kitchen or elsewhere in the house as not a scrap of food was left and dirty plates were everywhere. The final saga was the sleeping arrangements. The servant slept on the floor at the foot of the Prince's bed. An ADC outside the bedroom door and, again, the remainder of the party scattered through the house with blankets and pillows raided from the linen cupboard. We were not aware of this part of the drama until the following morning when it was worse than rush hour at Waterloo station tripping over somnolent bodies. I must add as a tail piece to this visit that, throughout, the affair was conducted with great courtesy and the Prince's doctor in particular was a man of considerable charm, erudition and culture with a wide knowledge of English and European paintings and furniture.

"Prince Michael of Kent's recent visit to Bovington provides my last snapshot of the visitor scene. He is well known for his interest and knowledge of things mechanical so it was inevitable that he should be invited to drive **Challenger.** After a few minutes instruction in the controls he climbed into the driver's compartment and his private detective, suitably bedenimmed, gingerly placed himself in the loader's hatch. With no encouragement the tank left the hard standing for the training area as a Formula 1 leaves the grid at Silverstone. Within half a mile the back-up tank was 400 yards behind and rapidly losing the Prince and his steed. Then ensued a circuit of the area out of sight of the escorting party until the tank roared back into view and headed straight for one of the water filled hollows in the track. **Challenger's** suspension is excellent and the Prince took this obstacle at speed but the bow wave created by the glacis plate plunging through the deep pool of water totally soaked Prince Michael and even drenched the detective still hanging on grimly to the loader's hatch."

Today and tomorrow

AN EX-TANK CORPS soldier who trained at Bovington during the First World War would have great difficulty in relating the modern, spacious camp with the crowded hutments of "Tin Town". The same would apply to a pre-war RTC soldier, or to a not so-old warrior from among the thousands who passed through "Bovy" during the frenetic days of World War Two. Most of the old landmarks have now gone in the extensive post-war rebuilding programme. However, he would find no difficulty in identifying with the modern-day resident of the Garrison. The main tasks of the RAC Centre have remained unchanged over the years, namely to teach tank crewmen their jobs.

They say "old Soldiers never die" and we are extremely fortunate at the Tank Museum to be continuously visited by old soldiers of at least three generations. Last year for example, they included a veteran of Flers, who had commanded a tank in the first ever tank battle on 16th September 1916. He drove up from Torquay to see us on the 70th Anniversary of that action, aged 92 and still fighting fit! He marvelled at the firepower, protection and mobility of the modern main battle tank, but understood completely its "raison d'être", because it was no different from that of the old Heavy Mark I tank he had commanded all those years ago. The same applies to Bovington and Lulworth. The modern RAC Centre may outwardly appear very different to the Tank Training Centre of 1916, but its basic, raison d'être, remains the same.

Present status, mission and tasks

THE PRESENT status of RAC Centre is as an integral part of the United Kingdom Individual Training Organisation, under the Sponsorship of the Director, Royal Armoured Corps.

It is under command of the General Officer Commanding South West District, except for certain 'Special to Arm' functions. Its mission is to train for mechanised warfare, officers and soldiers of the Household Cavalry, the Royal Armoured Corps and other Arms (including Commonwealth and Foreign students as directed). Its principal tasks include the running of courses with the primary aim of producing unit instructors in tank gunnery and guided weapons, driving and maintenance, signals and radar, armoured tactics, AFV and weapons technology.

In addition, Young RAC Officers receive their Special to Arm Training, Crew Commander training is carried out and Junior Leaders are trained. As well as the basic job of training, the RAC Centre is responsible for a wide range of other tasks including technical training advice, armoured trials and developments, sales visits and demonstrations, technical and tactical publications, advice and assistance on RAC matters and liaison with other arms training establishments. In carrying out these tasks RAC Centre works under the direction of HQ DRAC and in conjunction with such supporting units as 18 Base Workshops, REME and Armoured Trials and Development Unit.

Modernisation continues

THE PROGRAMME of modernisation continues albeit at a slower pace than in the Sixties and Seventies, everywhere except perhaps at the Tank Museum where the spitit of 'free enterprise' prevails! The next few years should see Lulworth Camp modernisation progressing faster, while in Bovington the changes are mainly in the area of Camp amenities. For example, there is every chance that a Garrison Church will be constructed with in a couple of years; the now defunct cinema should be converted into a Sports Centre soon; while the RAC Memorial Hall has this year (1986) been extended to include more public rooms and offices for the Chaplains and others.

Alterations to the shopping area include a change of ownership at the supermarket, a facelift to the Bovington Insurance Services premises, the opening of a vetinerary practice in what was the old pre-war chemist shop, and the installation of a car wash at the Garrison Garage. A complex of new semi-detached houses and flats is in the final stages of completion behind the Garrison and Alamein Garages, backing onto the side of Higher Wood.

One casualty of the need for greater security has been the closure of both ends of Rhine Road with barriers, where it joins into King George V Road in the West and Cologne Road in the East, sealing the main military area of the camp from unauthorised vehicular access. All vehicles must now go in and out via a Provost-manned "Sleeping Policeman" road block outside the camp guardroom.

Another large detached house is being built at the southern end of Cologne Road, on the site of a much smaller bungalow. It is however, interesting to see that one of the old WWI railway carriage conversions still exists in Cologne Road. Bovington Farm continues to thrive, its fields, livestock and its thatched roof being an ever present rural reminder of Bovington's early days.

The end of the RAC Centre Regiment

IT HAS recently been decided that from March 1988, the ABTU Catterick and the RAC Centre Bovington will be manned by a single RAC Regiment. The basic reason for this change is to release another Regiment for service in BAOR. From March 1988 the single regiment will have its RHQ, HQ Squadron and two squadrons at Catterick, while the remaining two squadrons will be at Bovington and Lulworth respectively. Bovington Garrison will be commanded by RHQ Royal Tank Regiment – presently located in London – who will take over this responsibility when RHQ 3 RTR leaves.

Bovington Camp: proficiency with a Challenger on the Dorset heaths tests these who will man the front-line defences of a divided Europe.

The reason why

IN CONCERT with her NATO Allies, Great Britain needs strong conventional ground forces if we are to provide a realistic deterrent against possible aggression in Western Europe. The mainstay of the British Army of the Rhine is 1st British Corps, comprising four armoured divisions, one artillery division and supporting troops. These forces are equipped with over 600 main battle tanks and nearly 3000 other armoured vehicles.

If war ever came, then these forces would have to face an enemy who is superior in numbers of both men and armoured vehicles. If there is to be a balancing factor then it must rest in the combat effectiveness of every single soldier and his ability to get the best out of his armoured vehicle and its weapon system. This means first class training, by dedicated instructors who really know their job. A large proportion of these instructors are trained at the RAC Centre, so it can truly be said that the efficiency of our conventional deterrent relies, to no small degree, upon the efficiency of the Royal Armoured Corps Centre – could there possibly be a better reason for its continued existence than this?

7 THE TANK MUSEUM of the Royal Armoured Corps and Royal Tank Regiment

BOVINGTON HAS its own unique shrine to its beginnings and purpose. With the end of the Great War, Tank Corps units in Europe and overseas, as well as their training establishments at Bovington, Lulworth, Wareham and Swanage, began to reduce in strength upon demobilisation. Large numbers of tanks accumulated on the heath north of the Camp, where many remained until they were broken up and sold for scrap. Twenty-six specimens from the Tank Park — examples of each mark of current or experimental vehicle — were collected and moved to about half an acre of ground, fenced off with chestnut paling. These were the beginnings of the present museum.

In 1923, Rudyard Kipling during a visit to Bovington expressed disappointment that so little was being done to preserve these machines and in 1924 a start was made by housing a selection of them, including **Little Willie** and **Mother** in an open-sided shed in the Driving and Maintenance Wing of what was then the Royal Tank Corps Central Schools. In 1925, an equipment store was taken over to house souvenirs and relics, and the embryo museum, was considerably enlarged in 1928. It was not open to the general public but was kept up for instruction of all members of the Royal Tank Corps and selected parties and individuals from all the Services. Various experimental machines of the inter-war years were added to the collection whenever they had outlived their usefulness. A visitor to the Museum at this time wrote in the Tank magazine: "Down below I could see some large buildings, obviously workshops. But almost rubbing shoulders with them were a few — three or four — low tin-roofed shelters behind a red fencing, looking for all the world like a farm. And this likeness to a homestead was the more faithful by token of a flock, or small herd or whatever you call it, of a dozen or so beasts on the heath this side of the fence. Strong hump-backed cattle they looked rather on the big side. Bellies to grass and sterns to the wind they looked impervious to a monsoon.

"Calling the dog to heel I legged it pretty briskly for the big gate and shelter. Here I found "Ted". "Ted" looks like a jovial farmer in overalls, he said he was N.C.O. i/c Museum.

"He isn't. He's the curator of the Wonder House, I know. I spent two topping hours in his company "doing" the museum, which my farm proved to be. It is the Royal Tank Corps Museum. The old building at Lahore fascinated Kim, this one just absorbed me. In a few minutes the rain was forgotten in my interest, and I found it an afternoon well spent. No charge either. A chap doesn't even have to leave his brolly at the door. The exhibits of things historical and heroical are there to be seen and Ted's there to show 'em."

1939 saw the formation of the Royal Armoured Corps, comprising the Cavalry of the Line, the Royal Tank Corps (thereafter called the Royal Tank Regiment) and certain Yeomanry and Territorial Army units. It was decided to enlarge the scope of the existing Royal Tank Corps Museum, to cover the interests of all the regiments then making up the RAC, but the project had to be abandoned on the outbreak of war, when the museum closed for the duration.

During the invasion scare of 1940, **Little Willie** guarded an airfield in Gloucestershire and a number of other museum exhibits were used for local defence schemes. The **Mark V** was stationed on the Wareham road, while the **Vickers Medium,** with the **Independent,** covered the road from Bovington to Wool. Other machines were positioned on the coast near Lulworth Cove. These and a number of other tanks were thus saved from the drive for scrap steel which destroyed many irreplaceable relics; among them was **Mother,** others were the experimental electricity-driven tank, Gen Martel's own home–made light tank, the Medium 'C', and many other unique machines.

In 1945, space for about 50 vehicles was again found at the Driving and Maintenance School but the buildings were not very suitable, so between 1947 and 1952 the present central hangar was taken into use. The Museum was first opened to the public in 1947 and some 2,500 persons visited it in that year. A collection of Allied and Foreign AFVs which had accumulated during World War 2 came to the Museum in 1951. The Jolly Hall was added in late 1970, the new Entry Block in 1983, the Gauntlet Restaurant and Sultan of Oman Theatre in 1984 and the George Forty Hall (to house the World War 1 exhibits) in 1986.

The modernisation and expansion of the Museum is still continuing the Jolly Hall being divided to form the Evolution and Interwar year halls, while a new Postwar hall is now under construction in the yard. For this reason not all the collection is on show at the present time. The museum premises still house the Royal Tank Regiment Museum, which co-exists with the collection of RAC exhibits. The Household Cavalry and the Cavalry regiments of the RAC all maintain their own separate regimental museums in their home recruiting areas, however, a small cavalry room is shortly to be added at the Tank Museum to cover all mechanised cavalry regiments.

The present collection contains over 180 major exhibits and illustrates the historical and technical development of the armoured fighting vehicle (AFV) from the turn of the century to modern times. The museum acts as a storehouse where examples of past and present ingenuity in the automotive, armament and armour aspects of AFV design may be studied in detail and engineering and tactical lessons learnt.

All the Services and a number of Government and official agencies take advantage of the display as a means towards improving their knowledge, as also in a slightly different context, do increasing numbers of school parties. This is in full accord with the museum's charter, which may be summarised as charging the trustees with the responsibility of providing technical and historical recreation for them and for the general public, on all aspects of the development of the armoured fighting vehicle.

Bovington Camp: His Majesty George Vth is shown 'Little Willie' by Major General Sir John Capper (left), first Colonel Commandant of the Royal Tank Corps, in the 1920s. These redundant wartime vehicles became the nucleus of the Tank Museum collection.

Bovington Camp: Mark I tank of the Great War at the saluting base outside the Tank Museum, in the 1950s.

149

Tank Museum: Post-war arrangement of the fighting vehicles of both sides facing each other, with the Germans (left) showing superior firepower throughout the conflict.

Tank Museum: Ferret Scout Car in the foyer, with dummies by Anne Forty, co-author of this book and Museum Display Officer.

Tank Museum: Centurion Tank, cut in half, vividly shows its workings, gun controls and armour.

Lulworth Ranges: Heavy Mark V of the Great War on an excursion from Bovington Tank Museum to the heathland tank gunnery ranges, where it poses beside a Chieftain main battle tank.

Tank Museum: HRH Duke of Kent preceded by Lieutenant-Colonel George Forty, the Curator and co-author, with General (now Field Marshal) Sir John Stanier being glimpsed behind the Duke. They are seen at the opening of the Entry Block in July 1983.

8   VIP VISITORS

Bovington Camp: Monty at Bovy, 19 April 1944. General Bernard Montgomery (centre), wearing his famous beret, visited the Driving and Maintenance Wing of the Armoured Fighting Vehicles School in his rôle of overall land-force commander responsible for the planning and execution of the D-Day assaults in Normandy that would take place on 6 June 1944.

Bovington Camp: HRH Duke of Kent arriving at the Tank Museum, in a Rolls-Royce Armoured Car, to open the new Entry Block, in 1983.

Bovington Camp: HRH Duchess of Kent inspecting a guard of honour of the 17th/21st Lancers in January 1979.

Bovington Camp: HRH Princess Anne presenting prizes at the Spring Pass Off for the Junior Leaders' Regiment in 1971.

Bovington Training Area: Prince Michael of Kent at the controls of a Challenger, the Army's main battle tank, 24 September 1986.

Bovington Camp: HRH Duke of Gloucester on a tour of the Driving and Maintenance Wing in 1956.

Bovington Camp: HRH Princess Margaret meets her Regiment – the 15th/19th The King's Royal Hussars – in August 1985.

Bovington Camp: Lord Louis Mountbatten inspecting the Junior Leaders Regiment, December 1971.

Bovington Camp: HRH Duke of Edinburgh visiting the Queen's Royal Irish Hussars in March 1969. He is seen in the WOs and Sergeants Mess.

TANK CORPS ROLL OF HONOUR

Somme

Arras

Messines

Ypres

Cambrai

Amiens

St Quentin

Le Cateau

1916 · 1918
Killed   879
Wounded   5302
Missing   935

Commanders at Bovington

Tank Corps Training Centre

Brig Gen	FG Anley CB, CMG	9 Nov 16	–	24 Jan 17
Brig Gen	WJT Glasgow CMG	25 Jan 17	–	1 Aug 18
Brig Gen	EB Matthew Lannowe CMG, DSO	2 Aug 18	–	6 Aug 19

Tank Corps Central Schools

Brig Gen	Sir HJ Elles KCMG, CB, DSO	7 Aug 19	–	14 May 23
Col	EB Hankey DSO	15 May 23	–	17 Oct 23

Royal Tank Corps Central Schools

Col	TC Mudie DSO	18 Oct 23	–	16 Aug 27
Col	KM Laird DSO	17 Aug 27	–	30 Sep 29
Brig	WD Croft CMG, DSO	1 Oct 29	–	30 Apr 31
Brig	CA Bolton CBE	1 May 35	–	30 Apr 35
Brig	WM Sutton DSO, MC, ADC	1 May 35	–	31 Mar 37

Army Armoured Fighting Vehicles School

Brig	WM Sutton DSO, MC, ADC	1 Apr 37	–	30 Apr 39
Brig	HL Evans MC	1 May	–	31 May 41
Brig	R Naesmyth DSO, MC	1 Jun 41	–	30 Sep 43
Brig	ECN Custance DSO	1 Oct 43	–	29 Nov 46
Brig	NW Duncan CBE, DSO	12 Jan 47	–	31 Dec 47

Royal Armoured Corps Centre

Brig	NW Duncan CBE, DSO	1 Jan 48	–	13 Aug 49
Brig	RP Harding DSO	14 Aug 49	–	2 Dec 51
Brig	HJB Cracoft DSO, ADC	3 Dec 51	–	8 Oct 53
Brig	R Younger CBE, DSO, MC	9 Oct 53	–	8 Dec 54
Brig	WB Radford MBE, MC	9 Dec 54	–	2 Jan 57
Brig	AW Brown CBE, DSO, MC	2 Mar 57	–	17 May 58
Brig	RN Harding-Newman MC	18 May 58	–	30 Jan 61
Brig	RE Coker MC	31 Jan 61	–	12 Dec 62
Brig	GTA Armitage MBE	13 Dec 62	–	31 Oct 65
Brig	HC Walker MBE, MC	1 Nov 65	–	6 Mar 67
Brig	HBC Watkins MBE	19 Jun 68	–	18 Dec 68
Brig	DVL Allott (KILLED IN FLYING ACCIDENT)	9 Dec 68	–	14 May 69
Brig	HG Woods MBE, MC	8 Jul 69	–	20 Dec 71
Brig	PB Cavendish OBE	21 Jan 71	–	2 May 74
Brig	RMF Redgrave MC	3 May 74	–	28 Sep 75
Brig	CH Robertson	29 Sep 75	–	22 Mar 78
Brig	AR Douglas-Nugent	23 Mar 78	–	19 Mar 81
Brig	SC Cooper	20 Mar 81	–	10 Dec 82
Brig	RJ Rhoderick-Jones	11 Dec 82	–	12 Dec 84
Brig	RS Webster	13 Dec 84	–	25 Jan 87
Brig	ABJH Gooch	26 Jan 87	–	to date

Regular Regiments who have served as RAC Centre Regiment (1968-88)

Arrived	Departed	Regiment
Aug 68	Aug 70	Queen's Royal Irish Hussars
Aug 70	Aug 72	2nd Royal Tank Regiment
Aug 72	Aug 74	13th/18th Royal Hussars
Aug 74	May 76	The Queen's Own Hussars
May 76	Nov 77	14th/20th King's Hussars
Nov 77	Nov 80	17th/21st Lancers
Nov 80	Nov 82	16th/5th The Queen's Royal Lancers
Nov 82	Nov 84	1st Royal Tank Regiment
Nov 84	Nov 86	15th/19th The King's Royal Hussars
Nov 86	Mar 88	3rd Royal Tank Regiment

THE ROYAL ARMOURED CORPS CENTRE

circa 1980

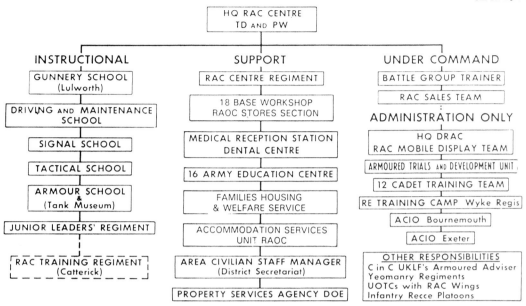

HQ RAC CENTRE
TD AND PW

INSTRUCTIONAL

- GUNNERY SCHOOL (Lulworth)
- DRIVING AND MAINTENANCE SCHOOL
- SIGNAL SCHOOL
- TACTICAL SCHOOL
- ARMOUR SCHOOL & (Tank Museum)
- JUNIOR LEADERS' REGIMENT
- RAC TRAINING REGIMENT (Catterick)

SUPPORT

- RAC CENTRE REGIMENT
- 18 BASE WORKSHOP RAOC STORES SECTION
- MEDICAL RECEPTION STATION DENTAL CENTRE
- 16 ARMY EDUCATION CENTRE
- FAMILIES HOUSING & WELFARE SERVICE
- ACCOMMODATION SERVICES UNIT RAOC
- AREA CIVILIAN STAFF MANAGER (District Secretariat)
- PROPERTY SERVICES AGENCY DOE

UNDER COMMAND

- BATTLE GROUP TRAINER
- RAC SALES TEAM

ADMINISTRATION ONLY

- HQ DRAC RAC MOBILE DISPLAY TEAM
- ARMOURED TRIALS AND DEVELOPMENT UNIT
- 12 CADET TRAINING TEAM
- RE TRAINING CAMP Wyke Regis
- ACIO Bournemouth
- ACIO Exeter

OTHER RESPONSIBILITIES
C in C UKLF's Armoured Adviser
Yeomanry Regiments
UOTCs with RAC Wings
Infantry Recce Platoons

Acknowledgements

THIS BOOK began as the germ of an idea, following on from a photographic display of "Old Bovington", held at the Tank Museum three years ago. It aroused so much local interest that we felt it would be a good idea to try to put it all down on paper. Fortunately Mr Rodney Legg thought so as well, so he is the first person we must thank. It has been a difficult book for him to edit, because so much material and photographs were available that inevitably it has meant leaving out a great deal, however, perhaps it all could be included in a future enlarged edition! We must also thank Mr George Lanning for allowing us to quote from his excellent work "From Rifle Range to Garrison", which charts the early years of Bovington Camp.

Next come the host of soldiers, both serving and retired, and civilians, who have lived in Bovington and Lulworth Camps over the years. We thank them all for their generous assistance, in particular the following whose contributions have been included: Major Generals Geoffrey Armitage and Simon Cooper, Colonels Tony Blad, Dick Everard and Clifton Rayment, Majors Chris Gray, John Rix, Bert Starr, Captain Edward Body and Messrs Chuter, Cooper, Chadwick, Evans, Hammersley, Hunter, Morley, Munns, Payne, Rundle, Roper, Stimpson, Tharme, Wilton-Jones and Dr Waldie; also Mrs Beryl Cornish, Mrs Sylvia Wood, Mrs Denise Wright, Miss Bettina Hockey. Sadly, our good friend Mr John Wright passed away earlier this year.

We must also thank the members of the Tank Museum staff who have helped us in this "labour of love", in particular Mr Roland Groom, our photographer who has produced most of the photographs, including the splendid cover, Mr David Fletcher our overworked Librarian and last but by no means least, Mrs Paula Green, who nobly typed the manuscript while her husband was serving in the Falklands.

We hope that everyone will feel that the end results justify their efforts.

George and Anne Forty
Bryantspuddle Dorset
November 1987

Footnotes

1 — as quoted in "From Rifle Range to Garrison"
2 by George Lanning (published privately)
3 — all these quotations are taken from bound
4 copies of the "Tank Corps Journal", "The RTC
5 to 10 Journal", "The Tank Magazine" and "Tank"
inclusive which are held in the Tank Museum Library
11 and 12 — extracts from letters received from Mr Glyn
Evans of Swanage
13 — extract from letter received from Captain
Edward Body of Deal
14 — extract from letter to "The Tank Magazine"
15 to 19 — taken from the Official Diary of the Tank &
inclusive Central Workshops a copy of which is held in
the Tank Museum Library
20 to 22 — taken from the Official Diary of 1st (Depot)
inclusive Battalion RTC a copy of which is held in the
Tank Museum Library
23 — extract from article in "The RTC Journal"
24 — as quoted in "From Rifle Range to Garrison"
by George Lanning
25 — lodged in Tank Museum archives
(Accession No 21378)
26 — "History of the Royal Armoured Corps
1945-75") by KJ Macksey
27 — taken from the "Tank Magazine" 1946 but
first published in "Blue Flash"
28 and 29 — taken from the "Tank Magazine" of 1947
30 Fenn continued to work at Bovington after his
retirement and was employed as a civilian
gardener in the RAC Centre Officer's Mess. He
was killed in a road accident on 6th January
1969, aged 73 years

31 — it had by then been agreed that all Regiments
of the Household Cavalry and Royal Armoured
Corps would take their turn at the various
tasks and duties required of the RAC, thus
Cavalry Regiments operated tanks as
armoured car role. It was done on a strict rota
basis, including providing cover for the ABTU
at Catterick and the RAC Centre
32 — "PULHEEMS" was the way in which a soldier
was medically classified, each letter standing
for a part of the body (eg: U = upper limbs),
while HO stands for "Home Only", ie: not to be
posted outside UK
33 Cambrai House was at that time the residence
of the Commandant RAC Centre, now DRAC
does occupy the house, while Commander
RAC Centre lives in Swinton House
34 — extracted from an article in the QRIH
Journal, 1970
35 — extracted from various handouts kindly
supplied by Dr Derek Waldie, PRO Junior
Leaders Regiment, RAC
36 — taken from "They Also Served, a pictorial
antology of camp followers through the
ages" by George and Anne Forty
37 — sadly in recent years unscrupulous poachers
have sought to make easy money killing deer
in both areas. The army is endeavouring to
"police" both areas in order to stamp out such
activities

Index